Blood and Fire

The Duke of Windsor and the strange murder of Sir Harry Oakes.

Another Royal Revelation

John Marquis

Revealing the truth about Sir Harry Oakes' murder and the involvement of the Duke of Windsor

LMH Publishing Limited

© 2006 John Marquis
First Edition
10 9 8 7 6 5 4 3 2 1

All LMH titles, imprints and distributed lines are available at special quantity discounts for bulk purchases for sales promotions, premiums, fund-raising, educational or institutional use.

Executive Editor: *Julia Tan*
Cover Design: *Jason Donald and LeeQuee Design*
Book Design, Typesetting and Layout: *Michelle Mitchell, PAGE Design Services*

Cover Photo (right): *Edward, Duke of Windsor (King Edward VIII)*
by Hugh Cecil Saunders, 1925 (NPG P503).
Courtesy of the National Portrait Gallery.

Published by: LMH Publishing Limited
7 Norman Road,
LOJ Industrial Complex
Building 10
Kingston C.S.O., Jamaica
Tel: 876-938-0005; 938-0712
Fax: 876-759-8752
Email: lmhbookpublishing@cwjamaica.com
Website: www.lmhpublishingjamaica.com

Printed in the U.S.A.   ISBN: 976-8202-14-9

ACKNOWLEDGEMENTS

I am indebted to The Tribune's publisher, Eileen Dupuch Carron, for permission to use information and photographs from the 1959 book, *The Murder of Sir Harry Oakes*, and to several Nassau friends and associates for insights into various aspects of the Oakes affair. These friends, for various reasons, wish to remain anonymous. Any views expressed, and conclusions drawn, are mine alone and do not reflect those of *The Tribune* or its owners.

FOREWORD

As a young journalist in Nassau during the late 1960s, I took a call at my desk one day and heard a familiar voice. It was a trusted contact of mine, one of many who kept me supplied with information about the social and political life of the Bahamas capital. "I need to meet you," the voice said, "and I'd like it to be somewhere quiet." Within the hour, the source and I were sitting across a table in a dark downtown bar, tucked away in a corner where no-one could hear and few could see. The information this person imparted in a lowered voice was stunning and – in the climate of the times – unpublishable. But I never doubted that it was true.

In journalism you learn to grade sources. Some you disregard as too reckless to be plausible. Others are sometimes right, but require caution. Yet more have a personal axe to grind. The Grade A sources, as I like to call them, are invariably honest and accurate, with no motive other than to expose the truth. This source fell into the latter category, which added a chilling edge to what they were saying.

Exactly what this person said can be left until later, and will be disclosed towards the end of this book when the reader will be able to appreciate the full significance of their words. However, the disclosure sparked an interest in the fascinating wartime murder of Sir Harry Oakes which has never waned during the intervening 35 years. During that time I have read several accounts of the murder and trawled through a tremendous amount of biographical material about the protagonists whose lives were forever touched – and in some cases blighted – by the brutal slaying of the British Empire's richest man. I have read all the theories advanced by policemen, criminologists, forensic experts and researchers about the supposed killer, his motive, and the means by which he murdered Sir Harry. At the end of it all, a mass of questions still hung in the air.

Since 1969, when my secret meeting took place, revelations about the Duke of Windsor's wartime sojourn as Governor of the Bahamas have added an extra dimension to the mystery. The Duke's known pro-Nazi sympathies, his alleged illegal financial dealing, his unusual and highly suspicious network of friends, and Sir Harry's unique role in Bahamian life, have all coalesced to cast new light on one of the most enthralling murder mysteries of modern times.

Was the Duke directly or indirectly involved in the killing? If so, why? Was his mishandling of the Oakes investigation another example of his ineptitude, or did he deliberately intend the inquiry to pose more questions than it answered?

The two biggest and most disturbing questions of all, about his role in this affair, go right to the root of the Windsor enigma. Was he really a doe-eyed weakling whose every decision was made for him by his wife, or was he a ruthless conspirator prepared to see an innocent man go to the gallows to protect himself and his friends from exposure?

In these pages, I intend to re-examine the suspects, lay bare the motives and throw new light on a mystery which, sixty years on, continues to excite the senses of all those with a taste for scandal in high places, where avarice and power combine to corrupt all, even it seems the former King of England and his dubious associates.

It is a story with everything – love, lust, treachery, greed, betrayal and, of course, tragedy. And all against a backdrop of Royal wealth and privilege in a tropical paradise, at a time when the western world faced its biggest crisis.

By the end of this book, readers will be able to review many of the preconceptions that have hampered a reasoned appraisal of this extraordinary case. They will also be able to view anew the fascinating array of characters, who found themselves ensnared by one of the great murder mysteries of the age.

Reputations will come under close scrutiny, not least that of the Duke and his Nassau friends, and few will emerge unscathed. A ruthless conspiracy was at the heart of the Oakes affair, and many lives were laid waste in its aftermath. Six decades on, the story retains the power to appal and enthral, as you are about to find out.

For Joan

CONTENTS

CHAPTER ONE
Death in the Night 1

CHAPTER TWO
Friends of the Nazis 19

CHAPTER THREE
Under Suspicion 31

CHAPTER FOUR
On the Brink of a Confession 45

CHAPTER FIVE
An Honourable Man 55

CHAPTER SIX
Private Eye 83

CHAPTER SEVEN
The Trial 92

CHAPTER EIGHT
The Defence 120

CHAPTER NINE
Persecution 141

CHAPTER TEN
Prime Suspect 155

CHAPTER ELEVEN
Aftermath 179

CHAPTER TWELVE
    Meyer Lansky 200

CHAPTER THIRTEEN
    Disquiet 209

CHAPTER FOURTEEN
    A Meeting 215

Afterword 219

Conclusions 227

Chapter One

DEATH IN THE NIGHT

It is high summer in Nassau and the humidity is intense. Clerks toiling under ceiling fans in the fierce heat watch their ink dissolve in sweat. Businessmen at lunch in downtown cafes fidget as their shirts stick to their backs. Huge black Bahamian women find shade under parasols, mopping their brows. Grizzled men with time on their hands doze in doorways. The air is motionless, leaden, oppressive.

In the heavy atmosphere of summer, the very rich fly out to find fresher air in Switzerland or Vermont, or head north in their yachts for cooler ports of call, on the eastern seaboard of the United States. Some will be found in Cape Cod, others in the Carolinas. Those left behind manage as best they can in the sizzling crucible that is Nassau town. It's the season for thundery weather when the sea is as flat as a platter, subdued by the heavy air. Only the mosquitoes, fat on blood, are on the move in this heat, siphoning sustenance from humans too tired to stir.

It was on a day like this that final preparations were in hand to kill Sir Harry Oakes, a man so coarse, so rude and so awkward to handle that he was often likened to a warthog. Rich almost beyond belief, he was nonetheless untutored in social niceties and frequently appalled society dinner hostesses by spitting grape pips across the table. He had a liking for loud-checked shirts and mining boots, neither of which were considered a suitable form of dress for the prosperous upper reaches of Bahamian society, and wide-brimmed hats which reminded him of his younger days as a gold prospector. An odd and ungainly character without doubt, but admirable in many ways, too, largely because of his phenomenal work ethic and the magnanimity that ran counter to his rough-and-ready demeanour.

1

In the summer of 1943, Nassau was a tiny, pink-washed colonial capital far from the insanity of the European war. Its main thoroughfare, Bay Street, was lined with half-empty shops and bore a striking resemblance to the fly-blown main streets of a hundred western movies. Hooded pre-war cars clanked alongside horse-drawn drays and donkey-carts; the stylish sedans were owned by the white merchants, lawyers and bankers who called the shots in this tiny sliver of Empire, the drays and carts by black men scuffling for a living. On the island's northern shore were the villas and mansions of the wealthy white elite, their terraces overlooking a turquoise sea. Over the hill in Shantyland, black families lived dirt poor in broken shacks, with buckets as lavatories and standpipes in the streets. The alleyways of Grants Town, lined by petty shops and busy yards, were full of barefoot urchins and lice-ridden dogs. The Bahama Islands were in the midst of another depression; most local men were out of work, and an eerie torpor had descended on the people. Times were hard.

Nassau had known much better days. Eighty years before, it had experienced the glorious bounties of the American Civil War, when the embattled southern states relied on blockade-runners from the Bahamas to keep them supplied with food. During the 1920s, the parched victims of Prohibition looked to Bahamian bootleggers for relief and the islanders were only too eager to oblige. With a long history of ship-wrecking, piracy and smuggling behind them, Bahamians were never averse to making a living by nefarious means, and shipping illicit liquor was very much their line. The islands' moral framework, such as it was, tottered on shifty foundations. While religion provided an opiate for an impoverished people, it offered little by way of a behavioural template. Traditionally, Bahamians had resorted to a devious trick or two to get by. In the 1940s, the poor hustled for a living as best they could, in a society which did its best to ignore them. Some fell foul of the police for petty theft, but most Bahamians accepted their lot and existed in a state of resigned inertia.

Since the Prohibition boom, Nassau had been forced to fall back on the fruits of the sea. Sponging had for years been its salvation, but a fungal blight put paid to that, and for most of the depression years, poor blacks were at subsistence level. Those who could acquire a boat hauled conch and grouper from the sea; others tried to coax edible vegetation out of limestone rock. Children collected seagrapes and split coconuts for sustenance. In season, mangoes and paw-paw grew wild, but never in abundance. Sometimes, there were stunted, under-nourished bananas to be had. In difficult times, New Providence island, on which Nassau stands, was an unforgiving place. Sparse soil, few trees, a soggy wasteland of mangrove swamps at its western end, heavy squadrons of mosquitoes to suck what life they could find in the long-suffering former slaves...this was not a place to be without money or the means of earning it. By contrast, the rich wanted for nothing and felt untouchable.

Today, Bay Street is lined with jewellery shops and liquor stores. It caters for the tourists who pour into town, from the towering cruise ships from Florida which stand in the nearby docks. During the war years, however, it was the principal shopping area for Bahamians, who bought groceries, hardware and dry goods from its stores, and fruit and vegetables from waterfront stalls. It was at the nearby wharf that mailboats from the Out Islands moored: simple, rough-hewn sailing craft pulled alongside, their cargoes of melon, mango, guava and breadfruit displayed in boxes on the dock. On days like this, their sails hung limply against their masts.

Only two events uplifted this benighted isle as the great powers waged war in Europe. One was the arrival of the Duke and Duchess of Windsor in 1940, he to become Governor of the Bahamas, she to carry on charitable work among the poor and needy. The other was an infusion of British military personnel for service training at the local airfield. The Windsors added a touch of glitz and glamour to a thoroughly depressed colony, while the servicemen were a reminder that the Bahamas had a role to play, however small, in the great events taking place in far-off lands.

As time went on, Bahamians would be confronted more brutally by the reality of war. German U-boats would lurk among the islands waiting to strike at Allied shipping in the North Atlantic. Occasionally, trainer planes lifting off from New Providence crashed into the bush or sea, killing their crews. An enclosure of tombstones bears witness to these tragedies to this day. These occurrences jolted locals into the realisation that, beyond the clear aquatints of Bahamian waters, lay a grim, grey ocean and a world of conflict and torment, where people were dying daily in the fight against tyranny. But for the most part, the Bahamas slumbered during these momentous days, an unregarded string of rocks far from the European theatre of war. No-one in Europe noticed, no-one in power in London seemed to care. Then dawn broke on 8 July 1943, and everything changed.

From Bay Street, a road heads west, flanking the sea on the island's northern edge. At one point, it reaches a sharp left-hand bend, which carries it round the fringe of a beautiful bay. On the far side of the bay is Cable Beach, now a spangled wall of luxury hotels, but then a scattering of pleasant colonial-style homes, mostly owned by wealthy foreigners who were in the Bahamas to evade the punishing tax regimes of their homelands.

At the eastern edge of Cable Beach, right next to Goodman's Bay, stood the pink two-storey home of Sir Harry Oakes. This creeper-clad mansion, with its external stairways and breeze-blown balconies, was considered one of the island's finest. It looked out over pristine waters to two off-shore islands and, to the east, the long curve of the bay round which the road ran to Nassau town. From here Sir Harry and his wife could watch sublime sub-tropical sunsets and the gentle to-ing and fro-ing of tiny island boats. It was a choice spot and they loved it, not least because it was so much in contrast to their home soil in Maine and, more recently, Canada, where the chill air and overcast skies created downcast spirits. Such a home in such a place was symbolic of Sir Harry's success. They could sit over cocktails in their seafront balcony and reflect how, in the end, hard work paid off and propelled them to unimagined heights. They saw the Bahamas as a highly desirable prize, confirmation of their new-found status.

The house was called Westbourne and it stood amid casuarina and coconut trees, with seagrapes fringing the beach. Alongside it stood the country club, where wealthy expatriates played tennis and sipped pink gins. In every sense it was symbolic of the colonial age, oozing quiet gentility and self-satisfaction. When the Windsors arrived in the Bahamas, having been banished from Europe by the British government, they stayed there briefly during the costly refurbishment of Government House, the colonial hilltop mansion in central Nassau, which they considered sub-standard for their refined tastes, but which had been the home of British governors for years. Over the next three years, they would come to know Harry and Eunice Oakes well, as all four would find themselves at the top of most society entertainment lists. In fact, the names of Windsor and Oakes would become forever entwined, in circumstances that would haunt them for the rest of their lives.

It was at Westbourne, during the early hours of that fateful morning, that Sir Harry died, murdered in bizarre and brutal fashion in his bed.

As managing editor of Nassau's morning newspaper, *The Tribune,* I feel a certain affinity with the Oakes case and all that followed. It was The Tribune's renowned publisher of the day, Sir Etienne Dupuch, who broke the story to the world. And it was his brother, Eugene Dupuch, then The Tribune's assistant editor, but later to become an eminent Queen's Counsel at the Bahamas Bar, who provided the most comprehensive account of the trial of Count Alfred de Marigny, Sir Harry's son-in-law, and the only man ever to be charged with his murder.

Oddly enough, I feel an affinity in two other, quite minor, ways. The eve of the murder came three months to the day before I was born. During the de Marigny trial, later that year, I was a babe in arms. Then, in the late 1960s, I attended a party at Westbourne, which had been converted into apartments. I forget who the host was, but I do recall that his apartment was on the upper floor in the part of the building where Sir Harry died. I was sitting on a couch sipping a Scotch and ginger ale, and, inevitably, the subject of Sir Harry's murder came up in conversation. As we talked, the host said casually: "You do realise, don't you, that you're sitting in the exact spot where Sir Harry's body was found." When later I studied photographs of the death scene, I realised that he was right. That, and the mysterious tip-off I received in early 1969, cemented my interest in what has frequently been called "The Murder of the Century".

In the mid-1960s, when I worked in Nassau for three years as a young political reporter, the Oakes murder was emphatically a taboo subject. It was generally mentioned only in whispered asides, with nods and winks and, in some instances, genuine trepidation. The upper reaches of Bahamian society were stoically silent on the subject and resented it being raised at all. More adventurous expatriates were quickly warned off any public discussion of the more lurid theories about the case, and the local populace at large knew better than to tread on dangerous ground.

There were powerful reasons for this. During the years following the murder, there were several unexplained killings of people directly, or indirectly, involved with the events of that thundery summer night in 1943. In the main, they were people who were believed to have seen too much or heard too much. In one case, the victim was a foreign investigator determined to crack the Oakes mystery and make her name. Her mission was misguided, for she failed to understand the sinister forces at work in the Bahamas at that time. Her body was found upside down in a banana hole. These deaths, all deeply shocking, sending tremors of fear through an already wary population, indicated the lengths some parties were prepared to go in keeping the Oakes mystery quiet. The Bahamas was then a sunny little land with some very dark corners, wherein lurked a privileged few who were considered beyond the reach of the law. It was, as one wag memorably remarked, "a sunny land for shady people."

The distinguished British comic actor Robert Morley, an expert in murder mysteries, once said the 20th century produced only two 'perfect' murders. One was the Kenyan Happy Valley killing which resulted in the celebrated film *White Mischief,* the other was the 1943 slaying of Sir Harry Oakes in Nassau. By 'perfect', he meant not only that the killer was never caught, but that the crime was of such historical and social interest that it would be discussed around the world for eternity, especially among criminolgists, thriller readers with a taste for the bizarre, and high society figures appalled at the brutal destruction of one of their own.

Exactly 60 years have passed since Sir Harry's body was found, yet speculation about the way he died, those responsible, the weapon they used, and their motives is as rife as ever. And still no-one, even those closest to the late protagonists in the drama, appears to be any closer to an indisputable conclusion. Among Nassau's older whites, there are still whisperings about who knows what, but those with secrets are likely to take them to the grave. This silence is no longer caused by fear, but loyalty to the old order. Since the death of Sir Harry Oakes, the Bahamas has undergone a quiet political revolution, and those who once ruled, while retaining their financial strength, have been sidelined by events. For the die-hards, protecting old secrets has become a defensive mechanism, and their silence is absolute.

Robert Morley's son, the film critic Sheridan, said the Oakes murder, like the Happy Valley mystery, had the "snobbery with violence" element that gives crimes of this type their special allure. Everyone expects brutal death among the riff-raff, but when the victim is a multi-millionaire baronet, and the number one suspect is a Mauritian count, the story benefits from being not only unusual, but almost unprecedented, certainly in modern times. Morley described Sir Harry as "a larger-than-life gold prospector who was the uncrowned King of the Bahamas". That is, more or less, an accurate appraisal of Oakes and his special status, in the Bahamas, during the early war years, and it probably offers the single biggest clue to his killing. Several books have been written about the Oakes case. All of them offer different motives for the crime, and every one points a finger at a different killer. But the version that carries more credence than most suggests that Oakes, the quick-tempered gold digger from Maine with a baronetcy from the King, was becoming too powerful for his own good in the then extremely enclosed society of small-town Nassau. It was by no means the only reason for his murder, but it was a powerful factor.

Imagine the Bahamas in those distant days. It was a miniscule, and relatively insignificant, outpost of an enormous empire. Its upper crust, though of little account alongside the movers and shakers of the mighty dominions, felt inviolable on their sunny rock, comfortably in charge of their own lives, politically and financially dominant, and secure in the knowledge that the raging war was four thousand miles away. Into this cosy, self-serving little world strode a colossus of the gold-prospecting fraternity, a Yank-cum-Canadian with more money than all of them put together and the social decorum of a buffalo. It was not long before Sir Harry, who moved to the Bahamas to keep his huge fortune away from the Canadian taxman, was involving himself in practically every aspect of Bahamian life.

He bought large tracts of land, dabbled in local politics, became renowned for his philanthropy and won respect for the financial muscle he possessed. He was accepted by the worthy and well-to-do the world over, and inevitably, came to be a dominant force among the less worldly folk around him in the Bahamas. This mesmerising combination of financial power and mental toughness, and the added spice of high-flying international social connections, made him a formidable and fascinating figure. Whatever he lacked by way of savoir faire, he made up for with the sheer weight of his wealth. His money gave him gravitas in whatever he said or did. Though small in stature, he had an imperious presence which was somehow reinforced by coarseness of manner. He was a prickly man who instilled wariness. Fiercely individualistic, he cared little for the social mores of the day, and, in polite company, he was rated uncouth, scoffing food like he was still out there in the wilds, searching for that elusive mother lode.

"He learned his table manners on the Klondike," sniffed one critic haughtily, "And, of course, there were no tables on the Klondike."

What he lacked in refinement, however, he made up for in energy. Social graces were at a premium, but he had ideas in abundance. Sir Harry provided the money for the first Nassau airport at Oakes Field, which he envisioned as a gateway to a more accessible Bahamas. He foresaw ambitious hotel and marina developments in some of the islands' choicest locations. He viewed himself as a dynamic force who could propel the sleepy colony into a new era. As a self-made success, he possessed vision and self-assurance aplenty, and set about making himself the main man in his new-found fiefdom.

Though his money was welcome in what was then a very small, insular and not especially enterprising backwater of the Empire, his assumption of power and influence posed a threat to some of those whose family links with the Bahamas stretched back two centuries or more. There was a growing feeling among some that Sir Harry, with an hereditary honour from the Crown, and a dynasty in the making, was getting much too big for his mining boots. The story of his buying the British Colonial Hotel in downtown Nassau, and promptly firing a senior employee who had barred him for improper dress, reinforced this impression. The Oakes family seemed poised to become a quasi-regal presence in the Bahamas, with Sir Harry as the monarch. Inevitably, such a unique status would give rise to tensions, not just among entrenched white Bahamian interests, but also at Government House, where King George VI's brother, and official representative, went about his colonial duties with barely concealed resentment, having been summarily despatched from Europe by the British government.

So was the killer a member of Bahamian society, eager to be rid of a man who was creating a social imbalance in Nassau, which threatened their own position? Was Sir Harry seen as a growing threat to those who felt their long association with the islands, in some cases stretching all the way back to the first settlers, entitled them to unchallenged power? It is among the likelier of all the scenarios on offer, but if that were so, why was Sir Harry killed in such a bizarre way? That is one of the many questions hanging over what continues to be a wholly enthralling mystery.

On the day before his death, Sir Harry was in buoyant mood. Though he had a reputation for irascibility, he could also be cheerful when the mood took him. At one point during the morning, he was seen walking jauntily along Bay Street, swinging his arms in his usual purposeful way despite the summer heat. In the languid atmosphere of Nassau, his energy was always considered one of the most remarkable things about him. In a colony of talkers, he was a doer. While lassitude was commonplace in these parts, Sir Harry remained a busy little terrier of a man, always looking for things to occupy him, whatever the time of the year. One of the enduring images of Oakes during the 1940s is of the ex-prospector atop a bulldozer, levelling scrub on his vast acreage in western New Providence, or wielding a cutlass to cut down bush, or cracking limestone rock with a pick-axe. He had always been a physical man, and money did not change him. He was physically as hard and compact as a gold nugget. Despite unimaginable wealth, he remained in touch with his past. It was this lack of pretension, and his empathy with life's underdogs, that endeared him to the island's blacks. He took upon himself none of the airs and graces of the colonial dignitaries sent out from London. There was no assumption of superiority. He was blunt and transparent, as unlike the archetypal baronet of the realm as you could imagine. What you saw was what you got, and what you got may have been unpalatable to his detractors, but sat well with those who saw him as a sincere, self-made man with no side.

Later that day, July 7th, he was at Westbourne with his friend, Harold Christie, a real estate agent who, like him, was eager to promote the Bahamas as a playground for the wealthy. Sir Harry and Christie, a white Bahamian whose family was part of the tight social milieu that dominated Bahamian affairs at the time, were associates whose business interests were closely aligned. They had much in common, including quite humble beginnings when money had been tight, and an unquenchable desire to ensure they were never poor again. More importantly, they both identified the immense potential of the Bahama Islands long before anyone else. They developed a passion for acquiring and selling land, and both were convinced that the Bahamas had a future as a haven for people like Sir Harry, who resented their hard-earned fortunes being decimated by tax demands in their homelands, and squandered by irresponsible governments. If more of the world's wealthiest people could be lured to Bahamian shores, there would be the makings of a stable economy, something the colony had always lacked. The men's interlocking financial interests were reinforced by what appeared to be genuine friendship. Sir Harry and Christie spent a lot of time together. They were certainly buddies, and possibly soulmates, who shared common goals and spoke the same financial language. It was noted that they even began to walk alike.

On this hot summer day, the Oakes family was away, the eldest daughter Nancy in Vermont, and her mother and siblings at Sir Harry's Bar Harbour home, in Maine. They had escaped the stickiness of Nassau for cooler northern air. Sir Harry and Christie had planned a not too strenuous game of tennis, at the Bahamas Country Club courts, just east of Westbourne. The following morning, Sir Harry and Christie were due to meet Etienne Dupuch of the *The Tribune* to tour the Oakes sheep farm, an enterprise set up to help overcome the island's meat shortage, during the severely rationed war years. Dupuch wanted to write an article for his paper, but also shared Sir Harry's enthusiasm for such self-sufficiency, and was actively pursuing his own home produce scheme at his hilltop home at Camperdown, in eastern New Providence. After this appointment, Sir Harry intended to set off the next day, for Bar Harbour, to meet up with his family. The appointment was never kept – and, of course, that trip to Maine never materialised. A killer put paid to both.

On the evening of July 7th, Sir Harry hosted a small dinner party at Westbourne. While ill at ease in more formal settings, he enjoyed the company of close friends in his own home. Like most of his kind, Sir Harry – though a beneficiary of the British honours system – had an instinctive aversion to the world of privilege. He had little time for those who had not earned their wealth, as he had, and recoiled from the patrician airs of colonial officials. Among plummy expatriates, he always felt under scrutiny, judged by people he didn't respect by standards he didn't uphold. But with those he trusted and liked, he could be affable and amusing, and that was undoubtedly his demeanour during the last few hours of his life. All three of his guests that night were, he thought, well-disposed towards him, and he was in relaxed and expansive mood. There was good food, spirited conversation and an undeniable air of conviviality. Their laughter rang out across the deserted beach outside, where the soft ripple of the sea was the only other sound, apart from an occasional growl from distant electrical storms, which danced behind clouds far out to sea, like a magic lantern show laid on for their entertainment. Occasionally, the casuarinas would sigh in a sudden breeze. Otherwise, silence.

Apart from Sir Harry and Christie, the dinner guests that night were Charles Hubbard, owner of Labourchere Estate at Cable Beach, a near neighbour of Westbourne, and Mrs Dulcibelle Henneage, wife of a serviceman who was posted overseas. Hubbard was not a frequent visitor at Westbourne, nor even a close friend of Sir Harry, but he had been glad to accept a late invitation to the dinner, which had been casually convened following the tennis party in the afternoon. Mrs Henneage had lunched with him and been invited, too. When they arrived at Westbourne around 6pm, Sir Harry, Christie, a Miss McMahon and Miss Sawyer were still playing tennis. About half an hour later, they all went inside, where Sir Harry served drinks on the upper floor verandah overlooking the sea. He proudly showed off some trees he had planted on the waterfront, then settled down to chat while they all watched the sun go down.

By now, Miss McMahon and Miss Sawyer had departed. As day quickly turned to night, and shadows fell through Westbourne's spacious rooms, Sir Harry and his three remaining guests went in to dinner, which was cooked and served by the Oakes' domestic staff. The meal was pleasant but uneventful and came to an end some time after 9.30pm. Then the foursome settled down to a game of Chinese checkers, which continued until about 11pm. By now, the evening had reached its natural conclusion and Hubbard and Mrs Henneage rose to leave. Hubbard was planning to drive her to her home on the Eastern Road. When they left, Sir Harry was said to be "jovial and high-spirited".

Comfortably replete from dinner, slightly flushed from drink, Sir Harry went back into the house with Christie and they climbed the stairs. They went immediately to Sir Harry's bedroom where the baronet's bed had already been prepared for sleeping. The pair chatted for ten or fifteen minutes before Sir Harry put on his pyjamas and got into bed, surrounding himself with his mosquito net to fend off the many flying insects – and especially sandflies – that plagued Cable Beach. When Christie left the bedroom, Sir Harry was reading a newspaper. It was about 11.15pm and all was well.

Christie, who frequently stayed overnight at Westbourne, went to his room three doors away, with a magazine and a pair of spectacles he had borrowed from Sir Harry. He got into bed immediately and read for between 30 and 45 minutes. Everything was quiet. Eventually, he turned off the light and fell asleep for a couple of hours, when he was awakened by mosquitoes, which had got under his net. He fell asleep again until a heavy rainstorm made him stir a second time. The storm was a typical summer squall, quickly whipping up high winds and depositing huge amounts of water in minutes. According to Christie, that's all he remembered until after sunrise when he awoke to a bright Bahamian summer morning. He went on to the northern porch where he and Sir Harry usually breakfasted. As Sir Harry was not there, he went to the door of his friend's room, which also opened on to the porch. He called out "Hi, Harry!" through the screen but got no reply. What happened next was to set in train a series of events which had a resounding impact on many lives, not least those of the entire Oakes family, the Duke of Windsor, the people of the Bahamas and, of course, Christie himself.

It was to have repercussions throughout the British Empire, even dislodging war news from the front pages of newspapers in the dominions and colonies. At a time when many soldiers' lives were being lost at war, when Jews were being gassed in their thousands in

Europe, when men were dying painfully on the Burma railroad, and families perished under falling bombs in Britain and Germany, the demise of Sir Harry Oakes still ranked high in public interest. So here was one man, among many, whose life was brought to a premature end in those dark days, but his fate commanded attention for a number of compelling and extraordinary reasons. Not least was that Oakes himself was a rich, powerful, colourful and commanding figure. But more significant still was that his murder, and the investigation that followed, fell under the jurisdiction of the Duke of Windsor, who gazed down on the life of Nassau town from his sitting room at Government House, where he and his wife Wallis were spending their miserable wartime exile.

When Christie entered Sir Harry's bedroom, he first saw the burnt wooden frame of the mosquito net round Sir Harry's bed. He dashed to the bed and saw Sir Harry lying on it. The baronet's pyjamas were burnt, there was soot and a raw spot on his face and his pyjamas were scorched away over his chest, exposing a large raw burn in that area. He lifted his friend's head, shook him, poured some water in his mouth, propped up his head with a pillow and used a towel to wet and wipe his face. By doing this, he hoped to revive him. When he achieved no response, he rushed to the northern porch overlooking the servants' quarters and called for help. At first he got no reply, so returned to Sir Harry's room, ran to the southern window and shouted for the watchman. He then telephoned to Mrs Madeline Kelly, who lived in a cottage in the Country Club grounds. He also called his brother, Frank Christie, and told him to get a doctor and come quickly. Then he called the police commissioner, Lieut Col R A Erskine-Lindop.

First on the scene was Mrs Kelly, who dashed upstairs to Sir Harry's bedroom. Next came Dr Hugh Quackenbush, followed by the dinner guest Mr Hubbard and Frank Christie. Dr Quackenbush did a quick examination of Sir Harry and formally pronounced him dead.

The scene confronting this group was extremely unusual, even given the extraordinary nature of most murder mysteries. There had clearly been a fire, though of limited scope, which had left burns on the bed, wardrobe, a Chinese screen and the carpet near the door. There were also a number of feathers which had stuck to Sir Harry's corpse. Later medical examinations would reveal that Sir Harry had received a blow, or blows, to the head which had left four unusual puncture holes in his skull near his left ear, all triangular in shape. Although the body was on its back, blood had run from the wounds across the face, suggesting Sir Harry had been moved after the fatal blow or blows. There were also several marks on the screen and walls. The fire, the wounds, the blood on Sir Harry's face and the marks in the room were all to become enormously significant in the weeks following Christie's gruesome discovery. But for now, those at Westbourne that morning were struggling to come to terms with the enormity of what had happened. Nassau and the Bahamas were about to absorb the full impact of their most notorious and baffling murder. And the Duke of Windsor was about to make a decision that would cast doubt on his allegiances and his integrity.

When the Duke and Duchess arrived in Nassau, there was jubilation on the waterfront. The police chief, colonial officials and leading Bahamians were there to greet them, as they stepped ashore. Acting Governor W L Heape, the police chief Lieut Col R A Erskine-Lindop and a guard of honour formed by local officers were all decked out in splendid white pith helmets and tunics, with medals and scarlet braid on full display. The day, 17 August, 1940, was oppressively hot and the Duke, in army khaki uniform and peaked cap, looked uncomfortable in the stifling humidity of a Bahamian summer. The Duchess, in floral dress and light cape-like coat, seemed more at ease and smiled broadly when a young girl, Sonya Duncombe, presented her with a welcoming bouquet of flowers. For the Bahamas, their arrival was seen as a social coup. Local socialites were ecstatic that a couple so steeped in international glamour, so much at the centre of things, and subjects of the most enthralling romance of the age, should have opted to live among them. But, as *The Tribune* reported in its special centenary edition more than 60 years later, the dockside clamour that summer day took place against a backdrop of many unanswered questions, about the couple and their new role in life.

In the world of high society and power politics, things are rarely what they seem. In the case of the Duke and Duchess of Windsor, nothing was quite what it seemed to the Bahamian people when the couple stepped ashore to take up their official duties at Government House, in the merciless heat and humidity of a Nassau summer.

Those, now of advanced age, who recall that heady day, retain the images of the occasion as vividly as ever. They remember the crowds massed on the waterfront, the glamorous couple making their way to Government House, the palpable excitement of having figures of such international renown in their midst.

At the time, the couple were viewed by most – and this was certainly true of ordinary people throughout the Empire – as victims of official stuffiness. The Duke's love and devotion for Wallis Simpson was so powerful, so overwhelming, that he was prepared to give up everything, including the Throne, to spend his life by her side. Theirs was, indisputably, the romance of the century, according to the prevailing wisdom of the day.

The fact that they spent more than 30 years together as man and wife suggests there was certainly an enduring quality to their relationship. But behind the glitz and glamour, the lavish lifestyle, and the romance inevitable in any story of forbidden love, lay deep undercurrents which caused enormous tension during their Bahamas sojourn. For them, the five years they spent in Nassau were a far from happy time.

The undercurrents were, indeed, many and varied, but none – apart from the obvious reverberations of the abdication four years earlier – was even vaguely suspected during the dockside ceremonials. The Duke and Duchess were not in Nassau because they opted to be there, as the people of the Bahamas chose to think, but because the British government could no longer countenance the prospect of having them on the loose in Europe, where they were seriously undermining the Allied war effort, and causing deep disquiet among civil and military leaders. It was not the couple's choice to be posted to a distant isle, far from the salons of Europe and the centre of power, to spend the war's duration undertaking duties they considered beneath them, among people they secretly despised. The decision had been forced upon them by Winston Churchill, whose concern about

15

their obvious Nazi sympathies and alarming political indiscretions made firm action imperative. Once it became clear that exîle was the only serious option for this reckless pair, it only remained for a location to be chosen. In an Empire so large, with territories of all sizes in every latitude, the options were evidently many and varied, but when all was taken into account, the Bahamas emerged as the only realistic choice.

Firstly, it was far enough away, with an entire ocean between Nassau and London, 4,000 miles of treacherous water patrolled by German submarines. Secondly, it was climatically benign, its humid summers off-set by glorious winters of gentle breezes and incessant sunshine. Thirdly, it was near enough the Windsors' well-heeled Florida friends for them to be able to retreat from their exile from time to time. And fourthly, the governorship of a distant possession offered at least a trace of Ruritanian regality for the former king. All in all, it was not a bad posting for someone who had turned his back on the responsibilities for which he was groomed, but – not surprisingly – the Duke and Duchess did not see it that way. From the outset, they were affronted and appalled by the Bahamas appointment. The Duke saw it as the colonial equivalent of a county council lord lieutenantship, a meaningless job offering a plumed helmet, a ceremonial sword and little else. The Duchess, with her soaring social ambitions and regal pretensions, was candid in dubbing it her Elba, the isle to which Napoleon Bonaparte was banished, after his defeat in Europe, in the early 19th century. To be exiled on a limestone reef among former slaves and their dim-witted masters was, for her, the ultimate indignity. Together, they saw it as falling short in most key areas, but specifically in its social limitations and the paltriness of the duties it offered. In spite of everything that had gone before – the blow he dealt Britain and the Empire when he quit as king in 1936, and his willingness to cast duty aside at a dangerous point in his country's history – the Duke felt he was entitled to higher office, with important ambassadorial responsibilities and all the deference his status demanded. His inability to grasp reality, and acknowledge his own inbuilt deficiencies, not to mention his frankly hazardous political views, was one of his many defects at this time, and it was made all the worse by the Duchess's willingness to encourage his absurd delusions.

The smiles offered the Nassau crowds were, therefore, a shallow camouflage, for their deeply hurt feelings of rage and resentment. When they arrived in the Bahamas, the Windsors were boiling in more ways than one, but the summer heat was nothing set alongside the searing disgruntlement they were to suffer for the rest of the war.

What the British and Bahamian people did not know, at the time, was the extent to which the Windsors had been compromised, by their political dealings in Europe, during the four or five years immediately preceding the Second World War. At the time of the abdication, there is little doubt that the so-called "ordinary" people, and specifically the British working class, saw the Duke as something of a hero. There were several reasons for this. In the context of the times, he was seen as quite liberal-minded, especially when it came to acknowledging the plight of the poorly-off. His oft-quoted remark after visiting unemployed miners – "Something must be done" – was taken as incontrovertible proof of his compassion, concern and sincerity, especially at a time when the problems of working men were considered, by Britain's rulers, of very low priority. His shabby treatment at the hands of the Establishment, and all because of his love for a twice-divorced American, also endeared him to those who felt similarly victimised by a stuffy, elitist society in which emotions were considered secondary to duty, conformity and the rigid demands of tradition. After stepping down as king, he was also out of a job, a predicament in which millions of his countrymen found themselves at the time. And his defiance in the face of official hostility gave the people an additional cause to feel affinity with the former king: he was rebellious and recalcitrant. All in all, he was seen as an all-round good egg and the people wished him well. This attitude had traversed the Atlantic via the airwaves and news wires, so Bahamians also saw him essentially as a glamorous, romantic and slightly raffish and rebellious figure, a man unfairly denied the chance to become a great monarch of the people, and all because of his admirable love for an attractive woman.

If the people felt they had much in common with the Duke, it was merely one of the many illusions they harboured about him. In fact, it would be hard to imagine anyone more distant in every conceivable sense from the common herd. The Duke was privileged beyond reason, living in aspic amid the vacuous denizens of the British upper-classes. His refusal to take on the job for which he was trained was seen by those in the know, not as an admirable act of defiance but a wilful abnegation of duty. His self-inflicted unemployment bore little resemblance to the degrading plight of his former subjects, for their joblessness meant hunger and real poverty. His did not. The one aspect of the Windsor myth that was to survive scrutiny in the years to come was the Duke's love for the Duchess. There can be little doubt that it was deep and heartfelt. Whether it was returned in full measure by the Duchess is still open to question.

Chapter Two

FRIENDS OF THE NAZIS

From this distance in time, it is interesting to speculate on how the Duke's admirers would have responded had they known the truth. It is difficult to imagine that those whose sons were being sacrificed on the battlefields of Europe and North Africa would have warmed to his pro-Nazi beliefs. Yet these were the predominant components of his thinking at the time.

The Duke was of German background and was markedly teutonic both physically and psychologically. During his time in the Bahamas, traits emerged which left many with the impression that he was more than ready to embrace the principles of racial supremacy. Bahamians of mixed blood were particularly sensitive to what they saw as his routinely dismissive attitude towards the coloured races. The Duke regarded blacks as fundamentally untrustworthy and dishonest, while the Duchess was proud of what she regarded as her southern heritage. "We southerners know how to treat coloured people," she was fond of telling friends.

It is the German in the Duke which is frequently overlooked. A contemporary regarded him as "more German than Hindenberg", a characteristic most evident in his love for rigid protocol and regimentation. He was openly and quite aggressively proud of his German heritage, and inwardly lamented the casualness and indiscipline which he felt was contributing to Britain's decline. He also had a keen sense of history, and was eager that the higher orders should heed the mistakes of the past.

The Duke was appalled at poverty among the people, and appeared to genuinely care, but it was difficult to assess just how deeply his sentiments ran, and whether they were entirely altruistic. In every other area of his life, the Duke was notoriously selfish, and his critics were inclined to believe that his views, on the alleviation of poverty, represented a strategy more aligned to self-preservation than deep-felt compassion for the masses.

The Duke was acutely aware of the lessons of history, and especially those political convulsions of the past, which had directly affected his own kith and kin. The Russian Revolution of 1917 had shaken royal courts throughout Europe, and the slaughter of the Russian royals unnerved their many cousins, especially in London. For anyone who accepted that the revolution was as much a product of Tsarist despotism, and indifference to people's welfare, as of Bolshevik ambition, there were clear issues to be addressed. The Duke recognised that a well-fed, well-clothed proletariat, whatever their ethnic origins, were less likely to revolt against the established order than those who were almost literally clinging to life. He believed even a modicum of fairness would stave off the horrors of Moscow and Paris where monarchies and entire systems, based on privilege and preferment, were overturned by revolutions because of rampant public disgruntlement.

The Duke's much-publicised compassion for the unemployed in Britain did not extend to any active involvement, in improving their status or general well-being. He was in no sense of the word a far-seeing radical. His main interest appeared to be to keep them in a state of moderately comfortable compliance, and it was this benevolent paternalism which led him into Hitler's camp.

What the Duke and others in the British upper classes feared more than anything was Communism. The transfer of power to the State, and the rise of the workers, was anathema to them for all the obvious reasons. Communism would have meant an end to the kind of life the Duke enjoyed. Among western democracies, Britain was almost obscenely elitist and unjust. There were rigid class divisions which gave emphasis to the social prejudices that abounded among the country's ruling classes. Well into the post-war era, the master–serf attitude persisted, and working people were expected to know their place in a society which was forever conspiring against their interests. The rise of trade unionism was seen by some as a prelude to Communism. And this prospect struck fear into the privileged classes, who felt the foundations of their lives begin to quake beneath them. The Duke and others like him would have been jettisoned by communism, and their networks, lodges and fraternities dismantled. The murder of the Tsar's family in 1917 had pierced to the heart all the off-spring of Queen Victoria, for it seemed to signal the emergence of an unacceptable new order, which put all the established monarchies at risk.

Hitler was, of course, virulently anti-communist and therein lay his primary appeal to the Duke's pampered coterie. That, and his known hostility to Jews, whose most powerful families posed an economic threat of a different kind to the established order. There is a certain irony that people like the Duke should identify their "saviour" in this shrieking Austrian upstart. He was not of the right class or even the "right" racial type. It was simply that his poisonous ideology was most in keeping with theirs, and that he appeared to have the drive, and personal magnetism, required to make it prevail. Hitler's hostility to the Russian communists, and the Jews en masse, was founded primarily on heartfelt contempt for them as people, but he also recognised the economic implications were they allowed to achieve dominance in Europe. The twin objectives of eliminating Communism and the Jews congealed into a deathly, all-consuming mission. The discipline, sense of order and no-nonsense militarism of the Nazi system, plus its rampant anti-semitism, were an intoxicating cocktail for those right-wingers who feared the old social structures were under threat in free Europe. The Fuhrer also glorified a racial type that Europe's aristocracies could identify with. It is little wonder, therefore, that the Duke found himself under Hitler's spell.

There is no doubt that, based on disclosures made public in recent years, the Duchess was, if anything, even more fervently pro-Nazi than him. This was due, in part, to her strong feelings about rank and breeding. Wallis Simpson, though in fact of modest origins, had always seen herself as of superior stock. The lumpen hordes were, for her, mere riff-raff, of no account. It's no surprise, therefore, that the supremacist philosophy of the Nazi hierarchy appealed to her. She admired their arrogance, their strutting and posturing, their goose-stepping and Heil Hitlering. They offered a properly structured and well-stratified system to uplift the strong and subdue the weak. The masses would be fed and watered but kept in their place and that suited her perfectly. When the couple met Hitler on a visit to Germany in 1937, their admiration for the Fuhrer grew enormously, and helped crystalise their views. They felt he had shaken life into a demoralised nation, and were forced to draw unflattering comparisons with Britain, which they considered down-at-heel and poorly managed, with little hope of imminent revival. At the time, the Windsors were close to Oswald and Diana Mosley, whose fascist sympathies and blackshirt followers appeared to give Nazism a British dimension. The four were undoubtedly close, and their twisted ideology was a binding creed, deepened by an almost slavish regard for Hitler himself. He was an icon, a talisman, a beacon of hope in troubled, uncertain times.

The Windsors were on record as saying that the dictators Hitler and Mussolini were far superior to their political counterparts in Britain and other countries of western Europe. They did nothing to soften the deadening impact of their right-wing views and were quite flagrant in their contempt for other western European leaders. All in all, they were an enormous liability, a negative force whose many indiscretions were a propaganda nightmare for the Allies at a time when the future looked bleak.

The Duchess' pro-Nazi position was reinforced by genuine dislike for the British Establishment, which she regarded as an emotionally constipated collection of dreary nonentities. She never forgave the London government or the Royal Family for rejecting her as a prospective queen. Nor would she forget the way they had, in her eyes, effectively deprived her husband of the job for which he had been groomed. The Establishment's subsequent treatment of them both, and specifically their refusal to grant the Duke a job commensurate with what she imagined to be his talents, fanned the embers of her hostility, which flared up at regular intervals for the rest of her life.

Bitterness existed, too, over protocol issues. There was the personal slight of being denied the title Her Royal Highness. British courtiers went out of their way to point out, in advance of the couple's travels, the absolute requirement of Buckingham Palace that any such courtesy should be denied her. The archaic rituals of the Royal Family insisted that the Duchess should be referred to as "Your Grace", and no more, and that the traditional curtsy should not be afforded her on any account. The Duchess, to her credit, placed much less importance on these trivialities than the Duke himself, who saw them as a calculated insult. He never got over the indignity of it all and felt the slight intensely. To those of us who regard such nonsense as of little or no consequence, it is hard to understand the pain he appeared to endure. But he was the product of rigid Germanic stock for whom order, regimentation, status and discipline were all. To undermine his wife, and therefore him, was to tamper with a centuries-old social structure upon which the glory of empire was founded. Fundamentally, the Duke was an arch-conformist, whatever the popular view following his abdication, when he was seen as something of a social rebel.

In the Windsors' eyes, the Queen was the prime architect of their discomfiture, and she became the butt of their scathing humour. The couple frequently shared cruel jokes about the Royal Family, and especially Queen Elizabeth (later the Queen Mother) who they referred to mockingly as "Cookie" because of her homely shape and dimensions. Inevitably, the unflattering soubriquet had class connotations. Elizabeth Bowes-Lyon, as she had been, was depicted as of inferior breeding with a 'below stairs' presence, greatly at odds with the superior airs of the Duchess, who saw herself as an icon of style and elegance. In the eyes of the Windsors, the Queen was without such qualities, and they were happy to belittle her behind her back to their society friends as a Scottish bumpkin from the glens who lacked the polish for her role.

It is only now, following a string of disclosures since their deaths, that the ill-feeling between the Royal Family and the Windsors can be properly assessed. Before their banishment to the Bahamas, the Windsors had made a series of potentially embarrassing gaffes on their travels through Europe. The thrust of their views was that Britain should forget about the survival of democracy in Europe and negotiate a separate peace with the Germans to preserve its own future. This was a message few in Britain, and especially the government, wanted to hear. Churchill's post-Munich stance was emphatically upbeat, and the Windsors' defeatist whining was no help to the Allied cause. They had also worked assiduously to discourage America's involvement in the war, a tactic calculated to harm Britain's interests. A solution had to be found, and quickly, in neutralising the negative impact they threatened to have on public morale.

When Churchill chose the Bahamas for the Windsors, their response was far from ecstatic. They were appalled at the prospect of exile on what they regarded as little more than a limestone reef. In fact, his decision caused displeasure elsewhere, for the incumbent Governor, Sir Charles (later Lord) Dundas, was far from pleased at being unseated to make room for a rogue Duke and his highly dubious wife. However, the plans went ahead, Dundas was transferred to Uganda, and by the time the Windsors steamed into Nassau aboard ship from Lisbon, via Bermuda, an acting Governor was in situ and their future for the next five years had been settled.

August was a bad month to arrive in Nassau for the first time. Even the locals find the weather hot and humid during midsummer. For the Windsors, both bred in more northerly climes, the damp heat was unbearable. It was noted as the Duke went through the formalities of signing in as Governor that perspiration was seeping through his tunic. The Duchess was also feeling the heat, but remained elegantly composed, a faint smile playing on her lips.

At Government House, things were even less to their liking than the climate. The colonial mansion, standing aloft on Mount Fitzwilliam, its windows looking out over Nassau harbour and the rooftops of the downtown area, was in a rundown state. There was a fusty shabbiness about the place, with its drab curtains, threadbare carpets and peeling paintwork. On its walls were sombre oil paintings of long-forgotten colonial dignitaries, cracked relics of the Bahamas' past. The entire structure looked like a creaking banqueting hall for termites, its balconies flaking in the scorching sun.

Having been summarily banished and humiliated, the Windsors had clearly decided that there was only so far they were prepared to go in lowering their sights. The Duke, after all, was once a king and emperor, monarch of the greatest empire in the history of mankind. He had been educated to think on a large scale, in international terms, and was sensitive to the nuances of diplomatic rank. To find himself Governor of the Bahamas, a necklace of tiny isles and rocks on the fringes of the Caribbean Sea, was bad enough. To be forced to suffer untold indignity in sub-standard accommodation was intolerable. He demanded costly refurbishment of the house and landscaping of the gardens, the money to be found by the local Assembly, and promptly moved elsewhere until the work was done. In fact, he and the Duchess found temporary shelter at Westbourne, which within three years was to feature in their lives in ways they could never have imagined.

Those who ran the Bahamas at the time were somewhat put out by the Duke's high-handedness, but in London his attitude came as no surprise. One of the Duke's most irritating characteristics was a petulant insistence on having his own way, with no regard for the practicalities or consequences of his demands. It was a legacy of his over-indulged childhood, and as natural to him as the ease with which he accepted the deference of the people. Unreasonable demands had been a feature of his life. Now those demands were given additional impetus by the discomfiting realities of his new position. If his dignity were to survive, he must protest. And protest he did.

Churchill had shown admirable forebearance in the face of the Duke's childish impetuosity in the past, but grew increasingly annoyed when he placed his own convenience and comfort above the more important issues of the day. Churchill felt, with reason, that wartime by its nature necessitated a certain frugality, even in the upper reaches of society. If the Duke's brother and his wife – both forced into unwanted regal responsibilities by his abdication – were prepared to endure the London Blitz, with German bombers putting their lives in danger night after night, was it really asking too much for the Windsors to make do with the faded grandeur of a colonial mansion in the tropics, far from the falling bombs? The contrast between the relative comforts of his own job and the irksome and dangerous duties of his shy brother's new role in London were evidently lost on the Duke, whose own welfare was secondary only in importance to his wife's, which to him was paramount.

This selfishness, and arrogant disregard for reality, were to become increasingly irritating features of the Windsor style. They were unconcerned about the sacrifice of others, but wanted their own needs taken care of instantly. In later life, long after their Nassau sojourn was over, these traits would become even more marked as they traipsed from one soiree to another around the world, living a worthless life among air-headed socialites and titled nonentities. Self-indulgence seemed to be their life's mission, compensation no doubt for the more substantial treasures they had missed, by having neither jobs nor family of their own.

Even with its facelift, Government House, Nassau, was far from their ideal as a home. Its furnishings were less than opulent, its rooms less than grand in the European style. Whatever embellishments it acquired during refurbishment, it was essentially an official residence for a relatively low-ranking colonial administrator, and bore all the modest features of such. For a man whose life had been lived largely in magnificent palaces, with liveried flunkies all around, it fell well short of the salubrious. By far its best feature was its outlook, a vividly coloured vista taking in the busy life of Nassau harbour, the quiet offshore Hog Island, and a great sweep of aquamarine sea stretching away towards Florida in the north. Many times, the Duke would stand at an upstairs window and gaze out, contemplating no doubt the great events taking place beyond the distant horizon. Events in which, had he done his duty, he would have been very much involved. Instead, he was in charge of affairs on a distant, sun-bleached rock. It must have hurt deeply.

New Providence island, on which Nassau stands, is twenty-one miles long and seven miles wide, most of it bush and scrubland with virtually no soil. Formed of honey-coloured rock, with swamps at one end, the island has few natural assets apart from its splendid beaches, gin-clear seas, almost perpetual sunshine and, of course, its location only a few miles off Florida's shoreline. Its place on the map has, in fact, been its fortune, for it is difficult to imagine any island of its kind surviving in the way it has, had it been placed in less hospitable latitudes. Proximity to the United States has blessed it with untold opportunities, not all of them legal, but invariably lucrative. Many of its inhabitants have built considerable wealth through nefarious schemes. And it was largely the descendants of wreckers and blockade runners who ran the Bahamas when the Windsors arrived.

As Governor, the Duke was more than a titular head. Although the Executive Council was, in effect, the "Cabinet" of the day, he wielded considerable power over the islands' affairs, in theory at least. The problem was that the Bahamas, a neglected outcrop of empire with little to commend it but a stunning climate and incomparable seas, had been allowed to go its own way for so long that it had developed an irritatingly mulish attitude towards London's authority.

With low outgoings, and enough in import duty to keep life ticking over, the Bahamas was in a position to reject London's financial support and preserve a measure of independence. With little leverage, London was impotent in the face of the ruling whites' intransigence. Tension between Nassau and London centred on social development – or, rather, lack of it. Bay Street was against public spending to elevate living conditions for the blacks, and London was in no position to enforce it. Windsor's predecessor, Dundas, was acutely aware of this impasse and vented his views on it. But his protestations had little or no impact.

In the 1940s, Nassau's population was around 40,000, most of them descendants of the negro slaves brought to the islands during the 18th century. These people had, over the centuries, developed gradations of colour that were to determine their place in Bahamian society. To be ebony black was rated right up to the late 1960s as the least enviable hue, for it meant you were almost invariably an unskilled worker, in the bottom rank of the social order. To be brown, with possibly a hint of whiteness in your complexion from some long forgotten sexual union, was undoubtedly preferable, for it meant your blackness had been diluted. If your facial features were recognisably European, with a bone structure distinctive from a pure African countenance, so much the better. The mulattoes, people of mixed blood with an undisputed trace of whiteness, were higher still in the racial ranks. And those who professed to be white, with a direct line of descent from the early settlers, were the summit of Nassau society, a mutually supportive grouping who had become the colony's merchants and professionals. In later days, a black politician called Clarence Bain was to emerge, who would sum up Bahamian racial consciousness in a simple three-line rhyme. "If you're white, you're all right, if you're brown, stick around, if you're black, stand back." This became a kind of mantra during the days of political change in the 1960s, and was used to inflame the racial tensions that powered the moves to majority rule, and, ultimately, independence.

But until then, the councils of power, including the Assembly itself, were dominated by the white group, who used their economic might to wield authority in ways that must have surprised the Duke. In fact, the prevailing social order in Nassau offended the Duke's political sensibilities and cut across the basic principles he embraced, about keeping the lower orders in a state of well-fed compliance. The ruling elite were not only totally self-absorbed and offensively avaricious, they showed scant regard for democracy, and were happy to keep the black majority pinned down in their filthy slums, with neither economic nor political power. Though there was a democratic framework in place, courtesy of British colonial traditions, the actual mechanics of balloting were so corrupt that the whites seemed destined to retain power forever. Gerrymandering, vote-buying and intimidation were commonplace. In later years, I was told categorically, by a surviving member of the Bay Street Boys white merchant clique, that five pounds per vote was the going rate in the years preceding the rise to power of the blacks in 1967. There was no hint of shame when he described the system, for morality had little meaning in Bahamian politics, either before or after the "quiet revolution" of that significant decade. The blacks learnt well from their white masters and devised their own means of securing votes during the 1970s and 1980s. While money and other material gifts were undoubtedly part of the story, their inducements were more aligned to victimisation, the denial of jobs and government contracts.

As a young reporter, I recall covering Out Island elections when party workers would disappear into the humble shacks for ten minutes or so at a time when, I always assumed, the illicit transactions would take place. The gullible islanders, fearful and poor, were happy to accept the election-time largesse of their white masters and did not seem to see it as selling their rights. What were "rights" anyway when impoverishment was the norm? Five pounds was enough to add extra spice to life for a week or two, maybe a bottle or two of rum, and that was important for people who subsisted on a diet of fish and grits and little else. The whites, meanwhile, grew increasingly complacent, happy to keep the Bahamian electoral process literally decades behind the times. Incredibly, women were denied the vote until 1962.

When the Duke arrived in Nassau, therefore, he was confronted by a system which was egregiously unjust. The white merchants not only had the entire electoral process sewn up to their advantage, they were in a position to exploit the black majority commercially without mercy. Living on an island with no means of feeding itself from its own meagre resources, the blacks were a captive market for traders, who brought in goods from America and the Caribbean, and lived grandly off the handsome profits they squeezed from their poorer countrymen. The whites saw themselves as an immoveable force and did little to restrain the arrogance that became the natural by-product of their smugness. One observer was to describe the white Bahamian rulers of this period as even more crassly elitist than their counterparts in Africa and Asia. Their attitude was typical of those who would eventually lead the British Empire down the road to ruin. But in the 1940s, the Nassau clique's position looked impregnable.

Add to all this the problem of blatant racial discrimination and you can begin to imagine that the Bahamas, though outwardly calm, had the potential to explode. There was no doubt that white Bahamians perpetuated the slavemaster mentality right into the middle of the twentieth century. While the blacks had technically been liberated from slavery in the 1830s, they were still effectively denied access to political or economic power. In the 1940s, they still constituted the labouring classes and lived at a markedly lower level in every sense than the whites, who saw them as genetically inferior. There was a strong belief among the most bigoted of them that blacks were idle, feckless, dishonest and incapable of running their own affairs.

Until 1956, blacks were denied access to downtown hotels, restaurants and theatres. The colour bar was as real, if not quite so fraught and explosive, as that in Alabama or Georgia, with all the same and wholly understandable feelings of resentment and anger that went with it. Though basically docile and forgiving, showing none of the volatility of their Haitian brothers to the south, black Bahamians were becoming increasingly uncomfortable with their lot, and the first sure sign of their restiveness came within two years of the Duke's appointment. In 1942, Nassau experienced its first street riots, an event which sent a chill down the Governor's back, for here was a disturbing vindication of his belief that despotic and heartless governments spawn revolution. The riots quickly petered out, but a template had been laid for the future and ought to have forewarned the colony's rulers of the likely consequences if reforms were not forthcoming. However, although racial discrimination was formally ended by a parliamentary resolution in 1956, and all public facilities were opened up to blacks for the first time, the Bay Street Boys continued to control affairs as they always had, with self-interest the dominant dynamic and social equality so far down their agenda that it was out of sight. It suited them to keep the blacks down educationally and economically. To do otherwise, they reasoned, would probably fragment the system which kept them in power over an ethnic majority which outnumbered them eight or nine to one.

The Windsors found little to interest them among the white Bahamian elite of the day. They considered them dim, insular and incestuous, with little time for anything beyond the shoreline of their tiny reef, except those events that might affect their own well-being. To ease their feelings of social claustrophobia, the couple sought temporary escapes to Palm Beach in Florida, where some of their well-heeled friends lived far from the deprivations of war. For the most part, though, they fulfilled the humdrum duties of a minor colonial administrator and his wife, the Duke attending to the formalities of governorship, the Duchess engaged in voluntary work, mainly with the local branch of the Red Cross and the Allied service personnel who were in Nassau for wartime training.

There were, however, three Nassau residents who caught the couple's imagination, and these formed the foundation of whatever social life they were able to enjoy during their Bahamas sojourn. One was Axel Wenner-Gren, a Swedish industrialist who founded the Electrolux empire and had set up home on Hog Island, a limestone outcrop lying across the harbour from Nassau. The second was Harold Christie, a thrusting young white Bahamian real estate merchant who was keen to market the Bahamas to the wealthy of the world. And the third was Sir Harry Oakes, a straight-talking former prospector with lots of money and no class who was to become the central figure in the murder mystery of the age.

These friendships were to play a crucial role in the events of summer and autumn 1943. They were to cast shadows of suspicion over the Duke which were never dispelled and remain even more damaging to his name today than they were in his lifetime.

Chapter Three

UNDER SUSPICION

W HEN the Duke of Windsor received news of Sir Harry's death on the morning of 8 July, 1943, he responded in a way which left behind an odour that has never been wholly dispelled. His first move was to impose a news blackout, a tactic he never explained but which deepened all the misgivings his critics harboured about his judgment. His second was to bring in two detectives from Miami whose investigations were to raise more questions than they answered. His third was to jump to hasty conclusions and point to a Mauritian playboy and philanderer, Count Alfred de Marigny, as the only realistic suspect. His fourth was to thwart, seemingly at all costs, any attempt to cast suspicion on the local realtor, Harold Christie.

There are apologists, including one or two authors who have written books about the case, who say the Duke's handling of the Oakes investigation was merely another example of his ineptitude. Here was a man, they say, who was unused to taking life's big decisions, who flunked his chance at kingship, who had known little outside the closed world of the Royals and their aristocratic friends, was almost childishly preoccupied with his wife and their relationship, and found the enormity of the Oakes case simply too much to cope with. The picture that emerges is of a woebegone, hapless soul who, having been given a small job in a distant land, had unexpectedly been confronted with a gigantic problem with serious and wide-ranging ramifications which were beyond him. All of this constitutes an extremely charitable view which fails to stand up to scrutiny.

The Duke's response to the Oakes murder, in the light of information which has surfaced over the last thirty years, is really capable of only one plausible interpretation: that he was involved in a enormous conspiracy and cover-up and that he was prepared to send an innocent man to the gallows in an attempt to save himself, and his friends, from the kind of intense scrutiny that might well have resulted from a full and proper investigation. One would need to be extremely ingenuous to think otherwise, and in this chapter we can set about examining the reasons why.

Once apprised of the details of Sir Harry's demise, the Duke pondered his options. It took him some time to act, and by the time the news blackout was imposed, the basic details had already been sent to the wire services – Reuters, Associated Press and United Press– by Etienne Dupuch, The Tribune editor who was to have discussed subsistence farming with Sir Harry on the day he died. It could be that the blackout was the instinctive response of an ex-king used to the kind of press manipulation that was common in Britain at the time. In the upper reaches of British society, there was an entrenched belief that the public should be told only what was good for them. Although a free press existed in theory, it never enjoyed the constitutional protection American newspapers, for instance, took for granted. Among British editors and proprietors, there was a good deal of deference, and especially towards members of the Royal Family, who were considered more or less inviolable during an era when everyone was expected to know his place. As with much else in Britain, decisions on what should or should not be revealed were taken behind the closed doors of gentlemen's clubs. There were a number of unspoken rules that everyone was expected to obey on the pain of exclusion. The Duke himself had benefited from this arrangement as the abdication crisis loomed. The lords and ladies who ruled the London press of the day relished gossip which they resolutely declined to share with their readers. The Duke would, therefore, have felt on safe ground, with arbitrary censorship well within his remit. However, as time passed, the considered opinion was that he was buying time to collect his thoughts and devise his strategy. Eventually, after a delay of some three hours, he duly informed the Colonial Office in London of the calamity on his doorstep, and prepared himself for the fall-out.

The Duke's action baffled the Americans. Newsmen in New York kept asking their Nassau contacts why no information was forthcoming. In a country where the press's constitutional rights were enshrined in the First Amendment, journalists were perplexed by the British colonial administration's apparent taste for secrecy. Having already gauged the dimensions of the story, with its American, Canadian and British angles, its high society flourishes, and the reluctant involvement of the Windsors, the news agencies were eager to go to town on the details. All the western world's major titles were waiting to run banner headlines on the brutal death of the Empire's wealthiest man. It was a welcome break from the daily diet of war, and possessed an element of celebrity glitter, which readers craved in such grim times. But the Duke remained unforthcoming. A tight cordon was drawn around the case, giving rise to often fanciful speculation. The press, with little to go on from primary sources, had to make do with secondary sources and even hearsay. Rumours ran wild. In the climate of the times, it was assumed by some that wartime restrictions were merely being rigorously enforced, and that the Duke was doing no more than one would have expected of him. But time has changed that perception. The conclusion now is that he had something to hide.

By calling in the detectives Melchen and Barker from Miami, the Duke was safeguarding himself from the kind of unwelcome probing that would almost certainly have resulted had he summoned either Scotland Yard from London, or the FBI from Washington. The former could have been relied upon to snoop on behalf of the British Establishment, which had no time for the errant Duke, and the FBI, under the redoubtable J Edgar Hoover, was already a known enemy of the Windsors, primarily because of their Nazi connections. With no faith in the local force, largely made up of inexperienced black officers headed by a colonial commissioner, the Duke opted for the Miami duo, later to be called "the Laurel and Hardy of crime detection" because of what appeared, on the face of it, to be incompetence of majestic proportions.

As we shall see, the activities of Melchen and Barker in this affair can no longer be dismissed as mere incompetence. It would be stretching credibility well beyond breaking point to suggest that two experienced officers could be so dumb, or careless, or both. Given Melchen's previous social contacts with the Duke, and Barker's deep-seated dishonesty, which was later to be exposed in full, the likelihood of collusion appears convincing, if not overwhelming. The only realistic conclusion to be drawn is that both men were caught up in a larger conspiracy, and instructed to organise the evidence in such a way that it pointed to a single, unchallengeable conclusion. And the prime mover in that conspiracy was, we can safely assume, the Duke of Windsor himself.

To understand why the Duke would find himself in such a predicament, it is necessary to appreciate his state of mind at the time, and the attitudes of the British and American authorities towards himself and his wife. While their banishment to the Bahamas was an expedient for removing them from Europe, and thus keeping them out of trouble, it was by no means a case of "out of sight, out of mind." Although the British public at large was allowed to cherish its romantic notions about the couple, seeing them as wronged lovers who had fallen foul of an emotionally constipated Establishment, those in the know considered them dangerous, unpredictable and potentially treasonous. The Americans, renowned for their paranoia, especially in political matters, were even more disturbed by them. To have to contend with left-leaning college intellectuals was bad enough (and there were many of them around at the time), but that was nothing to the job of containing, and possibly neutralising, a right-wing Royal, his outspoken wife and their fascist friends.

In the Bahamas, the Duke was, by his own admission, under-employed. Not only did he feel the governorship was beneath him, he regarded the work as routine and uninspiring. In the diplomatic hierarchy of the day, when the Empire was still a real force in world affairs, and the great Dominions were emerging as powerful units in their own right, the Bahamas governorship was very small beer indeed. To keep himself sane in exile, the Duke applied himself to his colonial duties with diligence. If there was one positive aspect to his appointment, it was that he undertook his administrative work conscientiously. Though the petty rituals and routines of colonial office in such a small outpost of Empire must have bored him intensely, he applied himself with impressive zeal. Judged purely on day-to-day performance, he was considered by Bahamians to be a success as governor throughout his five-year stay, with more drive and energy than some of the time-servers they had been burdened with in the past. At the time, the Duke was eager to please, not so much because of any special sentiments towards the Bahamas, but for future reference when he tried to move his career forward. He felt a high-ranking ambassadorial post was a natural objective, and a good showing in the Bahamas would help his cause.

Though not in itself onerous, the job of Bahamas Governor was no cakewalk. Its pressures were not so much related to workload as the unusual attitudes that prevailed among the white rulers. In every minor attempted reform, the Duke was thwarted. Milo Butler, a black merchant who thirty years later would become the first Bahamian Governor-General, an unlikely successor to the race-conscious Windsors, summed up the resentment of the masses by saying: "Men get tired of being debarred from happiness." Butler campaigned to raise the colony's minimum wage to four shillings a day, but the whites were characteristically bullish in their resistance. The lawyer, Godfrey Higgs, who would later figure largely in the de Marigny trial, used his parliamentary seat to voice the ruling class's concern. "Much of the labour employed in this colony is hired as a form of charity," he said. In fact, he was probably right, which added to the Duke's exasperation.

Inevitably, unemployment was his forte. His famous comment about the Welsh miners, when his rather superficial compassion was given expression for the first time, found an echo in the Bahamas, where thousands of blacks were out of work. One of the tasks the Duke set himself was to create livelihoods for the unemployed in a land where the economy was virtually non-existent. With no oil, no soil, no industry, and precious little commerce, the Bahamas was largely a land without purpose. In 1492, when he discovered the New World, Christopher Columbus stumbled ashore on the remote Bahamian island of San Salvador and quickly decided there was nothing there to detain him. He moved on to more promising terrain, notably the Caribbean island of Hispaniola to the south, which was to become a rich Spanish foothold in the free world.

Although four centuries had elapsed since the explorer's fleeting visit, little had changed apart from the forced departure of the Lucayan Indians, who were subsequently worked to death by the Spanish in their new Caribbean holdings, and the arrival of the Crown loyalists and their slaves, who were to build the modern Bahamas. Apart from the occasional boom period, when the islanders were able to cash in on nefarious schemes of one kind or another, such as blockade-running and bootlegging, there was little happening in the islands. It's true that cotton plantations were established in the southern isles after loyalists arrived from America in the 1780s, but a pattern of failure soon developed as various agricultural schemes were tried and abandoned. In the 1940s, much of the Bahamas was economically backward, with subsistence farming and fishing the only means of survival.

The book *Out Island Doctor*, by American settler Evans Cottmann, indicates just how real and deep Bahamian poverty was at this time, especially in the southern isles far from Nassau. In Crooked Island and Acklins, for instance, the unvarying diet consisted of dried fish and grits, with virtually no fruit and vegetables. This lack of nutrition had a physical impact, particularly on the digestive system. As Dr Cottmann was to discover, abdominal ailments were commonplace.

In Nassau, the Duke set about canvassing his high society pals for help in work creation schemes, and it was this initiative which brought him into close contact with the Swedish industrialist Axel Wenner-Gren, who had set up home on Hog Island, an elongated strip of prime real estate lying a few hundred yards off Nassau's waterfront. This friendship was to help deepen suspicions about the Duke and his Nazi ties, and, subsequently, his role in the Oakes affair.

Wenner-Gren was an enigmatic figure before and during the war, and remains one to this day. He was an imposing man, shrewd in business, and successful enough to imagine that his word was gospel, on the big events then engulfing western man. It was frequently said that he considered himself far more important than he actually was, and that his advice was often offered where it was not always welcome. That he had pre-war connections with Herman Goering and the Krupp munitions family in Germany is beyond doubt. Whether he shared their ideals is the point on which few can agree.

In the Bahamas, Wenner-Gren had indeed found his Shangri-la. In fact, that is the name he gave his home on Hog Island, which, many years later, would become the famous destination resort of Paradise Island, with its luxurious hotels and casinos. His beautiful yacht, *Southern Cross*, was frequently moored off-shore, and in it he plied the fine clear turquoise waters of the Bahamas and the deeper blue expanses of the Caribbean. In those days, there was no bridge to Hog Island from downtown Nassau (there are now two) and Wenner-Gren was able to regard it as his private domain, a splendid off-shore haven within sight and sound of the tiny colonial city, but cut off from the populace by the harbour itself. A small launch took him ashore whenever he wanted to leave his idyllic retreat.

It was inevitable that the Duke and Wenner-Gren would strike up a friendship because they had so much in common. For a start, they were markedly teutonic, with fair skin, blond hair and blue eyes. If one were to pick two characters to fit Adolf Hitler's physical ideal, this pair would be among the front-runners as archetypal Aryans. They were emphatically northern European in looks and manner, pallid products of colder climes with a slightly haughty air and a barely concealed contempt for their inferiors. Secondly, both had close contacts with the Nazi regime in Germany before hostilities began. Thirdly, both had an intense interest in money. And lastly, they badly needed like-minded company during the inconvenience of exile. They became firm friends.

Together, the Duke and Wenner-Gren conjured up a work-creation scheme, which was to keep the locals chattering, on and off, for more than sixty years, as they debated the "real" motives behind it. Wenner-Gren wanted Bahamian labour to help in the construction of two canals on Hog Island. Using hand-picks, the men would cut through the soft limestone rock to create deep channels, presumably so that the wealthy Swede could offer seaborne access into the centre of the island to his boating friends. When the labourers' gossip trickled through Nassau, more sinister motives were attributed to Wenner-Gren and his unusual scheme. As U-Boat activity built up in the Atlantic, some Bahamians believed that the canals were, in fact, secret hiding places for German crews and that Wenner-Gren was deliberately providing refuge for the enemy on British territory.

Right up to the turn of the twenty-first century, gossip about Wenner-Gren and the U-Boat crews persisted in Nassau. It flared up again in the Bahamian press in 2001, when part of a U-Boat was found on the seabed off the Bahamian isle of Abaco, in water generally considered a sea route between Nassau and the north Atlantic. This otherwise innocuous metal panel was cited as tangible evidence that Wenner-Gren and the Nazis were in cahoots, for the armed submarines would have passed that way from their Hog Island "base" into the Atlantic, where they would do their worst to Allied shipping. The suggestion was that German submarines would enter Hog

Island's canals, under cover of darkness, so that their crews could "rest up" between manoeuvres. With little boat traffic between Nassau and Hog Island, save for occasional ferry trips for staff, and no air traffic apart from training flights from the distant airfield, locals felt all kinds of clandestine activity could be going on behind the swaying casuarinas and seagrapes across the water. But no-one ever produced a shred of proof.

Even at that distance in time, the off-spring of Wenner-Gren's friends felt compelled to rebut stories that appeared in *The Tribune*, Nassau's respected daily newspaper, recording people's suspicions. Although Wenner-Gren himself was long dead, they were upset that such calumny should persist after so long and presented evidence to disprove the suspicions. It must be said that their arguments were persuasive. The canals were not deep enough, or wide enough, to accommodate U-Boats and, in any event, would the Germans seriously try to rest up on an island within five miles of an Allied airbase, from which training flights were taking off daily, to fly low over surrounding waters? It seems very doubtful indeed.

However, other suspicions about Wenner-Gren were less easy to disprove or dismiss, and these are the ones that most concern his involvement with the Windsors. While Wenner-Gren's apologists suggest he was emphatically anti-Nazi once hostilities had broken out, and that his sympathies lay entirely with the Allied cause, there are others who believe the Swede was much too astute to take up uncompromising positions before the outcome of the war was effectively settled. They argue that, with his pre-war business contacts in Germany, he would be much more likely to hedge his bets, and bide his time, before coming down hard on either side.

Wenner-Gren was, by any reckoning, an extraordinary man with prodigious gifts. He was more than simply a hard-working entrepreneur: he was both inspired and inventive, with a keen sense of what would work and what wouldn't. He also had an instinctive appreciation of whatever market he was seeking to enter, knowing what was required by the consumer and when. Alongside his business genius (and his admirers insist this was not too grand a term for him), he possessed an astuteness in identifying, and nurturing, useful contacts. The war would have thrown up a multitude of conundrums for any businessman with an eye to the future, but he was alert to them all, and was seeking ways to accommodate any eventuality.

When he first met the Duke, the war was far from being a done deal. Britain was under serious threat, the United States had still to enter the war, the German-Russian pact was still in force and France had fallen. There was a very strong possibility at that time that Hitler would continue his march across Europe and establish himself as an unassailable force. In such an eventuality, Wenner-Gren and his kind would have big decisions to make. It was not a time for burning bridges.

Even so, in 2001, long after his death, his supporters contended that all suspicions surrounding Wenner-Gren, during the early war years, were without foundation. When the U-Boat conspiracy theory re-emerged that year, Mr Orjan Lindroth, whose father Arne managed Wenner-Gren's financial affairs in the Bahamas, dismissed categorically any suggestion that the wealthy Swede dug canals to accommodate German submarines. And he maintained unequivocally that Wenner-Gren's sympathies were always with the Allies.

"The speculation makes no sense at all," said Mr Lindroth. It was preposterous to suggest that Nazi Germany would send a prominent industrialist on his 400-foot yacht to a distant British colony to act as an agent for Hitler. "Wenner-Gren did a lot for this country," he said, "It's all idle speculation and I would challenge anyone to produce one piece of evidence to support it."

Mr Lindroth went further and declared it was time to lay the matter to rest, once and for all. Wenner-Gren, he said, had been blacklisted by the Allies during the war to his considerable financial detriment, but two official investigations later cleared him of collusion with the Nazis. "I was a boy and he was a man in his seventies when we met, but my father worked for him in Sweden before being brought to the Bahamas to manage Hog Island. He was a very kind and imposing figure and very well-respected. He was bright, interested in ideas and very scientific. My parents always thought very highly of him. They thought of him as a very decent person. But he was really hurt by the blacklisting."

Dr Wenner-Gren was born into a modest Gothenberg family in the 1880s, but rose by hard work, inventive genius and great vision to become one of the premier international industrialists of his generation. He was the brain behind Electrolux, which marketed vacuum cleaners worldwide, buying into the former Lux Company, spearheading its sales drive and transforming the renamed business into a major success story, finally becoming outright owner. He was also involved in Saab and the Swedish telephone company but, said Mr Lindroth, he never traded with the Germans.

Wenner-Gren's activities were, however, enough to prompt the Allies' suspicion and their response was sufficiently drastic to cause him major problems. Their decision to "neutralize" him by freezing his assets wreaked financial havoc from which, according to Mr Lindroth, he never fully recovered. At the time of his death, he said, his fortune had been severely depleted.

According to all those who dismiss Wenner-Gren's alleged Nazi links, the Swede's meddling and "imperial" manner were his downfall. Like many highly successful businessmen, he fell into believing that he had all the answers, even in global politics. His know-all attitude, and unshakeable belief that he could succeed, where the politicians had failed, in securing solutions to the world's mounting problems, caused him considerable difficulties with both the Germans and the Allies. His pre-war meeting with Goering was a vainglorious attempt to act as peace-broker between the major powers, but diaries read out at the Nuremberg Trials showed clearly that the Nazis dismissed his ideas out of hand. In the Nazis' eyes, it seemed, he was nothing more than a tiresome meddler.

Dr Wenner-Gren came to the notice of the Americans early in the war, when his yacht picked up survivors from the passenger ship Athenia, which was torpedoed off Ireland by a German submarine. The Swede was heading from Stockholm to the Bahamas at the time, and in touch with the US Secretary of State, Sumner Wells, about the mass rescue, taking the opportunity to make known his own views about the conduct of the war.

According to Mr Lindroth, questions were then asked about Wenner-Gren – how he happened to be close by when the Athenia was hit, how he was a friend of the Krupp family, and how he was once in touch with Goering. Together with a "character assassination" by the US Ambassador to Mexico, where Wenner-Gren took refuge for much of the war, the circumstantial evidence against him became too powerful to resist, for those who wanted to believe in his involvement. Even though he enlisted the help of his friend, Herbert Hoover,

Wenner-Gren was never able to eliminate the disastrous effects of his blacklisting. With all his bank accounts frozen, he was forced to sell off Electrolux stock just to live. "The blacklisting meant that, as an international businessman, his hands were tied behind his back," said Mr Lindroth.

Yet, he added, diaries kept by Dr Wenner-Gren and Goering showed beyond any reasonable doubt that the Swede was not a Nazi sympathiser. "He was a dyed-in-the-wool capitalist. He was not a communist and not a fascist," he said.

"Everything he did was contrary to the belief that he supported the Nazis. He even moved his assets to Allied territories. The canal theory was similar to all the other allegations about him. Officially, there was no evidence," he added.

Mr Lindroth said Dr Wenner-Gren's name was hand-written into the Allies' blacklist, with no reasons given, suggesting it was an afterthought with no supporting evidence.

When the war was over, and the heat was off, Wenner-Gren returned to the Bahamas from Mexico, and eventually sold off his Hog Island properties to the multi-millionaire Huntington Hartford, who, in turn, sold it to Resorts International, as the renamed Paradise Island in the mid-1960s. Eventually, in the mid-1990s, the land was bought by Sun International, the South African family company which transformed it into the highly-successful Atlantis resort of today.

Mr Lindroth's final comment on the Wenner-Gren mystery states: "His roots were in the western economies, and it is a documented fact that he was **not** a friend of Goering, as some people have suggested. He was misguided and probably arrogant, but you can't accuse him of being pro-German. He did have a relationship with the Krupp family, but that was a personal one...if you are a successful businessman, you are going to meet successful businessmen from elsewhere. Are people going to be operating a sub in a canal when there are 20,000 British servicemen parading around Nassau? I would say categorically that it simply isn't true." His view is reinforced by a veteran American serviceman who paddled a canoe through the canals.

"There is no room for a U-boat in there," he said. "There's seven feet of water at most. It's an impossibility."

True or not, the gossip proved remarkably durable. But the submarine theory has less relevance, in the Windsor-Wenner-Gren relationship, than actions the Swede was taking, to rectify his financial affairs and lay the foundations for his future. These were to spread suspicion, not just about Wenner-Gren himself, but the Duke and his wife, and Sir Harry Oakes. For the Windsors, it was becoming increasingly clear that the gulf between income and outgoings was never going to be adequately bridged by the Duke's earning capacity in years to come. His abdication had made it difficult, if not impossible, for him ever to return to the United Kingdom. The suspicion of the Americans would block any career possibilities there. His unsuitability for anything worthwhile, coupled with his outrageous indiscretions, made him a natural candidate for the labour exchange, yet his unique status rendered such ignominy an impossibility. In the early stages of the war, the Duke was as aware of his predicament as anyone else. His meagre $3,000 a year salary as Governor of the Bahamas was inadequate for his needs. And, with scant prospects on the employement scene, the future seemed financially bleak.

But the Duke was not poor by any reasonable reckoning. As Prince of Wales before becoming king, he received substantial revenues from the Duchy of Cornwall (estimated at £250,000 a year), and was given £1.2 million by his grandmother, Queen Alexandra. The Cornwall connection also guaranteed him £30,000-plus a year for life, not to mention the Civil List contribution to his upkeep, which Royal discretion ensured was kept a secret. But more important still were the invisible benefits of being the Duke of Windsor. Even so, the couple were not spectacularly wealthy by the standards of those whose company they kept. Friendship with the likes of Wenner-Gren had its rewards. For a start, the Duke and Duchess were able to enjoy the lifestyle of the mega-rich without necessarily being mega-rich themselves. With their colourful backgrounds and impressive titles, they had something to offer in return, by way of social cachet and a certain raffish appeal. But all things are relative and titles, even spiced by a breath of scandal, did not put venison on the table, and it was the prospect of a life of relative deprivation, with his income failing to match his phenomenal outgoings, that prompted the Duke into his next spot of bother.

The Windsors were convinced, right up until the early 1940s, that Britain was going to lose the war. Their pessimism was unequivocal.

In such an eventuality, they would presumably have been well-treated by their Nazi friends, who had plans for them in a captive Britain as puppet monarchs. However, when the tide of war began to turn, and a German victory became increasingly unlikely, they had to give serious consideration to supporting themselves in the future, knowing that resources from Britain would be limited. This is where Wenner-Gren's friendship became really useful because, apart from the expertise in financial management he was able to offer, he also had a convenient hiding place in which to stockpile cash. This was a bank he had formed in Mexico, and it was now suspected, by senior intelligence officials, that this bank was used by the Duke to reinforce his own financial position, keeping money away from prying eyes by secreting it in private accounts. It is not difficult to imagine the appeal Wenner-Gren's banking arrangements had for the Duke and Sir Harry Oakes. Both were obsessed by money and the awesome responsibility of protecting what they had in troubled times. Both had eyes on the future. Mexico, it seemed, was less likely to be hit by the fall-out of the war than any of the countries more markedly aligned with either of the two sides. So the temptations were obvious.

As the Duke became increasingly interested in any investment opportunities he could lay hands on, Wenner-Gren accommodated him, by offering to transfer cash from Nassau into the Mexico bank. Intelligence agents suspected that the Swede's banking activities in Mexico were for the purpose of hiding Nazi money, which would then be used in the event of defeat to finance the lifestyles of any party leaders who managed to flee to South America, where right-wing regimes were waiting to offer refuge. The Duke would not have felt uncomfortable in such company. The transfer of funds from Nassau to Mexico would have breached British wartime currency regulations, but the Duke was ready to take the risk because of its importance to his future well-being. If Sir Harry Oakes was involved in similar illicit transactions, it was almost certainly in preparation for his threatened move from the Bahamas to Mexico with his family. Had they been caught, imprisonment would almost certainly have followed, but in the Bahamas – traditionally a haven for villains and brigands – morality had a way of becoming skewed. Ethics were an alien concept.

At the time of these suspected financial manoeuvres, Wenner-Gren was thought to be custodian of some $100 million in Latin

America, most of it other people's money. That the Duke had substantial deposits in the Swede's safekeeping is near certain, his attempts to camouflage his assets once again showing flagrant disregard for his homeland, and its understandable restraints on currency movements at a time of national peril. With his usual petulance, he deeply resented restrictions imposed by London, which used exchange control to protect assets for the war effort, and selfishly sought to circumvent them. He was easily led into Wenner-Gren's web of intrigue. Interestingly, German documents were later to reveal that the Duke during this period was maintaining contacts with the Nazis, a claim which, if true, had deeply disturbing implications. It gives rise to a worrying scenario, with the Duke and Wenner-Gren possibly involved in the hoarding of Nazi riches while the Allies were struggling to achieve victory on the battlefields of Europe, the Far East and in Africa.

It is against this backdrop that the Duke was obliged to make all the key decisions surrounding the Oakes murder. At the time, he was twitchy, anxious and up to no good. It is hardly surprising that he chose to hand the investigation over to Melchen and Barker, whose detection work in Nassau was to be cited, for years to come, as "how not to investigate a murder" in police academies throughout Britain and the United States. Unlike Scotland Yard or the FBI, they would ask none of the really troublesome questions, that were bound to arise in Nassau, regarding the Duke, Oakes and Wenner-Gren and the vast amounts of money being moved into Central America. In every sense, they were the least troublesome option. And, of course, they were compliant, a quality the Duke required them to have above all others.

Chapter Four

ON THE BRINK OF A CONFESSION

THE popular image of Melchen and Barker is of two blundering hick cops from Florida who were in well over their heads when they were summoned by the Duke to investigate the Oakes murder. But, it is an image that is difficult to accept, and for several compelling reasons. What transpired during the scene-of-crime inquiries, their interviewing of potential witnesses, and later at the trial of Count Alfred de Marigny, suggests that they were briefed, right from the start, as co-conspirators in a plot to frame an innocent man. And, if necessary, to send him to the gallows.

It's true that Barker had risen with puzzling speed in the Miami force. It's also true that his career pattern was unusual. The leap from motor-cycle cop to fingerprint supremo seemed to have been made with few of the troublesome intermediate steps. But, like Melchen, he had many years of first-hand police experience behind him, with both their careers stretching back to the mid-1920s. So he was no rookie. He was well-acquainted with the rudiments of investigative procedure.

If you accept that the Duke had something to hide, was eager to protect the self-serving clique who ran the Bahamas in those days, was disinclined to frame a black man because of the social disorder it might cause, especially bearing in mind the Nassau labour riots of the year before, then it is not surprising that the character who finally faced trial for the murder of Sir Harry Oakes was de Marigny, the Mauritian rake who had seduced and eloped with Oakes' teenage daughter Nancy in a manner which most found disrespectful, impertinent and irresponsible.

The flamboyant "Freddy" as he was known to his friends and intimates, was everything the Duke could not abide. On the face of it, de Marigny was a bogus nobleman from a distant Pacific isle with highly suspicious antecedents, who preyed on any woman impressionable enough to be taken in by his oily charm. The French connection added to his mystique, and deepened the misgivings of every husband in town who had the fortune, or maybe misfortune, to be married to a pretty wife. There were even rumours, never proved, that he dropped Spanish Fly into women's drinks, to make them more compliant in offering up their sexual favours. In any event, he was considered disreputable and possibly deviant. True to his type, de Marigny liked stylish clothes, fancy cars and fine wines, spoke in the mellifluous tones of the practised charlatan, and gave the impression he was a good deal wealthier than he was. In 1943, de Marigny was in his prime, his early thirties, with first-hand experience of the ways of the world, an insight into human frailties, and a habit of getting what he wanted. In the enclosed Nassau society of the day, he was regarded with suspicion, not just because he was obviously "foreign", but because of his silken, gallic urbanity, which the colony's upper-crust found distasteful.

When his sights settled on Nancy Oakes, all their worst fears were, seemingly, confirmed. Not only was Nancy half his age, and apparently ridiculously naive with it, she was heiress to the Empire's greatest fortune, estimated by some at $200 million, a phenomenal amount for the time. De Marigny's targeting of Nancy Oakes, their subsequent elopement, and the apoplectic rage of Sir Harry left one irresistible impression: that the Mauritian cad had, without the knowledge of his bride's family, tried to manoeuvre his way round the law, for his personal enrichment, by whisking their daughter away from their protective embrace, and buying legal access to their money for the price of a marriage licence. Even sixty years on, it's easy to see how this conclusion was reached.

Though the Duke's own premarital adventures were hardly beyond reproach, it was easy to see why he would dislike a man of de Marigny's kind. So far as was known, de Marigny was exclusively and aggressively heterosexual as he cut a swathe through society's young beauties. He had, in earlier years, ingratiated himself with English society, sniffing round the high-class fillies at Henley and Ascot. If the rumours were true, his score rate was high among these compliant wenches. But the Duke – he of the soft blue eyes and silken blond hair

– had always possessed a deep streak of sexual ambivalence. In society circles, his bisexuality was renowned. In de Marigny, he probably saw what he would have liked to have been himself, a red-blooded charmer and chancer whose way with the ladies was beyond question. There was something else that irritated him – de Marigny's title, which had its roots in Mauritian heraldry but cut no ice with sniffy British types like the Duke, whose insistence on the intricacies of society protocol was to stay with him for life. In de Marigny, he saw a man who pretended to be something he wasn't, a would-be aristocrat of dubious provenance who spent his life trying to muscle in on privileges, which were not due to him through birth, rank or inherited wealth. The man was clearly a bounder, an imposter and mountebank in the eyes of the Duke and his friends, including Sir Harry, though his choice of words would have been somewhat different.

Given the hostility generated by the elopement, and the harsh words that had passed between Oakes and de Marigny from time to time, it was relatively easy to pin a motive on the count. Here was a man who apparently disliked his father-in-law intensely, had argued with him more than once, and desired access to the Oakes money. Moreover, there was evidence – later to be produced in court – that de Marigny was actually near Westbourne on the night of the killing. It was, in the Duke's eyes, an open-and-shut case with the added advantage that de Marigny was seen by local society as utterly dispensable.

If all this were not enough, there was one other, highly personal reason why the Duke would have targeted de Marigny so readily. In addition to all his other perceived faults, the count had been highly provocative and offensive in his attitude towards the Windsors, who he saw as imperial cast-offs, with no real purpose in life. This flagrant lack of respect was crystalised in one sharp exchange he had with the Duke, some time before the Oakes murder shook the colony. During this encounter, de Marigny ridiculed the Duke by hinting, none too subtly, that if Windsor amounted to anything in the eyes of the British Establishment, he would not have been cast adrift on what he called "a windswept coral reef – a pimple on the backside of the British Empire". This was an affront to the Duke's sense of dignity and rank; it bruised his still buoyant ego. It was a time when, in spite of the reverses of the previous five or six years, he retained ambition, and to suggest he was worthless was unforgiveably offensive.

In pointing to de Marigny as the obvious suspect, the Duke was giving vent to a host of prejudices. Also, by identifying the suspect so quickly, he was eliminating any chance of media speculation and giving his bosses back home the impression that he was on top of the job. In every way, de Marigny was the custom-built fall-guy, the prize patsy. When Melchen and Barker flew in, all they were required to do was fit the evidence round the count. Meanwhile, Government House could go ahead and order the hanging rope.

It's only fair to say that the public persona of de Marigny was not wholly accurate. In fact, the Bay Street Boys had other reasons to dislike him, and these were all to do with the positive aspects of his character. Far from being an idling playboy, de Marigny was quite an industrious entrepreneur. In his own way he, too, had his eye on the Bahamas' economic future and was prepared to speculate on his ideas with his own money. His chicken farm on East Bay Street, Nassau, had objectives similar to Sir Harry's pig-rearing enterprise: at a time of rationing and deprivation, it was natural that self-sufficiency should become popular among those bright enough to see its advantages. He had also invested in an apartment complex on Cable Beach, a three-sided structure on a spectacular stretch of sand, which bore more than a passing resemblance to Westbourne. With its outer staircases, open balconies and handsome cupola, it was faithful to the colonial style then still very much in vogue, and survives today as Cable Beach Manor, where transient professionals enjoy a taste of beachfront life.

His foreignness, his enterprise and most damning of all his free spirit, and sometimes discomfiting frankness, all struck discordant notes with Nassau's ruling families. What's more, his quick intelligence was markedly at odds with their comparative dim-wittedness, a lethargy of mind induced by decades of comfortable living in a non-competitive environment. When Melchen and Barker had completed their initial inquiries, and inevitably reached the same conclusion as the Duke, that de Marigny was their man, he found himself up against formidable odds. Not only were the Bay Street Boys firmly against him, so was the local colonial establishment, headed by the Duke, who was enthusiastically supported by the Attorney General, Eric Hallinan.

If there was one type of person de Marigny disliked more than the Bay Street Boys, with their self-serving cliques and boundless avarice, it was the archetypal British colonial official, usually drawn from another self-serving clique – the old-boy network founded on England's public schools – and, in his eyes, equally dim-witted and boorish. For him, the two mutually supportive groups shared something he found intolerable: privileges which had nothing to do with merit. In the Duke, with all his odd sexual complexities and instincts for self-preservation, and Hallinan, an ambitious colonial flunkey eager to please his master, de Marigny had two committed foes, who would stop at nothing to destroy him.

In later years, long after he had been forced out of the Bahamas and condemned to wander the world as a virtually stateless man, de Marigny reflected frequently on the nightmare of that Bahamian summer. What irked him more and more, and was never eased by the passing of time, was the apparent eagerness of the Duke and Hallinan to condemn him while steadfastly ignoring the other, and more plausible suspect, Harold Christie. As a leading member of the white Bahamian establishment, Christie was considered bullet-proof, and at no point was he ever viewed as a potential defendant, despite disturbing evidence which was emerge as time went by. An invisible protective cordon was to ensure that he was never subjected to proper scrutiny.

In his 1990 book, *A Conspiracy of Crowns*, de Marigny recalls, touchingly, the ordeal of being unfairly accused of murder, in a land which was seemingly almost entirely hostile to him. He writes of being held, almost incommunicado, in a stinking prison cell during the unendurable heat of a Bahamian summer while the forces raging against him went about their business silencing potential witnesses, concocting evidence, and spreading falsehoods about him to besmirch his name still further. It would be easy for doubters to accuse de Marigny of paranoia, a wholly understandable condition in a man staring death in the face, but his suspicions were to be amply vindicated by events. There can be little doubt that de Marigny was the victim of a ruthless plot of which Macchiavelli himself would have approved: the elimination of a nuisance to protect affluent groups with much to lose and satisfy the petty prejudices of a spiteful Duke.

In his cell, de Marigny took stock of his position, analysing the motives of those who wished to condemn him, reviewing the evidence they might have against him, and organising in his mind the defensive strategy he might adopt to overcome seemingly insuperable odds. It was a time when his mind jumped from high moments of unrealistic optimism to deep lows of dejection. All the time he retained a touching, but wholly ridiculous faith in British justice, which he naively believed would work in his favour in the end. What he overlooked about British justice, and especially British colonial justice in an inconsequential speck of Empire, was that it always protected the Establishment, at the expense of everyone else. There had been times aplenty in history when innocent men of no account had been sacrificed by the judges to spare their own. It was one of the immutable rules of British justice at that time. De Marigny, a foreigner without the right connections, was expendable. It was as simple as that.

Melchen and Barker, following their brief, built a case against de Marigny on three key points: motive, which they were to base on his known hostility to his father-in-law; proximity, with witnesses prepared to testify that he was near Westbourne at the relevant hour; and a fingerprint allegedly found on the Chinese screen which had been in the Oakes' bedroom at the time of the killing. By eliminating all extraneous scene-of-crime evidence which didn't reinforce their theories, they could present a case against de Marigny that was nigh impregnable. As the accused languished in his cell awaiting a succession of hearings before a magistrate, public opinion in Nassau was hardening against him. There appeared to be no way out.

De Marigny saw Hallinan as the driving force in the mobilisation of the prosecution case. This British colonial official had only recently been appointed to the Bahamas post at the start of a four-year stint. For someone anxious to advance his career in bigger territories, the Oakes case was a dream assignment, a genuinely high-profile celebrity drama in which he could emerge as the star. De Marigny had plenty of time, during incarceration, to demonise Hallinan in his mind, and he began to recall all those little things he had noticed about him which, he imagined, would pitch the lawyer so enthusiastically against his cause. In the limited upper echelons of Nassau society, their paths had crossed socially from time to time, and de Marigny had noticed how resentful Hallinan had seemed when forced to park his Morris

Minor (all he could afford on colonial service pay) near the accused's rather lavish Lincoln Continental. There was a natural clash, too, between their character types: Hallinan the uptight British legal official, a stickler for regulations and colonial protocol, de Marigny the raffish continental with an insouciant view of life. It was Hallinan who, in de Marigny's eyes, was pulling all the strings during the investigation. But Hallinan was, of course, answerable to the Duke of Windsor.

Melchen and Barker, immediately after the murder, went through the motions of investigating Christie. It would have been unreasonably remiss of them not to have done so, for Christie was the only person, other than Sir Harry himself, sleeping at Westbourne on the night of his murder. Proximity, if nothing else, necessitated some questioning, however cursory. In quick time, however, they concluded he was out of the frame and Hallinan showed no reluctance to concur with their findings. As a leading light among the Bay Street Boys, and a member of the Executive Council, Christie was unassailable. From that point on, he was off-limits as far as the investigation went. Hallinan had his career to protect while the Duke, sitting aloft above the Nassau fray at Government House, had his own future to consider. Hanging a prominent local parliamentarian was off the agenda.

It struck the cynical as somewhat unusual that a black man was not pulled off the streets and framed for Oakes' killing. The bludgeoning of a rich man in his bed could well have been the work of an opportunist intruder, especially when there had been a crude attempt to burn the body and, it seemed, spread feathers on the scorched flesh. Nassau, then as now, had its share of rum-fuelled derelicts who hustled for a living and stole when they could. With the civil rights movement in America still twenty years away, there was no question of conscience being allowed to intrude had police decided on this course. But there was one thing which would have stopped such a scheme in its tracks: the 1942 labour riots in Nassau which had exposed an unexpected volatility in the ghettoes. This was not a time to hang a black man for a crime he did not commit. De Marigny, the unloved outsider, was a much safer option.

In addition to all his other perceived faults, de Marigny had offended Nassau's ruling elite in one way that simply couldn't be countenanced in those grim days of racial discrimination. He had actually emerged as a champion of the blacks, by demanding proper water supplies for deprived ghetto areas and, more specifically, in Eleuthera, where he had bought land. Moreover, he had campaigned for fair treatment for a group of castaway refugees from Devil's Island prison in South America, who had washed up on Bahamian shores. Both these actions were considered dangerous examples of pinko liberalism at a time when suppression of the "racially inferior" was regarded by colonial rulers as not simply acceptable but essential, if the status quo were to be preserved. The irony of this philosophy, given that the Empire was engaged at the time in trying to destroy a tyrant whose beliefs ran more or less parallel to their own, was lost on those whites who were left to formulate colonial policy.

There were few heartening developments for de Marigny during these dark days, but he was at least encouraged by the loyalty of his young wife, who had returned to Nassau from Vermont after first visiting her mother and siblings in Maine. While the case against her husband seemed to gather a frightening momentum, she remained resolute and steadfast in her support. Nothing the prosecution were alleging seemed even remotely plausible to her in relation to her beloved Freddy. For de Marigny, Nancy's courage at this crucial stage was important. It was a time when his depression could have degenerated into a loss of all hope. His wife, young as she was, showed commendable fortitude, in the face of what at the time must have seemed overwhelming odds. She never wavered.

Unfortunately for de Marigny, that was not true of Eunice Oakes, his mother-in-law. She was taken in by colourful accounts of the murder by Barker, whose lurid descriptions of Sir Harry's fight for life against a ruthless intruder reduced her to a state of tearful hysteria. He convinced her that Sir Harry died in great pain after being set alight while still alive. The pay-off line was that, amid the gore and mayhem, a fingerprint from de Marigny had been discovered on the Chinese screen. If his objective were to set Lady Oakes firmly against de Marigny, he succeeded, but in doing so he also sowed the seeds of his own destruction, as we shall discover later.

If things were not bad enough, they were to get worse for de Marigny as the legal process dragged on through the back end of that fateful summer. Four things happened which worsened an already grave situation. First came the sudden transfer to Trinidad of the

Bahamas police chief Erskine-Lindop, whose utter dependability would have been reassuring when things got tough. The deployment of Melchen and Barker had appeared like a calculated slight to this dedicated officer, and certainly gave the impression that he and his men were not up to the job. But his removal was not only a blow to the man himself, but all those who had a deep regard for his ability and integrity. Here he was, faced with the biggest murder investigation of his career, being transferred to another British colony just as inquiries were getting underway. Again, there was only one plausible explanation: Erskine-Lindop was too principled, too honest and too professional to allow himself to be part of the travesty now taking place in Nassau. He had to be swept aside if the right result were to be achieved. When he left the Bahamas, Melchen and Barker must have rejoiced inwardly, for the marginalisation of the local police force had been one of their key objectives. Now it had been neutralised completely.

Erskine-Lindop eventually retired from the colonial police service and lived on into his nineties, but not once did he discuss the Oakes affair, even with his closest family. There was, however, one occasion when he allowed a couple of pointers to slip out in conversation with a Bahamian friend who visited him in Trinidad some years later. One was that, had he been allowed to stay in Nassau and complete the investigation, he would have unmasked Oakes' killer. He supported this by revealing that he had a local suspect on the brink of a tearful confession shortly before his departure. The second was that he expressed annoyance and regret that the killer was still allowed to go about his business in Nassau society, free of the taint of his appalling crime. Pressed to name the killer, he refused – and that was as close as anyone ever got to cracking the former police chief's ironclad defences.

Even more disturbing was the strange disappearance of two watchmen at Westbourne who apparently saw comings and goings at the house on the night of the murder. These men would have been key defence witnesses, but their wives told de Marigny's representatives that they had gone to Andros, the westernmost Bahama isle, and were never seen again.

The third sinister development was that some people sympathetic to de Marigny's cause, and possibly in a position to help his case, began receiving mysterious and intimidating phone calls. Police cars were seen carrying out surveillance on their homes. Fourthly, and most worryingly for de Marigny, was the decision to call back to Nassau the plane carrying Sir Harry's corpse to Maine, his home state where he was to be buried. On arrival, the corpse was whisked away to Nassau Hospital, where it was hurriedly taken to a room protected by armed guards. The only people allowed in were Hallinan, Melchen, Barker and Dr Quackenbush, the physician who had pronounced the baronet dead and whose autopsy was considered far from adequate. Though it was unclear at the time what lay behind this extraordinary decision, and the goings-on inside that hospital room, it would later grow in significance for de Marigny as he pondered the measures being taken to prove his guilt and protect others.

De Marigny was to maintain in later years that the widely held belief that Sir Harry died from blows to the head was wrong. He felt strongly, and this, he said, was borne out by the evidence of a witness he met years later, that he had been shot repeatedly. When the Attorney General, the two American detectives and the medical practitioner gathered in that hospital room that day, they had but one mission as far as de Marigny was concerned. That was to clean out Sir Harry's skull and remove the bullets which would have put the issue beyond doubt. Astonishingly, Dr Quackenbush had not bothered to open up Sir Harry's head, having convinced himself that there was only one wound under the left ear even though there were, in fact, three more close by.

In all his statements to police and the courts, Christie maintained that he heard nothing untoward in Westbourne on the stormy night his friend died. In the event of a bludgeoning, that was just about credible, given the noise of wind and rain outside. But was it possible that he could have slept through the sound of four gunshots being fired only twenty feet or so from where he lay?

The highly secret operation carried out belatedly on Sir Harry's corpse in Nassau that day was, in de Marigny's mind, intended to safeguard Christie, and tighten the noose around his own neck.

Chapter Five

AN HONOURABLE MAN

WHEN news of Sir Harry's murder swept through Nassau on the morning of 8 July, 1943, the impact on the local community was immense. No-one in the Bahamas capital at that time was untouched by it because of the millionaire's imposing presence. Sir Harry was symbolic of so many things. To the ruling whites he was often considered unpleasant, but an undeniable asset nonetheless, given his readiness to live among them and invest in the colony's future. To poor blacks, he represented the more acceptable face of whiteness because he possessed the common touch and was magnanimous towards those less fortunate than himself. The familiar sight of Sir Harry stomping along Bay Street in his high boots and mining hat was part of Nassau life, and the blacks accepted him without reservation.

De Marigny was shocked, too, by the sudden loss of his father-in-law. Despite their quarrels, there seemed to be a grudging mutual respect. Though poles apart in many areas, they shared common characteristics, not least their individuality and bloody-mindedness. If there was antipathy, it was only the natural impatience of young for old, and vice-versa. Though de Marigny would not have been Sir Harry's first choice as son-in-law (he was far too exotic for Oakes' prosaic tastes), there was something the old man quite admired about him. Both men had acid tongues and were capable of causing offence, and both had a "don't give a damn" attitude towards those who were supposedly in authority. Their shared dislikes included British colonial officials, whose constipated attitudes and assumptions of grandeur were considered deeply irritating, and anyone who used their power to exploit the weak.

Although Sir Harry's view of the Windsors was not recorded, so far as I know, their relationship can possibly be best assessed by something the Duchess said, about the Oakes, to a visiting high society friend, during a reception at Government House. She called them "the Charlie Chaplins of Nassau society", a reference no doubt to their social awkwardness. There was something unquestionably comical about them: Sir Harry the short, rough-and-ready figure from the mines, Lady Oakes, his homely but much more sedate appendage. If the Duchess was out of step with the British in most areas of her life, the one thing she shared with them was snobbery, an unconcealed distaste for those she considered uncouth and unsophisticated. The Oakes clearly did not measure up, but then it's unlikely she and the Duke were to Sir Harry's taste either. Among the wealthy upper classes, friendship is often no more than an expedient and, in some respects, the Oakes and Windsors needed each other. The difference between Sir Harry and de Marigny was that Oakes recognised how high society worked, how "meeting the right people" helped to oil wheels and cut deals, whereas de Marigny had become immune to such considerations. In one exchange between them, Sir Harry chided de Marigny for failing to attend a cocktail reception at Government House, having been invited by the Duke and Duchess. "To hell with the Duke!" said de Marigny with the full support of his young wife. From that point on, the argument escalated, with Sir Harry calling them "asses" and threatening to horsewhip his son-in-law, and de Marigny issuing a counter-threat to kick his backside. However, there were no long-standing hard feelings. "You have to know how to deal with those Frenchies," Sir Harry later told his young son, Sydney, with a twinkle in his eye.

According to de Marigny, a conspiracy of silence and secrecy was evident from the beginning of the murder inquiry. The prison physician, Dr Ricky Oberwarth, told him he had been warned by the Attorney General to commit no medical details about the Oakes case to paper. All information had to be referred directly, and confidentially, to Hallinan. It was a situation which caused the doctor some concern. It didn't seem right, and he was reluctant to co-operate.

Meanwhile, de Marigny himself was in a dazed state, wondering how the killing would affect the lives of Nancy and himself. All the suspicion and uncertainty created an enormous burden for them. Then came a dinnertime visit by Lieut John Campbell Douglas of the

Bahamas police, who said Erskine-Lindop had asked to see him. They drove to Westbourne, which was overrun with people, including the usual army of rubbernecks and souvenir hunters. Rather than a crime scene, it bore a striking resemblance to the concourse at Grand Central Station. Little had been done to secure the site. It was at this point that de Marigny first met Melchen and Barker. The relationship was not to be a happy one. The heavily-built Melchen, every inch the American cop, with copious jowls and wire-rimmed specs, lost no time in getting to the point. He wanted to know where de Marigny was on the night of 7 July and during the early morning hours of 8 July. It was the beginning of a three-month ordeal which almost, but not quite, broke de Marigny's spirit. While waiting to see Erskine-Lindop, de Marigny was studiously ignored by the Duke, who had arrived to survey the scene. There was not even a word of sympathy. After an hour, de Marigny was led to into the presence of the Miami officers, one a bespectacled blimp, the other a slim B-movie cop lookalike, with a Sherlock Holmes spyglass and other paraphernalia of his trade. The room was sombrely lit with a single, intimidating floor-level light, which de Marigny felt had been so placed to achieve an atmosphere of intrigue and drama. At that stage, though, he was still unaware he was a suspect.

During Nancy's absence in New England, de Marigny had grown a Van Dyke beard. It was not a full naval set, but confined to his chin and lips. He had, he said, wanted to test her reaction on his return. His timing for such an enterprise was ill-judged because it gave Melchen and Barker another reason to suspect him. As will be seen in due course, singed hairs were to play a significant part in the Oakes mystery. After examining his hands and beard, Barker asked him to explain ash residue in his pores and clear signs of singeing on his face and limbs. De Marigny was able to offer several plausible theories, including the regular chicken scorching which took place on his farm, his liking for cigars, which he frequently relit, and his lighting of candles at a dinner party at his home in Victoria Avenue, where his clothing was examined. But none of these cut much ice with the investigation team.

On Friday, 9 July, the day after Sir Harry's body had been discovered, de Marigny was taken to Westbourne again. The house by now had become a sight-seeing attraction, with any number of unauthorised people being permitted to wander around at will. During this visit something happened which was significant in the light of subsequent events. Melchen invited de Marigny to follow him upstairs. They entered a small sitting room, where the officer began questioning him about the friendship between Sir Harry and Christie. He asked whether Christie owed Sir Harry money.

In retrospect, de Marigny was inclined to believe that the questioning, of which no record was kept, was merely a pretext for what was to happen next. It was a way of softening him up for the sucker punch. Suddenly, Melchen fell quiet and walked to a water-jug and two glasses on a small table. He invited de Marigny to pour them a drink. As they sat drinking the door opened. Barker appeared and asked if everything was okay. Melchen said "Yes" and Barker withdrew. In those few moments, the officers had acquired what they wanted – fingerprints that, properly presented as evidence, would place the suspect in the house. Without knowing it, de Marigny had effectively sealed his own fate. In criminal parlance, de Marigny had been trussed up like a turkey. The neck-wringing could wait awhile.

When de Marigny was formally charged with his father-in-law's murder, he tried to get the best legal representation available. In Nassau, distinguished criminal attorneys were rare, nigh non-existent, but the one man who stood above all was a living anomaly, an incongruity, called Alfred Adderley. A F Adderley, as he was more formally known, possessed a fine legal brain and represented some of Nassau's wealthiest residents. But he was anomalous because he was black: he was a successful professional black man in a white man's domain, at a time when black men were still barred from Nassau's downtown restaurants and movie theatres.

Even today in Nassau, there is still a keen awareness of colour gradations; the phenomenon of the "white thinking black man" is still remarked upon by more radical blacks. Younger Bahamians call them 'Oreos', named after tasty black biscuits with white cream interiors. The reference is invariably made with amused contempt, but rarely pronounced hostility. A F Adderley, whom lower-class blacks regarded as lordly and disdainful, would probably be regarded as an 'Oreo' of his day, a black man who thought white. One criticism made of him, though I cannot vouch for its accuracy, is that he always removed his hat for a white woman, but never for a black. Having been educated in English ways at Cambridge, he was keenly aware of upper-class elitism and how it worked. Like everyone else, a black professional had to know his place. His professional status placed him above fellow blacks, but below the whites, whatever their occupation or rank.

Adderley went through life in a quietly dignified manner, plying his trade at the Bahamas Bar with an astuteness and diligence that won him the respect and admiration of his legal contemporaries. Yet he was required to bear the black man's burden of the day: the realisation that, however distinguished in his field, he would always be considered inferior by lesser men on the grounds of colour alone. Had Adderley received de Marigny's call, he would have found himself, once again, trying to dig a white man out of a hole, but at least this time it would not have been a white man who secretly despised him. As it happened, Adderley never received de Marigny's message, which was supposed to have been passed on through the police. He was hired instead to help the Attorney General present the prosecution case. As de Marigny admitted long afterwards, he experienced a tightening of the throat when he heard of Adderley's role in his trial, and the callous way his own request for his assistance had been cast aside.

With the best spoken for, de Marigny was forced to turn to his second choice. The white attorney Godfrey Higgs had handled routine civil matters for him in the past and possessed the rare attribute in Nassau of trustworthiness and honesty, which de Marigny felt would serve him well in the predicament he now found himself. Engulfed by intrigue, de Marigny needed a representative who would give it to him straight, however unpalatable, and Higgs was someone he respected. Affable, approachable and fair-minded, Higgs was, in many respects, out of step with his white Bahamian contemporaries. He was much less obviously self-serving and acquisitive. In spite of that, he was fully accepted by his less scrupulous countrymen and had become a prominent figure in Nassau's political affairs.

Higgs was an honourable man, of that there can be no doubt. But he fell short in several crucial areas when it came to defending a man against a murder charge in a Nassau court. Firstly, he was not a crime specialist, or even a seasoned advocate. He had appeared in court only a few times before, and then only with reluctance. He was not a flamboyant denizen of the Bar, a man noted for the kind of eloquence that sets guilty men free, or turns cases on their heads. In legal terms, he was essentially a backroom boy, a specialist in dry civil matters who went about his work undemonstratively in chambers. He was a poor choice for another, even more potent, reason. As a member of Nassau's white elite, and a parliamentary member to boot, he was very closely associated with the forces ranged against de Marigny. Everyone in Nassau knew by now that, barring de Marigny, there was only one other logical suspect in town. That was Harold Christie, a close friend and parliamentary associate of the man now engaged to save de Marigny's neck. It was a far from ideal situation, but one that was almost inevitable in a society where the talent pool in all of the professions was so woefully shallow. Hiring a London barrister in wartime, and expecting him to brave the perils of a transatlantic crossing, was not an acceptable option. American lawyers were not trained in British law and procedure. De Marigny had to make do with what was available. So Higgs it was.

At just thirty-six years of age, Higgs faced formidable hurdles in handling de Marigny's case. He was unschooled in the intricacies of criminal law or, indeed, the whole business of jury handling which the best barristers were expected to have mastered thoroughly. He was effectively a tyro advocate in criminal terms, not much above the pupils who tout for briefs round the London courts. He also faced obstacles most barristers never have to consider: the possible repercussions of victory in such a small society, where he was hoping to spend the rest of his career. How far could he allow himself to go in probing, and possibly condemning, people he mixed with socially? How hard and uncompromising could he afford to be on a man's behalf, even when that man's life was on the line? Higgs' role was similar to that of a tightrope walker crossing a pen of pitbulls: a fall either way would be a disaster. He and his junior assistant, Ernest Callender, only two years younger, found themselves in a highly-pressured set of circumstances, made worse by the close attention of the world's press. Higgs and Callender were either about to suffer untold ignominy and anguish before the eyes of the world, or have glory thrust upon them.

What seemed certain was that never again in their careers would they reap the international headlines that were about to come their way. But standing between them and the plaudits of their peers was the revered Mr Adderley, whose brisk brain and silken, persuasive voice would be fully engaged in trying to undermine their cause. No wonder there was trepidation in the de Marigny camp.

Interest in de Marigny's trial among Bahamians was intense. At preliminary hearings, crowds gathered in the square near the courthouse to see the slim figure of the accused proceed, under guard, into court. There was a sizzling excitement in the air. There is a tendency in any court case for the public to assume, once charges are laid, that the accused is the culprit, and de Marigny was no exception. In those early days, opinion seemed to be against him. The usual outrage was evident, fired to some extent by the Duke's laudatory remarks about Sir Harry a couple of weeks after his death, and his emphasis on the impact it had made on the economy.

At a press conference in Miami, where he had been engaged in "private business", the Duke told American reporters that Oakes was "a very great benefactor, very much loved by everybody" in the Bahamas. He also alluded to the fate of Oakes' various business interests, in the colony, which had come to a standstill on his death. Sir Harry, he said, employed about two hundred and fifty men and paid them well. His death, therefore, was "a very great loss, not only in a material way, but because he was so very popular." If the Duke was seeking to alienate the masses from de Marigny's cause, this was an effective way to achieve his aims. Unemployment was the challenging issue of the day: it was a powerfully emotive topic which could rouse even the most even-tempered Bahamian to enraged indignation. With so few jobs around, Sir Harry's murder was an economic blow of alarming proportions.

The Duke also took the opportunity to explain why he had summoned two Miami detectives to investigate the case. It was not, he said, a reflection on the Nassau police, but an acknowledgement of the Miami officers' superior equipment and breadth of experience, which were not available in the Bahamas. Meanwhile, Melchen and Barker went about their business, noting that around a dozen witnesses remained to be called at the preliminary hearing, which had begun that week, and was expected to continue until 26 July. Melchen said, however, that the final chapter of the prosecution's case might not be made public before October, when the Supreme Court trial was expected to begin. Thus, Nassau was alerted to the prospect of a summer-long examination of the evidence, in a series of high-profile court hearings, even before the high court proceedings got underway. As Nassau's summer heat reached its height, so would the dramatic prelude to the trial proper. The city was abuzz with conjecture.

Barker said that Magistrate F E Field, who was presiding over the preliminaries, would be asked to hear the final three witnesses around September, and explained a postponement of the second hearing by saying: "We are getting down to the fine points now." He exuded an air of efficiency by saying he would return to Nassau from Miami in a week or ten days, after getting all the evidence "marshalled and organised."

He added sanctimoniously: "We don't want anything to go in that is unfair to the defendant. We can deal with him strictly by Marquis of Queensbury rules and feel confident that justice will be done." In light of what was to transpire later in the proceedings, these two statements are remarkable for almost breathtaking hypocrisy. Barker was anxious to present an image of a disinterested, proficient officer doing his job with characteristic even-handedness. Before the year was out, the world would know differently and understand what "marshalling and organising" of evidence was all about. But for now his facade seemed indestructible.

In building the case against de Marigny, the prosecution was eager to eliminate all suspicion that might fall elsewhere. *The Miami Herald* of 24 July reported that crucial new evidence had caused two of the principal investigators, Melchen and Major Pemberton, head of the Bahamas Criminal Investigation Department, to fly to New York, where they were to consult "an internationally eminent laboratory technician." This new evidence had been taken to Miami by Pemberton, but its precise nature was not disclosed. Barker, however, described this development as "very important in relation to this case." He would not elaborate, except to say "the new development further excludes the possibility of any other participant." He said his colleagues had flown to New York because the case "has developed to a point of such high technicality that we want the best advice to be had."

This strategy had a double effect in manipulating public opinion. It increased pressure on de Marigny, against whom they now had apparently important new and highly technical evidence, and took the heat off Christie, who had virtually been eliminated from inquiries. There was little wonder that de Marigny's mood sank, as he pondered his fate in his cell at Nassau Prison.

On 29 July, evidence was given before Magistrate Field which added considerably to de Marigny's load. The testimony of two women established his proximity to the murder scene at an unusual hour, about 1.20am, which was very much in line with the suspected hour of Sir Harry's death. Meanwhile, a young police officer was prepared to vouch for de Marigny's unusual demeanour on the morning the body was found. As it happened, the officer's evidence was so outrageous that it was never seriously considered, yet all three witnesses helped to turn public opinion against the luckless count.

On the eve of the murder, while Sir Harry was entertaining his guests at Westbourne, de Marigny was hosting a dinner party of his own at his house in Victoria Avenue, a palm-lined road linking Shirley Street with East Bay Street in central Nassau. When it was over, he drove Mrs Dorothy Clark and Mrs Jean Ainsley to their cottage near Westbourne. The women, both wives of RAF officers, gave detailed descriptions in court of their evening at de Marigny's home. Their relevance to the case was crucial because they established de Marigny's proximity to the murder scene at the relevant time. Medical evidence suggested that Sir Harry died in the early hours of the morning. However, neither woman had any idea where de Marigny went once he had dropped them at the cottage. At 7.30 the following morning, according to Constable Wendell Parker, de Marigny arrived at the police station on a routine traffic matter. He was, said the officer, "excited and wild-eyed" and his mouth was bulging. At this point, de Marigny must have felt the full weight of his predicament. The women, though perfectly truthful, had placed him literally within a hundred yards or so of Sir Harry's bedroom at a time when, according to Christie's account, the old man would have been tucked up in bed and possibly fast asleep. The women had not noticed lights on at the house as they drove past – indeed, one of them was unaware that the big house two doors away was Westbourne. But, as well-disposed acquaintances of de Marigny, with no reason to testify against him, their evidence was potent material for the prosecution to work on.

At this same preliminary hearing, the court gained an insight into life in the upper reaches of Nassau society, courtesy of Sir Harry's housemaid Mabel Ellis, who set the scene for the terrible happenings of that stormy night. She revealed how Sir Harry insisted that Westbourne should never be locked up, how his bedroom could be reached via three different routes, how she left a can of Fly-Ded and Flit in his room after preparing his bed. She told how Harold Christie had stayed at Westbourne the previous night (6-7 July) and breakfasted with Sir Harry, after which the two men departed for the day, returning at 5pm with a man and woman whose names she didn't know. She served drinks on the north upstairs porch and, at about 8.45pm, she served dinner. The meal finished at about 9.30pm when the party retired to the games room.

Mrs Ellis went upstairs to prepare Sir Harry's bed, tucking the mosquito net under the mattress. She "flitted" the room to rid it of mosquitos and put the can on the floor by the bureau near the door. She also left a small electric fan nearby. Sir Harry's bed, she said, was lying east and west, and south of the bed was a folding screen which was covered with "paper material." A small radio was on the table between the bed and the screen. At 10pm she left the room in perfect order. In line with usual practice, she did not lock the doors or windows. All the windows were screened except two on the south side which were fitted with Venetian blinds, both left up. The witness said she did not prepare a bed for anyone else that night because she was unaware a guest was staying. Christie's decision to stay over was, it seems, a spontaneous one. When she left, Mrs Ellis noted that Sir Harry and his guests were still in the card room. The cook, Edith Fernander, was the only member of staff still in the house.

Evidence given at this hearing also revealed the demeanour of the two men whose fates were to collide so dramatically. Sir Harry's guest Mrs Dulcibelle Henneage, an English evacuee living in Nassau with her two children, referred to her host's "very good spirits", as he waved goodbye at the end of the evening. Mrs Dorothy Clark, driven home by de Marigny, said her host was in a similar mood. It started raining at about 11pm or 11.30pm, she said, and as de Marigny's Lincoln Continental headed west, skirting Goodman's Bay towards Cable Beach, it was still drizzling.

If what de Marigny heard in court was enough to dampen his

spirits, it was made worse by the prosecution's call for an adjournment until the following week. De Marigny's lawyer, Godfrey Higgs, protested, and no wonder. Apart from the fact that the prosecution seemed sluggish in bringing the preliminaries to an end, de Marigny was having to live from hearing to hearing in the most appalling conditions. Even today, Nassau's prison is rated by the human rights organisation, Amnesty International, as one of the worst in the western world, with its small congested cells and shared slop buckets. Imagine, then, conditions in 1943, when prisoners' rights were seen as of even less account. In those days, the prison was a gaunt structure in East Street, not far from the bustle of Bay Street. It was old-fashioned and ill-equipped: so inadequate, in fact, that it was replaced ultimately by Fox Hill Prison at the island's eastern end. If today's prison is bad – and it is considered appalling – imagine the state of its predecessor, a harsh relic of centuries past, when prisoners were accorded no sympathy or compassion. De Marigny was detained in a cell reserved for "dangerous" criminals. Measuring only eight feet by twelve, it had a solid iron door, a small window so high that even a very tall man could not see through it, and a slop pail with all its attendant odours. As for many prisoners in today's jail, de Marigny was in solitary confinement for all but one hour in every twenty-four, and harsh lighting robbed him even of the comfort of darkness. To compound the humiliation and degradation he felt, he was actually kept in a cage when he finally came to trial. He felt like a circus freak, exhibited in a manner which was demoralising and unnecessarily demeaning. Had humiliation been the system's aim, it succeeded.

Under British law, an accused person is presumed innocent until proved guilty. But de Marigny felt, with some justification, that he was already deemed guilty until proved otherwise. There seemed to be no escaping the relentless persecution he was suffering. In his book, *A Conspiracy of Crowns*, he recalled nightmares he suffered in prison, and especially the spectre of the hooded judge condemning him to death, a visitation which caused him to grip his own throat and cry out.

Between the hearings, the night terrors, the feelings of desolation and the savage awfulness of his surroundings, there was only the tedium. "Like death, tedium can cause one's life to flash before one's eyes. And so at night, tossing on the thin bed I had improvised, I thought about the vagaries of fate that had led me, step by step, to this time and place." His only comfort was the soft lilt of native music drifting into his cell from the shanty settlements nearby. Deep, dark voices were coaxed along by the rhythm of drums. For the prisoner, this was an important link with real life, a message of hope.

Imagine, then, what must have been running through his mind, when at the resumed preliminary hearing on 3 August, Captain James Barker first formally presented the "scientific" evidence against him. The detective captain, at thirty-eight a ruggedly handsome man, likened by some to the screen star Robert Ryan, spent three and a half hours in the witness-box, during the morning, presenting evidence which was construed to seal de Marigny's doom. Barker said he discovered a print of de Marigny's little finger on the screen which was found drawn across Sir Harry's bed. He said microscopic examination revealed that de Marigny's beard and hair on his hands, head and forearm were scorched by fire. This stunning testimony was a double blow for the accused, placing him in Sir Harry's bedroom, and in close proximity to fire. Things were looking bad for the man in the dock.

Then attorney Higgs, during an inspired spell of cross-examination, established a point which seemed insignificant at the time, but was to prove the first shot in a blistering fusillade which was eventually to have a decisive impact on the case. He managed to establish that the screen was outside Sir Harry's bedroom in the hallway on the night of 8 July while de Marigny was at Westbourne with Captain Barker. The six-panel screen, which was six feet high and of pasteboard construction, with an oriental design, bore the print at the extreme top of one of the end panels. That placed de Marigny near the screen many hours after the murder. This had the effect of softening the impact of the fingerprint evidence. It created doubts about its origins.

From the start, the investigation into de Marigny's alleged killing of his father-in-law had attracted almost hysterical public attention. Now, the matter was taking on elements of showbusiness. The slim, bearded defendant, with his obscure French title and Mauritian background; his pretty young wife, devotedly in the wings as he endured the various indignities heaped upon him; the voracious appetite for information of the international press; all added a frisson of glamour to the grim reality. Nassau was taking on a carnival air and every morning there was an unseemly clamour for seats in the courtroom's public gallery. American visitors even tried to "buy" places in court from hard-up locals, offering two shillings a time to those prepared to vacate their places. This was good money, and some reluctantly relented.

Barker's testimony had been awaited eagerly, not least by the accused. After outlining his career background, and revealing that he had been with Miami police since 1925, Barker said he had appeared hundreds of times in Florida courts as a fingerprint expert. On the morning of 8 July, he said, he had been summoned by Miami's police chief, Leslie Quigg, to conduct an investigation into the death of Sir Harry Oakes in Nassau. He then spoke with Captain Edward Melchen, a detective assigned to Miami's homicide bureau, and assembled equipment needed for the assignment. Together they flew to Nassau on the 12.25pm Pan American flight, arriving at 1.30pm. There to meet them was Lieut Col R A Erskine-Lindop, the Bahamas police commissioner, and his CID chief, Major Herbert Pemberton. Under Colonel Erskine-Lindop's supervision, they drove to Westbourne, where they were immediately taken to Sir Harry's bedroom. Sir Harry's body was lying on the bed in a "semi-contracted" position, turned very slightly to the right side and very badly burned. The left side and frontal part of the body were burned, along with the legs and face. There were numerous ante-mortem burns which had blistered. Close examination of the head revealed an irregular wound on a line between the ear and nose. The wound proved conclusively that a firearm was not used, he said. Although he tested for fingerprints, and ruled out those of Major Pemberton, Harold Christie and Dr Quackenbush, all of whom had been in the room, he postponed further examination until the following day because of the extreme humidity, which affected print-lifting procedures.

During the afternoon of 8 July, he spent a considerable time inspecting the bedroom and noted the burned bed and rug. The hallway wall near the door showed signs of fire, smoke and smudging. He thought it probable that anyone in the room during the fire would have burned hairs. He, therefore, decided to examine everyone who had been in or near the bedroom. Both Christie and de Marigny submitted voluntarily to this process. Christie had no burnt hairs, but de Marigny was singed on his hands, forearms, eyebrows, beard and head. Asked about this, de Marigny said: "I have no idea how I got them." A few minutes later, de Marigny said he knew how he got them after all. At his chicken farm they often killed and scalded chickens and the scalding was done in a container of water over a fire. He sometimes did this job himself and may have received burns this way. Later, in his own home, he told Barker "I love candles" and showed him four standing in hurricane shades. He demonstrated how he used a match to light them and said: "This must be how I have these burns."

On Friday morning, Barker said he returned to Westbourne and resumed fingerprint tests. The screen had been folded, and moved the previous afternoon, to make way for the removal of Sir Harry's body, and protect the screen from handling. Several dozen impressions were raised of varying quality, nearly all illegible. But one was from the right little finger of Alfred de Marigny.

On 4 August, Melchen spent three and a half hours in the witness-box to corroborate his colleagues' evidence. He raised the possibility that Sir Harry had staggered into the hallway, his pyjamas aflame, and tottered against the wall, before being overtaken and dragged back to the bedroom. Melchen said that de Marigny was not allowed upstairs while the screen was in the hallway. He also disclosed that de Marigny had said he had not visited Westbourne in three years and had not seen Sir Harry since 29 March of that year.

In an interview with de Marigny a few hours before he was arrested and charged, the accused told him of the mutual antipathy between him and his father-in-law. De Marigny said Oakes hated him, and he in return hated "the stupid old fool." Melchen also claimed de Marigny had revealed that he and Nancy had once rejected a ten thousand dollar gift from Lady Oakes because it was like "a gift to a poor relative or an orphan child." The most interesting part of Melchen's testimony concerned bloodstains he found in the small bedroom used by Christie on the night of the murder. A small hand towel bore "considerable" bloodstains. There were also "bloody smudge prints" on the door. On the inside of the screen door he also found smudged and bloody prints which could not be raised.

The unfolding of the evidence during the preliminary hearings was merely a prelude to the grand drama to come. It also provided a colourful backdrop to the uneasy relationship between the de Marignys – the dashing count and his young, impressionable and headstrong wife – and Sir Harry and Lady Oakes.

When Melchen appeared for the afternoon session, the court was treated to riveting evidence of this turbulent family and the undercurrents which inflamed their lives. De Marigny, he said, had told him of a trip he and Nancy took to California. He said Sir Harry was very bitter and hated him for having married his daughter. He told of Nancy's illness, and of arguments between him and Sir Harry, over an operation that had either been performed or was to be performed. De Marigny, said Melchen, purported to hate Sir Harry because he was "a stupid old fool" who could not be reasoned with.

The strained relationship between them had been exacerbated further by Sir Harry's attorney, Walter Foskett of Palm Beach, who had received a letter from de Marigny's ex-wife Ruth Fahnestock which the lawyer showed to Nancy and Lady Oakes. He described it as a "filthy" letter and said Foskett had shown it to the women to break up his marriage. De Marigny admitted he hated Foskett for this, but made it clear he had no interest in Nancy's money or future inheritance, which had probably been implied in the letter.

By the time Melchen stepped down from the box, the odds seemed to be stacking up alarmingly against the defendant. His proximity to Westbourne on the night of the murder, the burnt hairs on his hands and beard, the all-important fingerprint, and his admitted hostility to Sir Harry all pointed to one conclusion. For those who, like me, believe that a conspiracy was afoot, there then came a devlopment which was extraordinary, given that a man was enmeshed in court proceedings with his life on the line.

With the apparent approval of the Attorney General, Eric Hallinan, Harold Christie gave a press interview, explaining circumstances surrounding his discovery of Sir Harry's body. With proceedings already underway, this was a most unusual development. Not only did such an exercise risk prejudicing proceedings, it also served to exonerate Christie who, anywhere else, would have been treated at least as an alternative suspect.

The Tribune of 10 August, 1943, reported Christie's press conference without comment, yet the irregularity of the situation must have been all too obvious. Again, Hallinan's co-operation in such an undertaking points to one conclusion: that the Nassau "establishment" was not only pinning guilt on de Marigny, but doing its level best to get Christie out of the frame. During the interview, Christie emphasised the extremely close nature of his relationship with Sir Harry, declaring that their association had even resulted in their having similar mannerisms. He said they both walked with "a slight rolling motion" and talked much alike. The discovery of Sir Harry, he said, had been "the shock of my life." He said he and Oakes were "inseparable friends" and they always had breakfast together, on the ocean terrace, when they stayed overnight at Westbourne.

In the interview, he was eager to explain how the bloody towels described by Melchen turned up in his bedroom. He recalled how he lifted Sir Harry's head, put a pillow under it, and took a glass of water and put some in his mouth. "I got a towel and wet it and wiped his face, hoping to revive him. I thought he was still alive."

In his room, he said, he tossed aside a towel and "washed away the bloodstains received when I lifted Sir Harry's head. By that time the discovery had so shocked me that I sat down for a moment. Then the doctor came."

By any reckoning this was an extraordinary development. It was completely at odds with British law, in that it highlighted, and explained, what could be construed as incriminating evidence, while proceedings were underway. For the Attorney General to have approved such a performanmce, one assumes at Christie's request, is almost beyond belief. The purpose, surely, was to counter the obvious implications of Melchen's evidence not, as one would expect, in the witness-box but in the pages of the local and international press. It was a flagrant interference with the judicial process, and an act which, in any other jurisdiction, would be rated contempt of court.

On 13 August, Christie had his chance in the witness-box, to elaborate on his friendship with Sir Harry. From his testimony, it was clear that they were unusually close. They had lived together, he said, in Bar Harbour, Maine, in Mexico, England and Palm Beach, Florida, as well as the Bahamas. In early July, Sir Harry was living at Westbourne, which was considered part of the Bahamas Country Club. His family was out of the colony, so Sir Harry was alone. He, Christie, slept in the house on July 4th, 5th, 6th and 7th. And on the final day of his life, Sir Harry had called at his office and they went to the security department at the Victoria Hotel, to obtain an exit permit for his trip to Bar Harbour two days later. At the Colonial Secretary's office, Sir Harry had his passport processed. Then they stopped at Seagate, Christie's home on the corner of West Street and Nassau Street, to collect a pair of tennis shoes.

It was at this preliminary hearing that Christie was first prompted to discuss the man in the dock. He said he knew de Marigny. "I think I have known him since he first came here. About a week after de Marigny's arrival in Nassau several years ago, he came into my office to inquire about real estate. I remember him telling me that he wanted a piece of land that Sir Harry refused to let him have. This was three to five months ago." The land was at Westward Villas on Cable Beach. "He stated that he and Sir Harry were not on friendly terms. I think perhaps there were a number of reasons. One reason was that he wanted the land and couldn't get it. I think that another reason was that Sir Harry felt he hadn't treated his former wife with due consideration and de Marigny was annoyed because Sir Harry would not listen to his side of the question." Christie also disclosed that de Marigny felt Sir Harry had not treated him properly and had been unduly severe.

To all the other evidence now on the stockpile was added the land dispute, Sir Harry's alleged thwarting of de Marigny's ambition, and the accused's belief that he was being treated unjustly by Nancy's father. If motive was considered a key component of the prosecution case, they were well on their way to establishing not one motive, but several. Not surprisingly, Higgs took the opportunity to question Christie about his press briefing, asking if the Attorney General had approved it. Christie said he told Hallinan he was going to give an interview, but the Attorney General neither approved nor disapproved. Higgs said he thought a press interview by a witness before giving evidence might be prejudicial. However, he chose not to pursue the issue in the lower court. It would not be the last time he would show mercy to his parliamentary friend.

The most important part of this hearing was the reading of de Marigny's first full statement to the police, in which he described the charges as "ridiculous" and said he had no reason to kill Sir Harry. It amounted to a full rebuttal. The statement, headed by his full name,

Marie Alfred Fouquereaux de Marigny, said:

"It is a ridiculous charge as I have no reason to do it. I had dinner at my house with my guests and the last ones were Mrs Ainsley and Mrs Clarke and I took them home in my car in the morning, car number 1383, between 1am and 1.30am. I returned home immediately. My servants were still there as it was raining heavily. I entered my car in the garage and went to bed. My servants apparently left, they told me, around 2.30am. Around 3.15am my friend Georges de Visdelou-Guimbeau took Miss Roberts home and the noise of the car passing woke me up. He returned about fifteen minutes later, entered on the ground floor through the dining room door and went into my room to get his cat, who was making quite a noise trying to get out. He left in a couple of minutes and I went back to sleep. I woke up early having some work to do and went to the farm with some chickens. I returned to town and went to the post office to see if there was any mail. I met Basil McKinney and Oswald Mosely on the corner of Bank Lane and Bay Street. We discussed, for about a few minutes, the races the previous afternoon. I left and returned to the farm where I stayed until roughly 11am. I returned to town to purchase some cheesecloth to make screens with. I met Mr J H Anderson who told me that Sir Harry had been found dead. We both went home and we announced the news to Mr Visdelou and Mr Anderson took me in his car to Westbourne House, and I can swear that I have not seen Sir Harry Oakes since the 29th of March. I have not been to Westbourne before two years for a short visit. This is all I have to say." It was signed M. A. F. de Marigny.

At this hearing, too, the prosecution tried to negate earlier evidence about the much-discussed screen, which Melchen said had been moved out of Sir Harry's bedroom, into the upstairs hallway, and was there when de Marigny visited Westbourne, on the day the body was found. Three detectives on guard duty testified that the accused was at no point allowed upstairs. Thus, the defence would have a difficult job showing that the all-important fingerprint found on the screen was left at any time, other than the frenzied moments when Sir Harry was killed.

As August dragged on, the weather grew increasingly sultry. It was Nassau's rainy season, and overcast skies threw shadows over the town. If the heat was oppressive for the man in the street, it was almost intolerable for de Marigny in his restricted cell. At this time of year, Nassau traditionally sank into a state of near inertia, its inhabitants mopping sweat from their brows and moving as slowly as life would allow in the heavy heat. In the magistrate's court on 17 August, tempers turned ragged. Everyone was feeling the pressure. The thundery weather unleashed a storm of harsh words. Penetrating questions, an explosion between lawyers...according to *The Tribune* "it was a rare scene for the magistrate's court because it carried the flavour of a full-dress Supreme Court skirmish."

At the centre of the clash was Major Pemberton, the CID chief, and the question of the missing towels. The blood-stained towels, which Christie had been so eager to explain away, in his press briefing, had seemingly gone missing until this very morning. Higgs was beside himself with indignation. The questions fired at Major Pemberton were sharp and penetrating. The witness replied in equally curt terms. The crowded courtroom was in a state of high tension. The heat was thick and unforgiving. Higgs was anxious to probe apparent contradictions in Major Pemberton's evidence. In a previous statement, Major Pemberton said he had seen the towels, one on Sir Harry's bed, the other in the smaller room used by Christie, but no longer knew where they were. In reply to Higgs' probing, he changed his tune. He did not know where they were until that morning. Christie's hurriedly assembled press conference and Major Pemberton's amended evidence suggested the prosecution had deep concerns about those towels.

When prosecuting attorney A F Adderley rose to request a week-long adjournment, Higgs' already heightened emotions exploded. Having argued before against prolonged adjournments, Higgs was upset that Adderley was apparently being so cavalier. As the two lawyers rounded on each other, de Marigny bent forward in his box, captivated. When the magistrate said he, too, favoured a week's adjournment because he had some cases to finish, Higgs knew his protest was in vain. Adderley twisted the blade by saying: "I have made a statement and I do not wish to gratify the defence by giving reasons for this and that." Then he challenged the defence's right to question reasons for an adjournment. He said it was out of order. At this point, observers sensed that Adderley, veteran of scores of Supreme Court criminal cases, was pulling rank over the relatively inexperienced Higgs, whose courtroom record was limited. The younger man was clearly being put in his place by the Bahamas' most able criminal specialist. "I don't intend to give any reasons," said a defiant Adderley, "I have not been instructed to say – and I will not say."

Higgs then asked the magistrate to record his objection. This seemed to create a procedural dilemma for Mr Field, who said it would mean opening a new minute book. Higgs suggested recording it in the depositions.

The magistrate said: "I guess I could do that. I can say that the prosecution asks for a remand and the defence objects."

Leaping up, Higgs said: "And that the prosecution refused to give any reason."

Adderley: "I don't think you should put down what my learned friend tells you to put. If you want it verbatim, you can have it, sir."

The magistrate declined the offer and granted the adjournment. De Marigny approached both lawyers, put his arms round their shoulders and said: "Next time, I will offer a trophy."

This gesture intrigued outsiders, especially foreigners who wondered at the apparent informality between the prisoner and the opposing attorneys. But they were unaware of the extreme intimacy of Nassau society in those days. As de Marigny was to record later, he was being tried in a town where everyone knew everyone else, where you were likely to bump into associates from every level of society in the course of a morning stroll. However, de Marigny's unruffled demeanour was a marvel to all. His morale was, on the whole, holding up well. The trophy reference would have come naturally to de Marigny, for trophies had always figured prominently in his life. He was a competitive sailor of quite exceptional ability, and well-known among privileged white Bahamians whose craft raced each other across the turquoise waters of Montagu Bay. Whatever the conflicting views of de Marigny during the late 1930s and early 1940s, and the hostility generated in some quarters by his elopement with Nancy Oakes, there was never any doubt about his prowess as a helmsman. In that area, he commanded great respect.

As prelimary hearings moved ahead, de Marigny's mood rose and dipped between high optimism and deep despair. His sense of humour helped him keep reasonably buoyant at times when he had little reason to be. Occasionally, his troubles overwhelmed him. Behind the scenes, his loyal young wife was working tirelessly on his behalf, though the results were not always entirely to his satisfaction. During August, she visited New York and her mother, Lady Eunice Oakes, in Niagara Falls, Ontario, telling the press that "what we have learned here will eventually be revealed in court. I am more than convinced – in fact, I can say I am positive – that Freddy is not the guilty party."

At various times during the early hearings, the petite heiress could be seen waiting under the portico of Nassau's Supreme Court, to see her husband arrive in the square under police escort. She always ensured she was in a position where he could see her, so that he might draw sustenance from her presence. At a time when he could be forgiven for thinking everyone but his own lawyers was conspiring against him, de Marigny felt uplifted by Nancy's commitment. At only nineteen, she was sufficiently in control of her own mind to be able to resist whatever propaganda came her way, about her husband and his alleged errant behaviour. She had always felt there was something colourfully roguish about him, but that was part of his attraction. Murder, she claimed, was an impossibility, incompatible with all he stood for.

"In the eyes of many people," she told reporters, "I suppose I am just the hysterical wife trying to save my own pride in defending my husband. But it is much more than that. I have always believed that Freddy could not have done this terrible thing. Now I know that he did not." She added: "This talk about Freddy's and father's disagreements has been exaggerated."

Whatever information Nancy de Marigny gleaned from her travels was not revealed. Had Lady Oakes disclosed something about her late husband's dealings and personal relationships? Had she spoken of his business arrangements with Christie? Were there fears and anxieties in Sir Harry's life about which he never spoke, even to his eldest daughter? Whatever she had learned, Nancy's mind had been made up by it. As the press pondered her comments, they picked up one piece of solid information. Nancy had engaged, at considerable expense, a private New York investigator to help her husband's cause.

His name was Raymond Schindler. Meanwhile, Walter Foskett, the Oakes family lawyer from Palm Beach, prepared to fly to the Bahamas for the climax of the most extraordinary murder story of the age. Lady Oakes was on her way from Canada. The big guns were descending on quiet little Nassau town.

Unfortunately for de Marigny, two of those big guns were trained on him. Walter Foskett's contribution to the preliminary investigation did the defendant no favours. His primary objective was to throw light on the estrangement of de Marigny and the Oakes family. Foskett was able to do this with rather more conviction than the average family solicitor, because his relationship with Sir Harry and Lady Oakes went far beyond a straightforward professional arrangement. Having practised in Palm Beach for twenty years, and known Sir Harry for at least a dozen of them, he was as much a close personal friend of the baronet as family legal adviser. It was for this reason that Foskett was able to take such a strong personal position with regard to de Marigny's involvement with Nancy Oakes. Foskett had known Nancy as a small girl. He had watched her grow into an attractive, self-assured, though some would say headstrong, young woman. He had followed the trials and tribulations of school and enjoyed insights into all the familial ups and downs of her early teen years. On Sir Harry's frequent visits to Palm Beach, he and Foskett spent time together. They had common interests. Foskett was to admit in court: "I considered Sir Harry my very warm personal friend."

As such, he was more than usually aware of the undercurrents which developed in the Oakes family due to Nancy's involvement with de Marigny. Foskett's interpretation of events was far from flattering to de Marigny, who emerged from his account of the affair as a seducer, exploiter and opportunist. It was no doubt Foskett's unique relationship with the Oakes family, as legal adviser, close personal friend and general factotum, that prompted de Marigny to seek his help when he was "frozen out" by his less than accommodating in-laws. De Marigny had felt, with some justification, that he was not fully accepted as part of his wife's family circle. There was, he thought, a frostiness in their relations which left him feeling uncomfortable. Nancy, too, was aware of her parents' lack of warmth towards her beloved Freddy and craved some kind of reconciliation. Without their full approval, she felt her marriage would suffer, and that she and her husband would feel embattled from the start.

On 25 August, Foskett appeared before Magistrate Field, to tell of an approach de Marigny made to him in February of that year (1943), with a view to easing relationships between the young couple and Sir Harry and Lady Oakes. It was one of two occasions when he and the accused had met. De Marigny had asked Foskett to "use his influence" with Lady Oakes, in particular, to get their relationship back on a more cordial footing. "I told him that that was a personal matter and something which he should attend to himself," said Foskett in court, "He stated that he was a gentleman and that he was not treated as a gentleman. I then told him that I personally disapproved of the manner in which he had married Nancy, that he was a man of mature years, much older than Nancy, who had been twice married and twice before divorced and who had pursued Nancy in her attendance at school in New York, at a time when she was but seventeen years of age, that he had invaded Sir Harry and Lady Oakes' home and had married Nancy two days after Nancy's eighteenth birthday, without the knowledge and consent of her parents."

"I further told him that certain information had come to me, by which his former wife was making certain charges against him, and that certain information which I had, was in the form of a letter in the handwriting of his former wife Ruth de Marigny and over her signature. He asked me to give him the letter or give him a copy of it. I told him I would not do that because it was addressed to Lady Oakes. He stated that his former wife would do anything to injure him or Nancy. He then made some very defamatory and ungentlemanly statements concerning his former wife, Ruth, and her family."

De Marigny told him, even before knowing the details, that the contents of the letter were untrue and he could disprove them. He wanted an opportunity to do so. When Foskett revealed the contents, de Marigny branded them "all lies" and said his ex-wife was trying to undermine his marriage to Nancy. Foskett said he had not told Sir Harry and Lady Oakes of the letter and would not do so, unless circumstances made disclosure "imperative." De Marigny then said he would go immediately to New York to secure proof that the allegations were false.

In those days, when divorce was still relatively uncommon, there was a widespread feeling among males – and especially so-called 'gentlemen' – that women were fragile, sensitive creatures at the mercy of their potentially caddish partners. It is a measure of Sir Harry's and Foskett's naivete that they were taken in by Ruth de Marigny's vilification of the count. Today, they would know better.

Though keen to characterise himself a gentleman, and not being too averse to the title "count", despite being reluctant to use it himself, de Marigny did not have the financial resources to sustain a lifestyle at the highest level. Though entrepreneurial by nature, and a property owner with a speculative streak, he was not cash-rich, and frequently found himself living off an overdraft. However, to say he was poor would be misleading. By his own admission, de Marigny was a quite assertive socialite in his youth, inveigling his way into society circles, being seen at all the "right" functions, and pursuing debutantes and their mothers with the kind of gallic intensity which made their fathers and husbands uncomfortable. He and his friend the Marquis were unquestionably of a kind, always oozing their way into society circles, winning over the women and causing the men deep irritation.

At Nassau Yacht Club, where he was quite a popular figure, due in part to his infectious humour, but mainly because of his considerable sailing ability, he was regarded as an aristocrat of dubious provenance and scant resources. Nassau had always attracted shadowy figures from distant lands, either fugitives from justice, or ne'er-do-wells on the run from themselves, and de Marigny seemed to fit the vaguely disreputable image of the expatriate misfit with something to hide. The name de Marigny was itself disturbingly exotic, and the title – which de Marigny sometimes brushed off, unconvincingly it seemed to some, as of no account – always came over as slightly fake, rooted in Franco-Mauritian nobility with little meaning in the modern world. He and his close friend, the Marquis Georges de Visdelou-Guimbeau, a sallow-faced character with a Chaplinesque moustache, were social oddities in conservative Nassau, where more conventional foreigners were even regarded with suspicion. With their sharp suits, Frenchified accents, and easy charm, they were seen as untrustworthy chancers with social aspirations above their means.

It was inevitable, therefore, that money, and de Marigny's

perceived need for it in abundance to sustain what many saw as his inflated view of himself, should be seen as the prime motive in this unhappy affair. There were several things the Oakes family disliked about de Marigny, but underlying everything was the suspicion that he wanted to use his marriage to lay claim to a slice of the family fortune. If there had been any doubt about this up to now, there was none once Foskett had delivered his evidence. The prosecutor, Fred Adderley, extracted this disclosure with a single question: "Did you prepare a document on Sir Harry Oakes' instruction after the visit of the accused to your office?"

Foskett: "I did."

Adderley: "On what date?"

Foskett: "On the 15th of February, 1943."

Adderley: "And what was that document?"

Foskett: "That document was his last will and testament. It was executed by Sir Harry in my office in the presence of myself, Lady Oakes and the witnesses."

Adderley: "And is that will in your possession?"

Foskett: "That will is in my possession in safe-keeping in Florida."

Higgs chose not to cross-examine him.

The impact of this evidence on all who heard it was considerable. It seemed to reinforce all the many misgivings about de Marigny that circulated in Nassau at the time. The implications of Foskett's testimony were clear: Sir Harry, suspicious of de Marigny's motives, drew up a new will to ensure that Nancy's inheritance would be sewn up legally in such a way that her husband would never be able to get his hands on it. Some suspected that Nancy had been disinherited, but this was not so. She was ensured an income with deferral of the capital sum.

Overnight, the gossip about Foskett's evidence was rife in homes throughout Nassau. It added tantalising extra detail to the portrait now emerging of de Marigny, whose defence seemed to be resting on increasingly fragile foundations. Having already been maligned as a cradle-snatcher, predator, seducer, exploiter and mountebank, de Marigny now had to square up to the most damning epithet of all. He was being depicted, by the prosecution, as a fortune-hunter, who was prepared to prey on the innocence of a teenage girl, to tap into her family's money. Higgs and Callender, the young barristers charged with defending de Marigny from the death penalty, were at this stage facing quite formidable odds. And their task was not made easier by the events of 27 August.

Until now, the people of Nassau had been left to imagine the full depth of grief suffered by Lady Eunice Oakes. Having been at the family home in Maine at the time of the murder, she had been distanced from the distressing scenes in Nassau. In those days, of course, there was no television to project grief-stricken faces into people's sitting rooms, so her first appearance in court came as a shock to many. The tragedy had clearly taken a terrible toll, for deep lines now marked what had always appeared a cheerful countenance. She was bereft, desolate. In the witness-box, she looked older than her years, burdened down by what had evidently been a grievous loss. Dressed in black, accompanied by her Nassau lawyer, A K Solomon, and business manager, H N Kelly, and the ever-present Walter Foskett, Lady Oakes entered the courtroom in total silence. She was met at the door by Nancy and they proceeded together to the magistrate's office to confer privately. Court officials spoke in hushed tones, noting her debilitating distress.

As the magistrate took his seat in court, a tearful Nancy walked quietly from his office to sit in the alcove near his dais. Then Lady Oakes, in what reporters described as a "severe black costume" and wearing dark glasses, entered followed by Mr Solomon, and took her seat in the lawyers' enclosure. The day was hot, very hot, and the magistrate moved his fan so that Lady Oakes could benefit from its cool blast. The packed court was respectfully silent as she took the oath. Lady Oakes was so unhinged by her ordeal that she was allowed to sit alongside Mr Solomon, who kept handing her a bottle of medicine from which she sipped, as if this tonic were vital for her survival. During the oath she sobbed, paused and swallowed, then asked the court orderly for water. There was concern throughout her appearance that she might not be able to continue. It seemed that grief had left her in a state of near disability. She removed her glasses, rested her head in her hand and closed her eyes. While these extraordinary scenes were taking place, Nancy sat bolt upright in her seat, watching her mother's face anxiously. Even Higgs and his client de Marigny were noticeably affected by Lady Oakes' appearance. While de Marigny gestured consolingly to his wife, who was visibly disturbed by what was going on, Higgs softened his usual combative tone when rising to object about alleged hearsay or to make other legal points. Indeed, at times he seemed almost apologetic to be making the points at all. Then Lady Oakes' quavering voice broke the silence.

After testifying that she was the mother of five children, of whom Nancy was the eldest, she said she was visiting Canada in May of 1942 when she heard of Nancy's marriage to de Marigny. "We were frightfully upset," she said of the family's reaction, "She was only a child, she was still at school. We knew that Alfred was divorced and was still living with his former wife – or whatever you call a wife that's divorced – but we decided to make the best of the situation and put up a bold front."

She admitted that when the couple spent a vacation with her in Bar Harbour, de Marigny was "very sweet" and tried to be nice to the children. In return, they liked him very much. From Maine they went to New York, then Mexico, where Nancy became very ill with typhoid fever. "She was desperately ill," she said, describing how stomach transfusions were necessary, "Oh, it was awful." This illness eventually led to trench mouth and gangrene which required a series of operations. Under questioning, Lady Oakes also revealed that her daughter became pregnant, but that termination was necessary because of her illness.

Lady Oakes admitted that the relationship with de Marigny was at this point "extremely strained, uncomfortable and unpleasant." It was made worse when he went into hospital to have his tonsils removed, and installed himself in a room next to Nancy, which had been reserved by Sir Harry. In a furious telephone call, Sir Harry told him: "If you don't get out of that room, I'll kick you out." He said there were other rooms he could use. This explosion led to total estrangement between the Oakes and the de Marignys, especially when the letter from Ruth de Marigny was sent to her by Foskett on her instructions. Nancy wrote to her parents saying she and her husband were cutting themselves off until de Marigny was accepted as a "full member" of the family.

However, Nancy's appeal did nothing to break down the wall of hostility. Asked by counsel if it changed anything, Lady Oakes said: "Certainly not! I considered him completely irresponsible in his care of Nancy and I knew he was trying to ingratiate himself with Sydney (the eldest of the Oakes' three sons) and trying to alienate the child from us. Furthermore, I did not approve of his treatment of Ruth de Marigny."

The awesome spectre of the gallows must have loomed in the defendant's mind at this point because the circumstantial evidence was accumulating against him at worrying speed. The framework of the prosecution case was now clearly delineated: on the evidence presented to date, they had de Marigny near Westbourne at the relevant time, they had testimony showing physical effects of fire, they had a fingerprint from the murder scene, and they had motive. Circumstantial evidence plus motive can together be sufficient to send a man to the gallows or electric chair, even in these supposedly more enlightened times. In the less sophisticated 1940s, and especially in a colony where liberal attitudes to crime and punishment were unheard of, circumstantial evidence, motive AND a fingerprint were considered conclusive.

As de Marigny was escorted back to his cell, it was becoming clear that something ingenious was required from the defence team to save his life. But, in bookmakers' parlance, they were a long-odds chance, as unlikely to win as a three-legged nag in the Grand National. Things were looking ominous for the count.

Only one decision was required of Magistrate Field at the end of the preliminary investigation -- to determine whether there was a prima facie case against the accused. Not surprisingly, he ruled that there was, and that de Marigny should stand trial at the October session of the Supreme Court.

Though expected, the formal committal of de Marigny to the October sessions sent tremors of excitement and trepidation through Nassau; excitement at the prospect of a high-profile courtroom spectacle, the glare of international attention and the drama all that implied; trepidation at the prospect of reaching a decision on de Marigny's guilt, which many thought unimaginable and implausible.

Chapter Six

PRIVATE EYE

Big murder trials have much in common with theatrical productions. They produce high drama and a compelling cast. Costumes and speeches add sartorial and vocal flourishes. The defendant, invariably, plays the lead, whatever his strengths or weaknesses, for most eyes are on him. Even the most nondescript of murder suspects is intriguing because everyone wonders what exactly goes on in his head. The victim, too, plays a strong supporting role. Off-stage, inevitably, but he or she often holds the key to the plot. The judge, the barristers, the witnesses, are all potential stars, depending on how they perform. Sometimes, there are bit players who steal the show.

The Oakes murder trial was remarkable for many things, but especially the richness, in every sense, of the cast. Yet one unusual figure insinuated his way into the Oakes affair in ways that added to de Marigny's already considerable burden. He was the New York private investigator Raymond Schindler. In theatrical terms, Schindler was emphatically off-stage. It's not even possible to characterise him as a back stage boy. He was a spectral presence most of the main players were barely aware of, yet he was unquestionably around, lurking in the wings, promising to emerge as significant to the plot.

Schindler, a New York-born criminologist with an international reputation, was hired by Nancy to confirm her husband's innocence. She wanted him to work behind the scenes to unearth evidence the police had missed. She wanted to be sure all the bases were covered. It was not surprising that Nancy found her way to his door because most wealthy people in some kind of difficulty did so sooner or later. Schindler's reputation was solid, yet few knew why.

This Alfred Hitchcock lookalike worked almost exclusively for the well-to-do. This was not surprising because his fees were Himalayan. He did nothing to encourage clients of modest means. He was a man of extravagant tastes whose jowls had been augmented by a million gourmet meals, mostly bought at other people's expense. It was said of him that, no matter how high his daily expense allowance, he would exceed it. With his personal meter running, Schindler didn't come cheap, but he was still in constant demand, and he reinforced his celebrity status among sleuths with impressive public relations skills. Cynics felt the image was bigger than the man, but this was no hindrance to his progress. For Nancy, money had never been a problem, or even a consideration, when there was something she needed to do. Hence, Schindler was engaged to get her husband out of a hole, whatever the cost. For the accused, this was meant to come as a pleasant surprise, a morale booster. The problem for de Marigny was that, not only had he not requested his help, he was the one paying the bill, which threatened to be considerable. Though Nancy, with the exuberance and impetuosity of youth, saw Schindler as the answer to all her husband's problems, de Marigny saw him as just another problem. The prospect of a $150,000 invoice did not excite him and he doubted if the super-sleuth would deliver the goods.

Schindler was a classic example of his kind. "I have not come to look for any one thing," he told reporters on arrival in Nassau. "I have been asked to confer with the Hon Godfrey Higgs, counsel for the defence, and to study the whole case. My job is to reconstruct the murder of Sir Harry Oakes in the light of conflicting circumstances and to make a private analysis of the case."

It all sounded ridiculously vague, but Nancy was impressed, and that was the main thing. He explained: "I was approached about this case before Mrs de Marigny enlisted my services. She was not the first person to discuss the matter with me." Hence, Schindler carefully constructed an image of himself as the shrewd "expert" in demand, the sleuth hired and trusted by the rich and discerning. Even his detractors had to concede that he was a cunning operator.

To dispassionate observers, it was difficult to see what could possibly be gained, by having Schindler prowling furtively around Nassau, while the Oakes investigation was in full swing. At best, police investigators would see him as an irrelevant irritant, a nuisance pushing his nose in where it was not wanted. But Nancy was convinced the portly, grey-haired figure could make some headway where others might fail. She was impressed by his self-assurance and comfortable presence. Among his proudest professional boasts was that he once saved a man from the electric chair. He also managed to track down the real killer in the case, a man the police had not even suspected. It was a triumph he milked to the limit. Much of his work, however, was more routine, like finding the "lost" beneficiaries of family legacies, and digging dirt in matrimonial scandals. He was an ace in the murky world of domestic intrigue among the rich.

Schindler was a law student who never practised law. Instead, he specialised in private investigations, first working for others, then setting up his own business, International Investigators Inc., which engaged sleuths to travel the world seeking information others didn't want them to have. By the first week in September, Schindler revealed he had unearthed a clue known to the prosecution, but not revealed by them because it did not accord with their preconceived notions of the case. He had volunteered information to the authorities which they did not regard as important. But he was unwilling to disclose what the information was. This tactic of throwing up supposedly significant disclosures, without ever revealing the details, was a classic Schindler move. He wanted people to believe that he operated at an elevated level, and that mere cops could not keep abreast of his intellect and investigative expertise. This 'clue' sounded like limp reward for his efforts to date, and poor value for money if the de Marignys' fears about his fees were to be believed. Schindler also made it clear that, under terms of his arrangement with Nancy, any information he uncovered would be disclosed, regardless of who was affected by it. No-one was holding their breath, it seemed. But he felt Mrs de Marigny's belief in her husband's innocence was clearly indicated by her agreement with this arrangement, which also created an illusion of high-mindedness in Schindler himself.

In all his deliberations, Schindler affected an authoritative air. He saw himself as the city slicker among the hicks, the man with all the answers. To Nancy, he was a formidable intellect, a reassuring presence, but to others he appeared more bustle and bluff than substance, a brush salesman who had somehow washed up in the more lucrative world of private investigation.

Schindler next surfaced in Nassau with Professor Leonard Keeler in tow. This was the man who gave the lie-detector to the world, an instrument which recorded pulse, perspiration, blood pressure and other reactions in determining guilt or innocence. The assumption was that de Marigny would be subjected to tests but, if that was the case, Schindler and Keeler weren't saying. Again, the super-sleuth was deepening the intrigue. However, Schindler – no doubt with one eye on his fees – said: "We can't say anything now except that we found some very interesting things and are very much encouraged."

These meaningless titbits of non-information were very much part of the Schindler game plan. They gave the impression he was privy to information denied to ordinary mortals. All the time, he wanted to appear to be on the inside track. Such comments were his safeguard against a terminated contract.

While the Schindler circus was keeping the Oakes case before the public during the lull between the preliminary hearings and the full trial, the Bahamas police chief, Erskine-Lindop, was transferred to Trinidad. This move was said, officially, to have been in the offing for some time. Erskine-Lindop had, it seemed, been demoralised by criticism he received after the 1942 riots and had drifted into a resigned and ineffectual state of mind, which was undermining force morale, according to those whose job it was to put a positive spin on his departure. This did not accord with later disclosures, which suggested that the commissioner, though marginalised by the Miami duo of Melchen and Barker, had been on the verge of cracking the case, taking a local suspect – through relentless interrogation – to the very brink of a confession. The removal of Erskine-Lindop at such a sensitive stage in the inquiries has always been a point for debate, and a source of genuine concern. The official line – that the move had been planned months in advance – was implausible, for even if it had been planned, no sensible authority would execute that plan when the commissioner was immersed in the biggest and most important investigation of his career. Once again, there is only one credible explanation: Erskine-Lindop, a veteran of the colonial police service, and a man of unshakeable integrity, had been moved because he was an obstacle blocking the conspiracy now in progress. There was no way the commissioner would allow himself to be part of a miscarriage of justice. Based on what he disclosed in later years, in one of the rare comments he ever made about the case, he was making real progress with his own line of inquiry at the time of his transfer. The trouble (though he didn't suggest this) was that his theories clashed with the Duke's cover-up. He had to go. And his dogged silence, right up to his death many years later, suggested he, too, might well have been pressured.

In today's climate, such a move would, quite rightly, provoke questions in the House, or at the very least a spirited debate in the press, but Erskine-Lindop's departure went virtually unremarked. This, as much as anything, points to the extraordinary power structure prevailing in the Bahamas at the time. The Duke, as Governor, exercised considerable authority, especially if that authority was being exercised wholly in accordance with the wishes of the Bay Street Boys. On this occasion, it was. The almost total power exercised by the Duke and those who formed the self-serving Nassau ruling clique of the day rendered grassroots dissent both pointless and inadvisable. The instinctive deference of the times would have muted feelings still more. Thus, colonial officials – whose entire careers could be jeopardised by the whims of local despots – were frightened into compliance. Though a man of firm principle and steadfast morals, Erskine-Lindop would have found himself severely undermined by the manoeuvrings of the Nassau ruling clique. He went silently and maintained that silence until the end.

Against these unscrupulous machinations behind the scenes, de Marigny seemingly had little hope. The comings and goings of Schindler, however fruitless, were all he had going for him. At least the private eye created an illusion of vigilance on the accused's behalf. But the count continued to entertain extreme reservations about him. To his mind, Schindler bore all the hallmarks of the kind of highly expensive snooper high society people engaged to hunt down errant husbands or faithless wives. He had little experience of high-profile criminal work. In a murder investigation of this magnitude, it was likely the sleuth was out of his depth, especially as he was expected to unearth clues against the backdrop of an extremely defensive police operation. Most disturbing of all was that three hundred dollars a day fee, plus expenses, which given his extravagant tastes and formidable appetite were unlikely to be modest. Later, de Marigny was to describe Schindler as a man who, given an unlimited budget, would exceed it. At the time, contrary to popular belief, Nancy had no money of her own, only the expectation of money. Schindler's bill, therefore, would be picked up by de Marigny, something for him to look forward to in the event of an acquittal. He was not amused.

Whatever his shortcomings as an investigator, Schindler proved to be a consummate public relations man. He was an arch-manipulator of the press and had the eloquence and eye-for-a-headline to ensure that his client's case remained prominently in the public prints. However, de Marigny was unsure how this would help his cause. He and Nancy began bickering over his role; she steadfastly convinced of his worth, de Marigny highly sceptical, believing Schindler to be little more than a high-class conman.

Flying back and forth between New York and Nassau, Schindler certainly appeared to be busy, but the sum total of his efforts to date was nothing that the defence could make use of. He had interviewed witnesses, annoyed local police, and hinted knowingly at new developments, but there was nothing to undermine the forbidding prosecution edifice which now stood between de Marigny and his freedom.

As he scuttled round Nassau pursuing his inquiries, Schindler dropped hints to the press suggesting he had established de Marigny's innocence. But he never produced a shred of evidence, nor did he testify at the trial. Instead, he made much of alleged police tapping of his telephone, leaving the impression among the gullible and credulous that he was a dangerous adversary the prosecution was anxious to neutralise. Meanwhile, Nancy continued to persuade her husband that Schindler would help counter the avalanche of propaganda now deepening his plight. "Ray is going to turn around this bad publicity," she said.

Her belief that Schindler was well-liked by reporters was undoubtedly true, and no wonder. On slow news days, when pressmen were finding it difficult to justify their expense accounts, Schindler was the kind of man who could spring a headline from a hat. He was shrewd enough, and glib enough, to burnish any fragment of fanciful speculation he could lay hands on, and present it to them as the genuine article. During that menacing hiatus between the preliminary hearings and the trial, he was a godsend for working journalists. Meanwhile, he was keeping Nancy happy by providing pseudo-authoritative interpretations of events to date. Those unschooled in the law, especially when they are not yet out of their teens, are easily taken in by a few arcane legal phrases, especially when uttered by an apparently successful middle-aged man, who was clearly on top of his trade. However, the truth is that Schindler turned up nothing that was remotely useful during the time he worked for the de Marignys. Yet right up to his death by heart attack in 1959, he maintained he possessed the key to the Oakes mystery. On his office wall were framed newspaper articles referring to the legendary private detective who had cracked the case.

By 'talking a good fight', a boxing phrase I love, Schindler gave the impression of being a superb operator. By stringing along clients with nebulous remarks like "There have been developments we can't discuss" he kept hope alive and guaranteed more fat fees. By using the press, and trading on his friendship with headline-hungry reporters, he was able to create an impressive image for himself. Soon, words like "legendary" attached themselves to him like lice. He gave every impression of being an effective fantasist, who came to believe the highly dubious concoctions of his own mind. For their money, the de Marignys got nothing but bluff and bluster, a little bombast and an encouraging headline or two. However, there were no answers. And that's what they needed more than anything.

Schindler carefully cultivated his own mythology. Working from a small office near Grand Central Station in Manhattan, he shrewdly used his assignments as exercises in self-promotion, hinting darkly at secret information he had uncovered, dropping names of prominent clients, nurturing his aura as a high society private eye. It seems most of his clients were women who were happy to off-load some of their husbands' fortunes, to hire this superficially reassuring, but not very effective, private detective. Nancy employed him "to get to the bottom of this case." Of course, he got to the bottom of nothing, but enjoyed many "conferences" over lunch at the British Colonial Hotel, then Nassau's most salubrious, where the bill was always charged to de Marigny's account. In fact, during the time Schindler was officially working on the de Marignys' behalf, a couple of disturbing incidents did occur which could have thrown new light on the case. Neither was investigated by Schindler, who apparently ignored a real opportunity to make a contribution, and they were allowed to fade from public consciousness. But in de Marigny's eyes, they were highly significant.

One of the most pressing theories about the Oakes murder is that the killing was carried out by a hitman, or hitmen, on behalf of another party. If any evidence could be turned up to support this theory, it would ease de Marigny's predicament because no-one was suggesting that he was assisted by anyone in the task of killing Sir Harry. While he was in custody, de Marigny received information from his friend, Basil McKinney, that he had talked with a caretaker and his assistant at Lyford Cay. Both men swore that, on the night of the murder, a vessel arrived there at about one in the morning. A car was waiting nearby to drive away two men who returned about an hour later and left aboard the cabin cruiser. Although it was a stormy night, the men were able to record the name and number of the boat. According to de Marigny, who referred to this matter in his book about the case, Godfrey Higgs was asked by McKinney to meet the men and take their statements. But he was off the island that weekend and never did. The men met mysterious ends; one drowned while the other was found hanging from a tree. Two watchmen at Westbourne, who lived in the pine barrens south of Nassau, left for a fishing trip to Andros and never returned. These extraordinary events were the beginning of a long sequence of unexplained killings, mysterious deaths and disappearances which pointed to a local conspiracy. Whoever killed Sir Harry Oakes, whether a local citizen or a foreign hitman, was being protected by plotters in Nassau. There were people at work who were hell-bent on ensuring that the truth about the Oakes murder was never told. Given the nature of Nassau society at the time, the relatively humble and powerless state of the blacks, and their overwhelmingly positive feelings about Sir Harry, it is a fair bet that this conspiracy was being orchestrated by powerful people, and that meant the Bay Street Boys and their Governor, sitting in his mansion on Mount Fitzwilliam.

De Marigny could have been excused for feeling despondent at this stage. News of the deaths and disappearances of four potentially crucial witnesses was relayed to him in his cell. It irritated him that Higgs had not responded with the diligence one might have expected in securing statements from the watchmen at Lyford Cay. The lawyer's excuse was that he was exhausted and needed rest, but de Marigny was to record years later that a swift response by Higgs might well have saved the men's lives and created a whole set of new problems for the prosecution. As things stood at this stage – the late summer of 1943 – Eric Hallinan and Fred Adderley held by far the better hand. Nothing seemed to be going well for the defence. De Marigny faced not only a formidable stockpile of evidence against him, but also the stark realization that unscrupulous forces were at work to eliminate anyone who might have information helpful to his cause. The climate of fear which descended on Nassau was to remain for many decades to come. Even now, in the early years of the twenty-first century, mention of the Oakes affair, to a friend in a Nassau restaurant, will often prompt a long-practised response, especially among older Nassau citizens of a certain class. They will glance quickly round the room, to check who's sitting close by and say whatever they have to say in a whisper. To declaim loudly on any aspect of the Oakes affair, and especially to declare one's theories about the possible killer, is still regarded as an unwarranted indiscretion.

As the trial of Count Alfred de Marigny drew near, there was but one factor that gave the accused a modicum of encouragement. That was the knowledge that the world's press were about to brave the perils of wartime travel and descend on Nassau in droves. De Marigny imagined, without much justification as it turned out, that the close scrutiny of leading journalists of the day would have the effect of controlling the excesses of the conspirators ranged against him. With the international press around, he thought, he would at least get a fair trial. Just how fair the trial turned out to be will be shown in due course.

For the moment, de Marigny was left to ponder his predicament. But, in spite of lapses into short spells of melancholy, he remained remarkably buoyant. There was an irrepressible element to the man. Even his own lawyers thought him roguishly upbeat in the face of such daunting odds.

Chapter Seven

THE TRIAL

On the day I was born, 7 October, 1943, *The Tribune* announced the opening of the Supreme Court session, during which de Marigny would be tried. It said the Attorney General would, on the following day, file cases due for trial, then summon jurors. Like many wartime babies, I have often reflected that I was born into a cruel, heartless and chaotic world. As I was making my entrance in the back bedroom of my family's home in Leicestershire, in the English Midlands, Europe was in turmoil as the Second World War moved inexorably towards its conclusion. Less than a thousand miles to the east of that cosy bedroom, as Hitler and his evil regime braced themselves for the final convulsions of the conflict they created, people were still dying in the most appalling and hideous fashion in the holocaust, and under falling bombs. My parents always told me that the last all-clear sirens were sounding in Wigston Magna, the village where I was born, as the midwife arrived to welcome me into the world. I've always liked to think of that as a good omen, but there was still a lot of dying to be done by servicemen and civilians in Europe, and the Far East, before this war was at its end. However, I was comfortably oblivious of it all, as I was of de Marigny's ordeal four thousand miles away, in a land of sunshine which, one distant day, would become an important part of my life.

Just ten days before the trial was due to begin, the prosecution announced that it wanted to reopen the preliminary investigation, to introduce new evidence. Five additional witnesses were to be ranged against de Marigny, a development that did little to hearten him. The key one was a near neighbour, Thomas Lavelle, who lived opposite de Marigny's home in Victoria Avenue. Lavelle, who was due to leave the island, was heard by acting magistrate Reginald Glanville, and his testimony was to reinforce accounts of hostility, between the accused and his father-in-law.

Remarkably, de Marigny emerged from his cell for this hearing looking fresh-faced and debonair, every inch the young nobleman of repute whose title pre-dated the French Revolution. It was the first time that he had appeared without his beard. Reporters noticed how youthful he looked. Considering the conditions he was obliged to endure during his remand, a cramped cell with a pee bucket in one corner which gave off a perpetual odour, he could be credited for retaining his morale and composure in trying times. Throughout Lavelle's evidence, de Marigny was his usual attentive self, leaning over the dock rail to absorb every word. Both his lawyers, Higgs and Callender, were present for the hearing.

Mr Lavelle, a guest house proprietor, was going abroad for surgery and would not be in Nassau for the trial. His contribution to proceedings was not crucial, but it served to buttress suggestions that there was, indeed, bad blood between de Marigny and Oakes. In March that year, he said, he was looking out of his window at his Victoria Guest House when he saw the pair arguing on the road. "You'd better not write any more letters to my wife," Sir Harry said, "You are a sex maniac."

Oakes, said the witness, was speaking in a loud voice, and at one point in the exchange mentioned his son, Sydney, who the family felt was being unduly influenced by the count. The boy emerged from de Marigny's house and was driven off. Mr Lavelle said Sir Harry appeared to be in "a mad state of mind" but de Marigny acted quietly throughout. Few of the words that passed between the two men were distinguishable, though it was clear that Oakes did most of the talking.

A few days before the trial began, Schindler reappeared, flying in from Mexico via Miami. As usual, he was full of vague, but supposedly significant, references to the case, saying his Mexican jaunt – that was not the word he used – had given him "some answers", but he didn't foresee any surprises from the defence, although there was some new information "which will be of value."

The vanishing watchmen from Westbourne, and the mysterious disappearance of the two men at Lyford Cay, seemed not to have exercised his investigative instincts at all: too much like real work, maybe, or perhaps he was scared of being similarly despatched. Schindler, after all, appeared to be much more interested in his own welfare than anything else, and the meter was still ticking over nicely, with some pleasant foreign trips thrown in, all at de Marigny's expense, of course.

As October 18 approached, the press began to gather like sandflies. Trilbied reporters flew in from New York, bringing a big city buzz to Nassau's central area, around which the courts and parliamentary buildings clustered in the sunlight. In many respects, wartime Nassau was a colonial toytown whose administrative offices were like a ready-made movie set. On this set were to appear some fascinating figures. To add an extra touch of glamour, the press corps was to include Erle Stanley Gardner, doyen of thriller writers, creator of *Perry Mason*, whose incisive prose was about to be engaged in describing a trial to enthral the world.

As the steam heat of that summer softened into autumn, a season in Nassau unrecognisable from the misty months of mellow fruitfulness known to all New Englanders and northern Europeans, the tiny colonial capital became the focus for unprecedented media attention. Nothing quite so sensational as the Oakes trial had happened to the Bahamas since the first colonial Governor, Woodes Rogers, cleared the pirates out a couple of centuries before. Every section of Nassau society, from the humblest black to the mightiest white, was in a state of excitement and high expectation, though their perspectives would have differed considerably.

Among the ruling whites, with their superior attitudes, de Marigny was seen as a slightly bogus gentleman with ambitions above his means. Fine competitive sailor that he was, and a charmer with it, he was irredeemably suspect, by virtue of his actions and his mysteriously exotic origins. The elopement with Nancy Oakes was near felonious in their eyes, especially as money was so transparently the motive, or seemingly so. The blacks, however, viewed things differently. Although Sir Harry was popular for his magnanimity, so was de Marigny for his compassion. Most white men in Nassau during the 1940s fell into two distinct categories: the racist Bahamian whites, with their absurd delusions of superiority, and the haughty British colonials with their braying voices and twitching moustaches. Neither was revered, or even liked, by the average black, who felt both types were hell-bent on preserving the status quo to their own advantage. The tragedy for them, the shanty-dwellers, was that Oakes and de Marigny both fell outside the stereotypes, and presented much more acceptable versions, of the caucasian ruling classes. They were so different from each other in so many ways, yet there was a human quality they shared, and that quality was a genuine regard for people less fortunate than themselves. De Marigny's campaign for water in deprived communities, and his admirable support for the Devil Island castaways would have made him a hero in these more enlightened times, but in the 1940s he was seen as a liberal upstart with preposterous ideals.

In the immediate post-war era, suspicion of "liberals" would reach panic levels in the United States, culminating in the Joe McCarthy witch-hunts, and the Un-American Activities Committee in the early 1950s. Among Americans, Communism was seen as a potent threat to the young democracy, and to big money interests. In the Bahamas, liberalism was seen as a dangerously naive philosophy which would undermine white self-interest. In both places, reactionary feelings were vehement.

The trial of Count Alfred de Marigny opened amid the full pomp and ceremony one would expect in a patriotic possession of the old British Empire. Pop-eyed Americans were transfixed by the spectacle, which reflected centuries of tradition going back, via the Great Reform Bill, the English Civil War, the Reformation and the Wars of the Roses to the Magna Carta and Norman Conquest. Every aspect of these proceedings had its roots in the deep dark loam of British history, much of it enriched by the blood of fallen soldiers and the living fibre of their high ideals.

Crowds besieged the law courts building, with its elegant portico and dark wood interior, forcing police to form a cordon to keep them back. A crier straight out of a Charles Dickens novel bellowed "Court!" and cracked his wooden staff on the floor. The public gallery, packed to capacity, was agog with barely contained excitement. From the rear, ascending the dais, emerged the Chief Justice, Sir Oscar Daly, in his shoulder-length wig and scarlet gown. He seemed to materialise from the floor like a spectre. "Oyez! Oyez! Oyez!" intoned the crier, "All manner of persons having anything to do before His Majesty's Supreme Court in the Bahama Islands draw near and give your attendance and you will be heard. God save the King!"

The judge acknowledged the bows of his bewigged legal brethren at the Bar and took his seat. For the highly cynical, highly sceptical New York reporters, this colourful piece of theatre was hard to comprehend. There was something extremely comical, yet undeniably impressive, about it. Two centuries ago, their forebears had shaken off the absurdities and pretensions of the motherland, but the Loyalists who fled the American Revolution had settled in this outcrop of British territory and retained the old country's rituals and finery. If there was something Vaudevillian about it, there was also something timeless and reassuring. The wigs, the gowns, the arcane legal terminology, the rigid courtesies and obsequies, all coalesced into something seemingly inviolable, free from the whims of fads and fashion.

As we shall see in due course, this phantasmagoric arena was not, alas, free from the taint of human frailty, but it preserved its integrity by exposing it with a ruthlessness and efficiency that was to be the talk of lawyers, for decades to come. Legal history was to be made in the trial of de Marigny, along with a young man's legal reputation, which would, from this case forth, carry the lustre of his triumph. Others, of course, would fare less well, for that is the nature of the courts. Winners beget losers, and the losers in the de Marigny case would live with their loss for all time, carrying the burden of defeat like stigmata. Not for the defeat itself, but the nature of their defeat. This would not be defeat with honour, but with everlasting shame.

The day, 18 October, 1943, was cloudy. De Marigny walked briskly from the nearby Central Police Station to the court across the road under close police escort. The accused appeared confident, purposeful, though there seemed little room for confidence considering the perils he faced. What he didn't know was that the hemp rope for his execution had already arrived on the island, ready to be looped over the gallows on which he would die. If bookmakers were taking bets on the outcome, de Marigny would not be given a prayer. The circumstantial evidence was powerful, the motives overwhelming, the fingerprint conclusive. The smart money was on a guilty verdict and de Marigny was an odds-on certainty to swing. That's how bad it was.

The constables flanked de Marigny as he stood erect in the barred dock he was later to describe as a cage. He felt like a menagerie exhibit, gawped at by the assembled throng. He looked straight at the court registrar, Clyde Roberts, as he read the indictment. "Marie Alfred Fouquereaux de Marigny, you are charged with murder under section 335 of the Penal Code (Chapter 60); particulars of the offence being that during the night of the 7th and 8th of July, 1943, at New Providence, you did murder Sir Harry Oakes, Baronet. Are you guilty?"

The moonless night on which Sir Harry died brought a spattering of summer rain. The wind strengthened to herald the approaching storm. At some time between about 11.30pm and early the following morning, Sir Harry was killed in the most horrific circumstances. Were there gunshots? Did he scream? Did he know his killer? Did he fight for his life? Or was he killed in his sleep, bludgeoned to death with a single blow? Surprisingly, none of these questions was answered conclusively in the court drama about to unfold. In fact, if there is one thing really strange about the trial of Alfred de Marigny, it is that it established so little. This was, of course, partly due to the idiosyncratic detection methods of Melchen and Barker, but the vagueness which characterised this celebrated trial was also the product of the Duke of Windsor's well-laid plans. Too much detail was inadvisable in a case where the suspect was so clearly guilty. Select the evidence that supported the prosecution case and destroy the rest. That was the Duke's highly simplistic approach to this troublesome affair. With Erskine-Lindop now safely out of the way, Melchen and Barker well-briefed, and Fred Adderley primed to do his considerable best before the bar of the court, this inconvenience could be safely disposed of. The hangman would do the rest, leaving an expendable playboy twitching on the end of the rope.

Meanwhile, not wishing to be troubled by the unpleasant details, the Duke and Duchess sent their regrets. They would be visiting friends in Washington, Baltimore and New York while the trial was on. As he proved in 1936, the Duke was one of life's runners. Untested in the harsh arena of life, pampered by nannies since birth, dominated by strong women, woebegone in the face of duty, the Duke found it hard to contend with the consequences of his own actions. Of course, he would be out of town for the trial. So characteristic, so like dear David. The whole thing was beneath Wallis, needless to say. It was one of those unpleasant tasks you hired servants to take care of.

Although Adderley was to be the Crown's criminal specialist in the case, a man who was expected to dismantle the defence in short order, it was the Attorney General, Eric Hallinan, who was leading counsel. He was a barrister-at-law of the Irish and English Bars and a former Crown counsel of Nigeria. He was very much of the colonial school. As with all the lawyers involved in this case, much rested on the outcome: for him, the prospect of professional advancement within the colonial legal service, for the rest the kudos that enhances the prospects of private practitioners. Hallinan's presence in the court did little to encourage de Marigny, who felt strongly that the Attorney General disliked him for reasons that had nothing to do with the case. He felt that Hallinan, an impecunious colonial functionary, disliked his flamboyance and lifestyle. Like many others, Hallinan scoffed inwardly at de Marigny's aristocratic pretensions. After all, the count's title was rooted in French nobility, who lost their heads in the 1789 Revolution. To still be using it, more than a century and a half later, was a cheap device to achieve social advancement, he thought. As an advocate, Hallinan was considered competent but unimaginative. He was very much a colonial service lawyer, who preferred the security of a regular salary to the rigours and hazards of private practice. Adderley was enlisted to assist him and provide the flourishes and jousting skills that could reduce witnesses to befuddled helplessness. As a barrister of Middle Temple, with two Cambridge University degrees, Adderley was well-qualified for the task ahead, but more important still were his twenty-five years experience at the criminal bar. He had figured in some of the Bahamas' biggest trials.

Of all the legal figures assembled for the drama, Adderley was probably the most interesting. He was a social incongruity, in that he was a black professional functioning with distinction in a colony where black professionals were not supposed to exist. This was a time when blacks were not permitted to frequent restaurants and other public facilities in downtown Nassau. They were barred from the Savoy Theatre in Bay Street. This injustice would continue into the mid-1950s when a parliamentary resolution put paid to the discrimination. Adderley was, therefore, a living contradiction: he was a highly regarded, and highly successful, professional black man in a society which rendered such a phenomenon nigh impossible.

The judge, Sir Oscar Daly, was an Irish King's Counsel who was also a former Great War intelligence officer. He arrived in the Bahamas after distinguished legal service in Kenya. The Irish lilt in his voice and impish humour marked him as a character among legal colleagues.

Alongside these experienced legal big guns, the defence team looked disconcertingly youthful. Godfrey Higgs, a barrister of the Inner Temple in his mid-thirties, was one of the youngest members of the Bahamas Bar. He was regarded as able, a good legal brain, but not necessarily as an advocate in a high-profile criminal case. His assistant, Ernest Callender, though slightly younger, had the advantage of seven years of criminal law behind him but was hardly the seasoned advocate such a life-and-death affair would normally require. By any reckoning, they were the underdogs.

As the trial began, the pressures on the defence were immense, and made more so by the press gallery, which was filled with the most distinguished collection of journalists ever to gather in a Bahamas court in the colony's two hundred years of history. Considering that the war was still at its height, this mass diversion of top-flight journalistic talent to a cramped courtroom in Nassau was proof enough of the case's importance around the world. All the major agencies were there, including *Associated Press, United Press International* and the *International News Service.* Erle Stanley Gardner was representing the *New York Journal–American. The New York Post* and the *New York Daily News* were there. Local correspondents served *Reuters, Canadian Press,* the *London Daily Telegraph* and *Daily Express,* the *New York Times* and the *Toronto Star.* The telephone and telegraph wires of Nassau would be hot for weeks to come, as messages encircled the globe..

It was now that de Marigny was given the chance to formally answer the charge. "Are you guilty or not guilty?" asked the registrar. "Not guilty," replied the prisoner in a firm clear voice. The public gallery braced itself for the fray.

First came the jury selection. There were challenges, legal exchanges, and a few rituals to be observed. Finally, twelve good men and true were installed to face one of the most onerous tasks in the entire legal process. For weeks, these ordinary Nassau citizens would hear the evidence, appraise the witnesses, then make an assessment and decide whether a man should die. In such a small community it was impossible to assemble a dozen citizens who did not know, or know of, the defendant in the dock. What defence lawyers had to ensure was that none of them had an ulterior reason for doing the prisoner harm. After being sworn in, the jury selected a foreman, businessman James P Sands, a well-known character who drove a painfully slow jalopy round the streets of Nassau, and the trial was underway.

Adderley's opening salvo set the pattern of the prosecution case. With his wig set forward on his head, a theatrical rustling of his black gown, and a jutting of his jaw, the lawyer set briskly about his task. It proved to be a stirring opening. The Crown was intent on depicting de Marigny as a near penniless fraud with a grudge, and an irresponsible philanderer to boot. Adderley's portrait was vivid. On the day before the murder, counsel said, the accused had a fifty seven pounds overdraft at the Royal Bank of Canada. In one sentence, he reduced de Marigny to penury. Adderley also dwelt on the hostility generated in recent months between Sir Harry and his son-in-law. Having disposed of his real estate holdings, and faced with a possible lawsuit for $125,000 from his ex-wife, de Marigny was, he said, in "desperate financial circumstances" with no means of sustaining his easy living. To penury he successfully added idleness. The prosecution case was, therefore, based on three key motives: deep-seated hatred, revenge for the family's contemptuous treatment of him and, most significant of all, gain from the family estate, to solve his financial problems and sustain his fecklessness.

From the start, the jury listened intently to the prosecutor's eloquent address. The word picture he painted was unflattering to the accused, to say the least. As Adderley progressed, their eyes wandered towards the dock, as though they were mentally fitting the defendant to the damning description now being laid before them. Was it believable? It would be for them to choose. De Marigny's face remained impassive.

Counsel then explored the background of the Oakes family's antipathy, and reminded jurors of the bad feeling, prompted by de Marigny's elopement with Nancy Oakes, just two days after her eighteenth birthday. This bad feeling was deepened when she fell pregnant: a condition the family felt inappropriate, given that Nancy had been ill with mouth and face problems for some months. This development led Sir Harry and Lady Oakes to change their wills in February, 1943, to ensure no capital from the estate could be inherited before the child's thirtieth birthday. All five offspring were to be confined to income alone.

In his spirited opening, Adderley was also insistent that any doubts the court had about the whereabouts of Harold Christie, on the night of Sir Harry's death, did not necessarily detract from the strength of the prosecution case. This was an early signal that Christie was to emerge as a key figure in the proceedings, a fact already evident from the preliminary hearings. And so it proved. Christie's credibility became a point for discussion throughout the trial. Yet the defence did not respond to those doubts as one would expect. You would need to be fully acquainted with the workings of Nassau society to understand why, but some pointers will emerge later.

As if the accused's problems were not severe enough, Adderley also dwelt on a couple of comments de Marigny allegedly made in the hours following Sir Harry's death. If true, these comments appeared to deepen his plight. While walking with a special constable called Douglas, de Marigny wanted to know if, in a British court, a man could be convicted if the murder weapon was not found. At the time this remark was made, de Marigny was unaware that he was a suspect. It is, therefore, possible to construe it as an idle question anyone might ask in the circumstances for enlightenment about the process of law. Adderley made much of it. "What did the accused know about the weapon at this time? Did he know that the weapon had already been destroyed? Would he have asked such a question if he was not certain that the weapon that killed Sir Harry could not have been found?" The questions were fired across the court like tracer bullets.

Looking directly at the jury, Adderley posed a question that would hang over de Marigny's head in the difficult days to come. "How can an innocent man ask such a question at such an early time after the murder?" Then, sarcastically, counsel provided the answer to de Marigny's question in a single word: Yes. Shortly afterwards, de Marigny asked the officer another question which seemed to tighten the noose round his neck. He wanted to know if a man could be convicted on circumstantial evidence. "How did he know that the case for the Crown was circumstantial?" asked Adderley, who said the killer was the only person who would have known such things at the time.

But the prosecution's most crushing disclosure centred on a single fingerprint, found on the Chinese screen, in Sir Harry's bedroom. As Adderley pointed out, de Marigny, by his own admission, had said the last time he visited Westbourne was three years before the killing. How, then, did his fingerprint appear on the screen, given that he had no access to it when he called at Westbourne after Sir Harry's body had been found? Upon that question turned the entire Crown case against Alfred de Marigny. It was the only evidence to place him in Sir Harry's bedroom at the relevant time. The jurymen moved uneasily in their seats.

To round off a devastating opening statement, Adderley listed fourteen points, upon which the prosecution based its case. They included de Marigny's anxiety to remove stockpiled gasoline from his home after the discovery of Oakes' scorched corpse, his failure to produce the shirt and tie he wore on the fatal night, callous references he had made about his father-in-law and, of course, his burnt hairs and his presence outside Westbourne at the crucial time. Fourteen points seemed formidable, some would say insurmountable. The jury's task was to determine whether such a case was enough to put de Marigny's guilt beyond reasonable doubt. Adderley seemed quietly confident that the defence would be found wanting in countering the Crown's claims.

From the outset, there were people in Nassau who believed the wrong man was in the dock. Among them were police officers who, knowing how Nassau society worked, sniffed a conspiracy in the making, with de Marigny the fall guy, the patsy. The man these officers felt was deeply implicated was Harold Christie, upwardly mobile son of an eccentric Bahamian family whose father was a dreamy poet and evangelist. If they stopped short at suggesting he wielded the killer weapon, they certainly felt he was somehow involved. But they also kept quiet out of self-interest and, it must be said, self-preservation. As Christie's close friendship with Sir Harry was well-known, no-one was able to pinpoint a motive. But the men were embroiled in land deals involving large sums of money. There was talk of unpaid debts. There was yet more talk of Sir Harry planning a move to Mexico which, if true, would seriously undermine Christie's ambitions as a realtor. When money, ambition and greed combine, the mixture can prove combustible, especially in Nassau, where money is everything.

If the "Christie did it" faction needed to reinforce their theories, they did not have to wait long. Christie's appearance in court as a leading prosecution witness on 20 October, 1943, was a revelation. Here was a man so deeply discomfited by the proceedings that the perspiration literally oozed from him, soaking his jacket. The courtroom was not especially warm on this particular day, now that autumn had arrived, but Christie was like a man in a midsummer heatwave. As he gripped the rail in front of him, he seemed to be on a white knuckle ride to oblivion. Several writers in court were to dwell on his extraordinary demeanour. If Christie was not guilty, he certainly looked it. His deep unease centred on two pieces of evidence, both of which served to challenge the vital part of his testimony, that he spent the whole night at Westbourne on 7-8 July. If the evidence of others could establish that he was lying, and that he was actually up and about during the night of Sir Harry's murder, it would prove he had something to hide. But what? The first obstacle for him to overcome was the evidence of Mrs Mabel Ellis, who made two points about Christie's car which contradicted his own version of events.

Although seemingly trivial, the position of the car in Westbourne's grounds, and whether Christie left it there during 7 July, were to prove deeply significant. It raised questions about whether the car was subsequently used for an illicit purpose, or at an unusual hour. Had he parked it away from the house, near the country club, instead of outside the main entrance? According to Christie, he had driven off in his own car on the morning of 7 July to attend an Executive Council meeting, but Mrs Ellis said he had left in Sir Harry's. That evening, said Christie, he had asked his driver, Levi Gibson, to bring the car to Westbourne in case it were needed to ferry dinner guests. But the more critical point for Christie was the evidence of Captain Edward Sears, the respected head of the Bahamas police traffic division. He said he saw Christie in a station wagon in George Street, in downtown Nassau, at about midnight on 7 July. If Christie is to be believed, he was by that time already ensconced in his bedroom at Westbourne. But Sears was adamant. There was no room for doubt.

"If Captain Sears said he saw me out that night, I would say that he was very seriously mistaken and should be more careful in his observations," said Christie, faced with the intense cross-examination of Godfrey Higgs.

"I put it to you," said the attorney, "that Captain Sears saw you in a station wagon in George Street around midnight that night."

Christie: "Captain Sears was mistaken."

Under further questioning, the witness accepted that Captain Sears was a reputable person, but reputable persons made mistakes, too, he said.

Sears, it seems, was doing his rounds at the time of this sighting. His vehicle passed the station wagon under a street light. There was no doubt in his mind that Christie was in the passenger seat, but he was unable to identify the driver. Later, Nassau was awash with rumours that the driver was, in fact, Christie's brother Frank. This was a version of events later revealed, long after the trial, by a woman friend inside Sears' vehicle, and a witness that de Marigny was to unearth during his own inquiries years later. There is now no doubt that the Sears' story was correct. Harold and Frank Christie were out driving that night, on a mission they wanted kept quiet at all costs. For those who believed all along that Christie was involved in Oakes' death, this was compelling supporting evidence. However, for those who insist upon Christie's innocence, another story emerged, and that revolved around adultery, not murder.

Christie, an affable character who was well-liked by most who knew him, was a "gay" bachelor at a time when the term had a different meaning from the one it endures today. He was a personable, quietly attractive man about town with a bit of reputation for the ladies. His wide smile and warm geniality made him a popular figure. One of his conquests was, it seems, Mrs Dulcibelle Henneage, a serviceman's wife, who had been a dinner guest at Westbourne on the eve of the murder. Mrs Henneage had been driven to her Eastern Road home by fellow guest Charles Hubbard. The suggestion is that

Frank drove Harold to Mrs Henneage's home for an assignation at an hour when her two children would be asleep. Meanwhile, Harold's car remained at Westbourne, where its presence would support his contention that he never left the house. Years later, evidence would emerge to suggest that Frank Christie drove into Westbourne's grounds later that night, in a vehicle which disgorged two or three unknown men. These figures dashed up the outer staircase of the house and, it is assumed, into Sir Harry's bedroom, in which flames were seen to flicker briefly, before being extinguished, possibly by the wind. If this story were true, and de Marigny insisted it was, did the killers include Harold, or would he have been there to show the way? Harold was never identified by the witness who made these chilling disclosures. It's just possible he was in bed with his lover while the evil deed was being done. Either way, it was important for Harold to insist he remained in his bedroom all night and that he had heard nothing to suggest his friend was being butchered by killers just a few feet away. Whether an adulterer or killer, it was so important to Christie that his real whereabouts remained a mystery that he was prepared to lie about it, and declare that Captain Sears was mistaken.

Higgs led Christie through other aspects of the case, including his actions immediately after discovering Sir Harry's body, and managed to unsettle the witness to such a degree that at one point Christie exploded impatiently. Christie's performance, his white-knuckled hands clinging to the rail, his constant brow-mopping, and the expanding stains on his clothing as sweat burst forth from every pore, did nothing for his credibility as a witness. De Marigny felt at the time that the cross-examination took a physical and psychological toll on Christie, which was evident as he stepped down from the witness-box at the end of his ordeal. He was moving like an old man. If Christie had been expected to add something to the sum total of the prosecution's case, he had failed. Adderley's response to his evidence was to invite the jury to discount it. It was the first serious reversal for the Crown.

De Marigny had become a curiosity to international readers. Press attention was now so focused on the man in the dock that newspapers sought more information about his past, his family origins and, most pressing of all, his title. Newspapers cabled their reporters in Nassau asking: "Is he a count or not?"

De Marigny always insisted that he did nothing to encourage the use of the title, even though he was entitled to it under the ancient laws of French and Mauritian heraldry. His friend, the Marquis Georges de Visdelou-Guimbeau, explained to *The Tribune* that he knew of at least twenty members of the de Marigny family who were entitled to call themselves count, but Freddy had not registered his because he didn't believe in titles. Mauritians, he said, had the highest "title count" in the world. When he had arrived in the colony a few years before, Alfred de Marigny had specifically asked *The Tribune* not to use his title.

With such comparative trivialities out of the way, the press was able to concentrate on more serious matters, notably the evidence of Dr Hugh Quackenbush, whose earlier findings had been remarkable more for their omissions than revelations. He had rushed to Westbourne after taking a telephone call at about 7.30am on 8 July and, having met Christie in his pyjamas in the hall, went upstairs, where he found Sir Harry lying dead on his bed. The body, he said, was badly burnt and there was a "perforating wound" in front of the left ear large enough to admit the tip of his left index finger. He believed Sir Harry had been dead for between two-and-a-half to five hours, and that most of the burning had occurred after death. Later, at the mortuary, he examined the body again and noted four wounds to the head which, he said, could not have been self-inflicted. This finally put paid to an earlier theory that Sir Harry might have committed suicide – one which, it has to be said, carried little weight with those who knew Oakes well. With the biggest fortune in the empire, the self-possession of a man who had done very well for himself, and a loving family, Sir Harry was not a convincing candidate for suicide.

Having been held incommunicado for several days, the jury was growing restless. Some members needed to sign cheques to keep their businesses going. A special concession was granted by the judge and they completed such transactions under close police guard. Then, as a diversion, they were taken to the local theatre where they saw a movie called *Above Suspicion*. One juror, Jerome Bethel, objected to going to the cinema on religious grounds, but he went anyway because, under court regulations, it was necessary for all twelve men to stay together. He also protested when a beach party was planned for a Sunday afternoon. However, rather than upset his fellow jurors, he went. One can imagine how popular Mr Bethel was, as authorities tried to find ways to make the jury's prolonged incarceration bearable. Each day they trooped under police guard to court from the Rozelda Hotel (later the Carlton House) in East Street. Then they trooped back at the end of the day's proceedings.

At one point, the jury foreman asked if court sessions could be extended into the evenings to shorten the trial. The judge refused. Then a juryman asked if they could see the chair that Rigor Mortis had sat in, a reference to earlier medical evidence. There is a dispute to this day as to whether this was a joke or a serious inquiry, but it has gone down in Nassau folklore as one of the trial's lighter moments.

Dr Lawrence Fitzmaurice, acting chief medical officer, detailed the head wounds suffered by Sir Harry, all four close to the left ear, and all of different depth and of "somewhat triangular" shape. There had been bleeding from all the wounds as well as the nose and left ear. He also referred to an unidentified dark liquid found in his stomach and estimated death had occurred between four and six hours after Sir Harry's last meal. He felt the murder weapon was a heavy blunt instrument with a well-defined edge and suggested that a series of rapid blows were delivered. The blows, he believed, were struck before Sir Harry was burnt. His skull was fractured.

As the trial went into its fifth day, the camera crews moved in. These were the 1940s equivalent of today's big news channels like *CBS* or *CNN*. *Paramount News* and *Movietone*, whose newsreels were popular in cinemas throughout America, set up cameras on the square outside the court, creating yet more public interest. In addition to those who wanted to see the key figures moving back and forth to the courtroom, there were now the starstruck wannabes jostling to appear on film. As proceedings gathered momentum, the precincts of the court were like a Hollywood movie set, with producers and technicians ducking under trailing wires and barking out orders. Cameramen strained to get the protagonists "in the can" as they made their way to court. Barristers preened themselves for unfamiliar international exposure. These were heady days for all concerned.

It was at this stage in the trial that the jury was entertained by the extraordinary evidence of Constable Wendel Parker, who said de Marigny had arrived at the police traffic branch at about 7.30am on 8 July to ask whether a car he had converted into a truck needed to be inspected. Parker said he was struck by the wildness of de Marigny's eyes and his bulging lips. Although Parker was called by the prosecution, they probably wished they hadn't bothered, for his evidence was regarded as highly suspect. Most who heard it concluded that Parker had been caught up in the post-murder frenzy, had thought de Marigny guilty, and was now allowing his imagination to run riot with fanciful notions about the accused's demeanour. He appeared to be saying what he thought others wanted to hear.

There was also testimony from Dr Leonard Huggins, the assistant medical officer at Bahamas General Hospital, about the mysterious dark fluid in Sir Harry's stomach which later scholars of the case would cite as some kind of poison or sedative to send him into a deep sleep. However, Dr Huggins detected no sign of poisoning and concluded the fluid was grape juice, which contained sediment like grape skins. Sir Harry was fond of grapes – his pip-spitting was legendary in society circles.

On 25 October, Lieut John Douglas recalled his conversation with de Marigny, in which he is supposed to have been asked whether a man could be convicted on circumstantial evidence. He also referred to the disputed remark "the old bastard should have been killed anyhow", which the defence claimed was uttered by Douglas, not de Marigny. It is doubtful if this officer's evidence, like that of Constable Parker, helped the prosecution cause. The question most intelligent people were asking was: "Would a man guilty of such a horrendous crime go into a police station of his own accord to inquire about vehicle inspections – and was it likely he would ask a police officer whether conviction was possible on circumstantial evidence and if no weapon was found?" Few thought these were the actions of a guilty man.

As the proceedings moved slowly forward, Christie again felt it necessary to give a press interview, this time to crush more rumours about his whereabouts during the early morning of 8 July. The damning evidence of Captain Sears was now being interpreted by many in Nassau as an attempt to protect a woman's honour. Christie admitted to the *Miami Herald* that his evidence before the court sounded implausible, but said he could not help that because it was true. He felt he was being smeared by gossip and worried that might affect his work, as a promoter of the Bahamas as a resort. "You might as well bury me as take my life work away from me," he told a reporter, "Nassau is my hobby and livelihood." He felt he would be stigmatised on the international scene and was keen to counter the suspicion which had fallen upon him.

Christie said Oakes' death was a personal and financial blow to him. "In addition to being one of my best friends, he was also my best client," he said. "He purchased more property from me than any other six persons." He revealed that Sir Harry wanted him to work for him exclusively, but he declined. He was reluctant to become an employee, and he felt such a position would prevent him carrying out other development plans he had in mind. "If you offer me a million dollars to go anywhere else I would not leave this country," he said.

The judge did not take kindly to witnesses giving press interviews, and made this point clear when Melchen gave evidence, and attention was drawn to comments of his being circulated by *United Press*. When Melchen denied giving an interview to correspondent John B McDermott, and branded McDermott a liar, there were indications of scepticism among jurors. Whatever the public thinks of the press, and especially the excesses of some tabloids, they are not foolish enough to believe that journalists, working for respected international agencies, simply make up stories and concoct bogus interviews. If anyone was lying, it was Melchen. The defence did not let him off the hook.

The cross-examination of Melchen by de Marigny's junior counsel, Ernest Callender, capitalised fully on the officer's dishonesty and exposed a major flaw in the prosecution's case. By the time young Callender had finished, the flaw had widened into a chasm through which he and Godfrey Higgs would drive not just a horse and cart, but an entire calvary division.

An extraordinary admission by Melchen drew gasps of astonishment from the court. It centred on the fingerprint that his colleague Barker had supposedly lifted from the Chinese screen. Melchen admitted that he did not know about this fingerprint until Barker broke news of it to Lady Oakes in Bar Harbour, Maine. They had been working closely on the case since the early afternoon following Sir Harry's death, had travelled together back to Miami, and then on to Maine and not once was the fingerprint mentioned. They had discussed other aspects of the case, but Barker had not referred even fleetingly to the single most important piece of evidence against de Marigny.

The disclosure to Lady Oakes came during the afternoon following Sir Harry's funeral. Throughout the officers' two-day journey from Miami to Maine, they had talked at length about every facet of the murder, including the scene of crime and the unusual nature of Sir Harry's injuries, but the fingerprint went unmentioned. Yet it would now become the focus for the defence. Higgs and Callender exploited it with ruthless efficiency.

The following day in court, Melchen asked permission to change his testimony on this point, explaining that he had been tired when he gave it. He had heard Barker mention lifting a print to Colonel Erskine-Lindop and that he was going to process it. At Bar Harbour, Barker told Lady Oakes about a print on which he was still working which he thought was de Marigny's. This was a significant change in testimony.

An irritated Chief Justice said: "That is very different from what you said yesterday. Don't you know the very great importance of this piece of evidence? Have you a good memory?"

Melchen said: "A fairly good memory."

Chief Justice: "Tell me, now that you are not tired, have you talked to Barker about this matter since you gave evidence yesterday?"

Melchen: "No. I talked about it in the Attorney General's office with the Attorney General, in the presence of Captain Barker, after I gave evidence yesterday."

This remark was not lost on the jury. It suggested that, having blundered in the witness-box, Melchen went into deep discussions, with the Attorney General and Barker, to see if his evidence was salvageable. There was a sniff of complicity in the air.

Chief Justice: "Now I want to know exactly what happened when you saw Lady Oakes and her daughter, Mrs de Marigny, at Bar Harbour."

Melchen: "Captain Barker told Lady Oakes and Mrs de Marigny that he had found a fingerprint or fingerprints of the accused on the screen."

Sir Sydney Oakes

Sir Sydney Oakes

Sir Sydney Oakes in his sports car

Utility pole broken in two by Sir Sydney Oakes' sports car. Note the imprint of registration plate.

Funeral of Sir Sydney Oakes, Nassau, Bahamas 1966

Pitt Oakes

Sir Harry Oakes

Lady Eunice Oakes,
widow of Sir Harry

Nancy Oakes

Pitt Oakes - Obsessed by his
father's murder

Capt. James Barker

Capt. Edward Sears

Capt. Edward Melchen

Chief Justice
Sir Oscar Daly

Marquis de Visdelou-Guimbeau

Alfred Adderley

Lt Col RA Erskine Lindop

Godfrey Higgs

Attorney General Eric Hallinan

The Private Eye, Raymond Schindler

Count Alfred de Marigny on his way to court

Godfrey Higgs, left,
and Ernest Callender
— defence team

Alfred Adderley addressing Supreme Court. Far left: Godfrey Higgs,
Front row, left: Attorney General Eric Hallinan.

The Jury, with Sir Oscar Daly, far right, leave de Marigny's house.

The officer's uncertainty was encouraging for the defence. It sent a tremor through the prosecution team. The defence tried to have the print withdrawn as evidence, recognising now that it was the most substantial weapon in the prosecution's case. If they could eliminate it from the prosecution's armoury, they would seriously weaken the Crown's case. They argued that the print was inadmissible, but the judge ruled against them. De Marigny was deflated by what he regarded as an incomprehensible decision, but the defence attorneys were unfazed. Attention was now focused on the authenticity of the print, and this proved to be a crucial tactic that paid off handsomely.

Melchen had been undermined by Callender's cross-examination. The experienced cop's natural air of authority foundered, as the defence picked away at the one point they knew could be decisive. Everything would hinge on Barker's testimony, and especially his ability to withstand the dogged, penetrating interrogation of Godfrey Higgs.

As the print, allegedly from de Marigny's right little finger, was formally admitted as evidence, the jury was about to witness one of the most famous courtroom exchanges in criminal history. The incisive questioning of Higgs was later to be cited by fellow lawyers as one of the most brutal, and effective, examples of cross-examination witnessed in a British colonial court. Although Higgs was not a natural advocate for a criminal trial of this magnitude, he was rising to the occasion. Of course, had Barker been an officer of solid professional integrity, no amount of incisive cross-examination would have been able to cut through his credibility. Higgs had sensed, though, that the Miami duo were up to no good, that they were not to be trusted. Once he had persuaded the jury to share those suspicions, he was well on his way to a successful conclusion.

In lifting what he claimed was de Marigny's print from the screen, Barker overlooked something so fundamental, to the sound principles of good detective work, that crime experts were left deeply perplexed. They wondered how a so-called fingerprint expert, with hundreds of cases behind him, could fall into such a deep trap of his own making.

Barker told the court he had taken rubber lifts from the top panel of the screen because his Scotch tape had run out. In the magistrate's court, he had marked in blue pencil the area from which he thought the rubber lift of de Marigny's print was taken. Now he was not so sure. In fact, Barker told the judge that, since re-examining the screen, he was not now prepared to say the print was definitely lifted from that area. It did, however, come from the top panel, he asserted. To have both Melchen and Barker wishing to amend key parts of their evidence at this crucial stage of the trial was deeply annoying for the judge, but encouraging for Higgs and Callender. If they could show that the fingerprint was a fake, and that Melchen and Barker were liars trying to frame an innocent man, they would not only save de Marigny's life, but strike a resounding blow for justice and the rule of law.

In the 1940s, the phenomenon of the crooked cop had not yet registered in the public consciousness. Automatic respect was accorded law enforcers, and there was a strong presumption in the courts that everything a policeman said was true. Three or four decades on, this would not be so. In the Bahamas, as elsewhere, the spectre of the crooked cop would hang over the judicial process, and attorneys would exploit it mercilessly. But the 1940s, though a decade of war and turmoil, was also an age of comparative innocence, and men in authority were taken at their word. The task facing the defence was, therefore, far from easy. Melchen and Barker looked the part: one a trilbied veteran with a long police career behind him, the other a handsome, no-nonsense character whose expertise appeared to be well-founded. The jury was, one assumes, suitably impressed, and especially since the Governor himself had secured their services. However, this facade of brisk efficiency and unshakeable integrity was about to be dismantled, right in front of the jury's eyes.

Questioned by Higgs, Barker repeated that he was no longer prepared to say that the latent print came from the area he had marked blue. He was sure, however, that it came from the top portion. The screen was carried to the witness-box so that Barker could see it more clearly.

Barker: "I wish to inform the court that the blue line which I now see on the screen was not made by me. There has been an effort to trace a blue line over the black line that I made myself on August 1st in the presence of the Attorney General in the Central Police Station. That blue line is not my work."

Then, astonishingly, he said he wished to correct this statement. Following the hasty amendments by Melchen, this had a profound impact. It seemed the prosecution's two star witnesses, far from being stars, were prize bunglers. First they said one thing, then they said something else. Jurymen shuffled uneasily. They were being forced to reassess whatever early impressions they had of the two men.

Barker: "I am sorry I have caused the court this trouble. I wish to withdraw what I said about the alteration of the blue line. I find my initials where the blue line is."

He said the area marked by him had been indicated twice – the first time in black pencil, then in blue. He had dated the find on 9 July, but only recorded it on 1st August.

"So until August 1st there was nothing on that screen to show where exhibit J (the fingerprint) came from?" asked Higgs.

Barker: "I relied on my memory only."

Higgs: "Yet on the 3rd of August in the magistrate's court you swore on your oath that 'I marked the spot on the screen, where the latent impression above referred to was found, with pencil and it is now within the area marked with blue pencil and signified by No 5 and initialled and dated 8/3/43 by me'."

Barker: "I did."

Higgs: "And you marked that area while giving evidence in the magistrate's court and said that was where the print came from?"

Barker: "I did."

Higgs: "You were certain then that it came from that area, weren't you?"

Barker: "I was."

Higgs: "And why are you not certain today, Captain Barker?"

Barker: "Detective Conway and I examined the screen carefully last Sunday and did not have sufficient evidence of ridges to enable us to say with certainty that it came from that area. I can only say now that it came from the top of the screen."

In a championship boxing match, a good fighter knows when his opponent is in trouble. The legs begin to weaken, the eyes become tired and glazed, the body suddenly ages and sags. It's then that that attacker displays the controlled aggression that makes champions. Barker was not yet sagging, but he was in retreat. If the all-important print was to have any validity, Barker needed to show beyond doubt that it came from the screen. A print of de Marigny's detached from its background was useless for prosecution purposes.

Higgs: "What made you re-examine the screen that Saturday?"

Barker: "I realised that I would be called on to produce the exact spot and I wanted to find that spot if possible."

Higgs: "Did Captain Conway tell you it couldn't come from there?"

Barker: "We examined it together and he agreed with me."

Higgs: "But realising that you would be called upon to find the exact spot, you didn't look until two days before the trial."

Barker: "That is correct."

Higgs: "Where would you say today that the print came from?"

Barker: "I can only say now from my memory that it came from some part of the top of that panel. I did not feel justified in isolating any area."

Barker, far from being the 'expert' he professed to be, was beginning to emerge as an oaf. He was asked to give a rundown of his career, and noted his roles as motor-cycle officer and emergency call dispatcher before moving into the realm of criminal investigation. He had a spell as a clerk and then returned to uniformed duties before his eventual elevation to superintendent of the Bureau of Criminal Investigation. It all sounded small beer alongside his present responsibilities.

Higgs: "Is it customary in Miami to appoint a superintendent with such small qualifications?"

Barker: "No."

Higgs: "You had only five months as a clerk before that?"

Barker: "Yes."

Higgs: "Why were you ordered back to uniformed duty in 1929?"

Barker: "Because the work had been brought up to date."

Higgs: "So you were an additional clerk in the office?"

Barker: "There were only two of us – the boss and myself."

Higgs: "You continued as superintendent of the BCI until March, 1939, when you were ordered back to uniformed duty?"

Barker: "Yes."

Higgs: "What for this time?"

Barker: "Insubordination."

Higgs: "And you remained out of that department for eleven months?"

Barker: "Yes."

Higgs: "You term yourself a fingerprint expert?"

Barker: "As the term applied, yes."

Sadly for Barker, he was now a markedly diminished figure in the eyes of the court. Having first been billed as an expert (by Royal appointment, no less), he was now exposed as little more than a jumped-up clerk, who had been promoted beyond his capabilities. Higgs' jabs, hooks and crosses had softened him up for the final fusillade.

Higgs: "Have you ever introduced as evidence a lifted print without producing photographs of the actual raised print on the object on which it was found?"

Barker: "Yes."

Higgs: "Are you certain?"

Barker: "Yes."

Higgs: "Will you give me the name of just one case in which you have done so."

Barker: "I can't do that."

Higgs: "Not one?"

Barker: "I could by inspection of my records."

Higgs: "Have you ever introduced that type of evidence in any superior court?"

Barker: "I have given evidence in cases where the sentence could be death."

Higgs: "Have you ever produced the object with the raised print on it?"

Barker: "I have."

Higgs: "Why did you do so?"

Barker: "In cases where the object was easily moved we found it advantageous to preserve the print on the object."

Higgs: "This screen is mobile?"

Barker: "It can be moved."

Higgs: "Why didn't you produce this moveable object in this court with the print on it?"

Barker: "The only equipment I had on the 8th and 9th of July was a small dusting outfit and tape. The use of tape expedited the examination."

Higgs: "You came prepared to look for fingerprint evidence, did you not?"

Barker: "Yes."

Higgs: "But you left your fingerprint camera behind?"

Barker: "I didn't know the nature of the case. I thought the kit I brought sufficient to take care of the average situation – even a murder case. A camera would have been desirable, but I didn't know the conditions."

Probed further, Barker was forced to admit he could have borrowed a camera from the local RAF base, or a local photographer. Again, he was made to look a fool, a man prepared to take short-cuts and settle for second-best, even when a man's life was at stake. It also emerged that several objects in the murder room, including a thermos flask, had never been tested for fingerprints.

Higgs: "I suggest, Captain Barker, that there were numerous articles in Sir Harry's room that you never processed."

Barker: "I quite agree with you."

Higgs: "If the accused had left a fingerprint on that screen, wouldn't it be likely that he left fingerprints on other objects?"

Barker: "Yes, under ordinary conditions. It is, however, my opinion that the nature of the crime and the extent of emotion or hurry would most likely prevent him from handling a lot of objects. In this case there was no necessity for the assailant to handle many objects."

Higgs: "Well, why did you dust the powder room downstairs?"

Barker: "We can't exclude anything in an investigation like this?"

Higgs: "But you did exclude a number of articles in the bedroom?"

"Yes."

If the defence had yet to put Barker's dishonesty beyond doubt, there is no question they had already exposed his intellectual shortcomings. Here was a man who set snares for himself, then walked right into them.

Higgs: "Did you exclude the possibility of accomplices?"

"I did not exclude the possibility of accomplices."

If Barker felt discomfited by Higgs' questioning, it was nothing compared to the ordeal he suffered the following two days, 29 and 30 October. This was the point at which Higgs decided to deliver the coup de grace, suggesting that it was impossible for the print to be lifted from the screen without some of its ornate pattern being lifted, too. When Barker was asked to demonstrate how he lifted the print, he allowed part of the lift to extend over the edge of the screen instead of over the design itself, which would have provided evidence of location. Barker said he did not think at the time that it would be important. The result was that the most vital piece of prosecution evidence was detached from its (alleged) original site with no proof it had ever been there. This revelation meant one of two things: that Barker was almost criminally incompetent or deeply dishonest. For it exposed the possibility, or rather the probability, that the print had been lifted from another object unconnected with the murder scene.

Higgs: "While you were working on that screen in the hallway on the 9th of July, didn't Captain Melchen bring the accused upstairs into the northern bedroom?"

Barker: "I understand he did."

Higgs: "Didn't you go to the door of that room and open it while they were there together?"

Barker: "I did not."

Higgs: "I put it to you that you did and that you asked Captain Melchen if everything was okay."

Barker: "I did not."

Higgs: "And I suggest that Captain Melchen said 'Yes'."

Barker: "I didn't even know Captain Melchen had been in that room until sometime afterwards."

Higgs: "Wasn't the accused's latent print obtained from some object in that north-west bedroom?"

Barker: "It was not."

Higgs: "But it was after they had left that room that you claimed to discover his print, was it not?"

Barker: "Yes."

Higgs: "I suggest that you and Captain Melchen deliberately planned to get the accused alone in order to get his fingerprint."

Barker: "No sir."

Higgs: "I suggest that exhibit J never came from that screen."

Barker: "It did come from that screen. Number 5 panel."

Higgs: "You can show none of the scrollwork on exhibit J, can you?"

Barker: "I cannot."

The court was transfixed by this electrifying exchange. Then came an interjection by the judge.

"When you were working on the screen in the hallway, was it spread out?"

Barker: "It was upright and spread out a panel at a time."

For onlookers, Higgs' cross-examination proved to be the dramatic high point of the trial. It read like a thriller script building to a crescendo. Barker was powerless in the face of what was to come.

Higgs: "Did you regard the rubber lift of this print as vital evidence in this case?"

Barker: "Definitely."

Higgs: "You never produced a rubber lift in the magistrate's court, did you?"

Barker: "I had it but was never asked for it."

Higgs: "You never told Captain Melchen of the discovery of the print, did you?"

Barker: "I told him when I discovered it on July 19th."

Higgs: "This is the most outstanding case in which your expert assistance has been required, is it not?"

Barker: "Well, it's developed into that."

Higgs: "And I suggest that in your desire for personal gain and notoriety you have swept away truth and substituted fabricated evidence."

Barker: "I emphatically deny that."

According to private eye Raymond Schindler, Melchen was so affected by Barker's ordeal that he left the courtroom, found a quiet spot behind the court building and vomited.

The effective demolition of Barker as a credible witness severely weakened the prosecution's case. Their plight deepened the following day when discrepancies in police evidence forced two more officers to change their evidence. This centred on the time Melchen was supposed to have taken de Marigny upstairs at Westbourne for an interview. Melchen told the magistrate's court that the interview took place between 3pm and 4pm. He was supported by Corporal Cleophas Knowles and Constable Eric Tynes of the Bahamas CID, who were on guard duty. Their testimony clashed with that of Lieut Douglas, who said he took de Marigny away from the house at 1.30pm.

Barker had previously disclosed that he lifted de Marigny's print from the screen between 11am and 1.30pm. It now appeared that Melchen, Tynes and Knowles had given the time of the interview as between 3pm and 4pm, to create the impression that de Marigny's visit was some hours after his print had been found, thus negating any suggestion of a false print plot. Douglas's conflicting testimony left them dangerously exposed.

For Hallinan and Adderley, things were beginning to look grim indeed. The officers on whom their case rested were unravelling under pressure. It now appeared that what seemed at one stage like an impregnable prosecution fortress was subsiding fast on loose gravel. The prosecution case was built on the evidence of no fewer than five liars.

More evidence was given about de Marigny's bank transactions, his reaction to being told of Sir Harry's death, and his decision to remove drums of gasoline from his premises in Victoria Avenue the day after the murder. Lady Eunice Oakes testified again on the family rift. On the fifteenth day of the trial, the prosecution closed its case. There is no doubt that what began as a powerful case against de Marigny was now looking far less formidable. The potency of Adderley's opening speech had been significantly defused by the dishonesty of the police officers, and their inability to cover their tracks. It was now up to the defence to stay composed and credible.

Chapter Eight

THE DEFENCE

On 4 November, 1943, Alfred de Marigny was freed from his cage to give evidence in his own defence. After two weeks of silently observing proceedings, it was a relief to be able to speak. His lawyers questioned him on his movements on July 7th and 8th, his relationship with the Oakes family, and his financial affairs. He closed the day's testimony by denying that he was at Westbourne on the night of the killing or that he was responsible for the murder. The appearance of the defendant is the climax of any high-profile murder trial. There is an air of high expectation as the court prepares to hear "the other side". How would de Marigny perform? Would his demeanour betray guilt or reinforce his claims of innocence? And how would the young attorneys, on whose skills his life depended, manoeuvre him through the ordeal? These were questions that spectators in court were aching to see answered.

Before entering the witness-box, de Marigny was visited in prison by his wife. As usual, she was offering moral support. For the accused, there would inevitably be tensions ahead, but he was remarkably serene. Nancy was apprehensive, but calm. It was to be an eventful day, with the courtroom packed with spectators, who filled the aisles and every square foot of floor space at the back of the court. During the lunch break, the public was reluctant to vacate the court, opting instead to eat sandwiches and guzzle soft drinks. The trial was a fascinating day out, a spectacle better than any movie. It was taking on a carnival air.

De Marigny opened by describing his past: his birth in Mauritius on 29 March, 1910, his first visit to Nassau in December, 1937, his purchase of a property in Governor's Harbour, Eleuthera, his first visit to Lady Oakes' house in 1938. It was at one of Lady Oakes' parties in 1941 that he met Nancy. In the spring of 1942 he and Nancy met up in New York, then travelled to California. A stomach illness forced him back to New York, where he was in hospital for five weeks. Nancy visited him every day. They agreed to marry. He did not discuss the matter with Sir Harry and Lady Oakes. The wedding day was 19 May, 1942, in New York. De Marigny also discussed his financial state at the time: between £7,000 and £8,000 in his personal accounts, a property in downtown Nassau, another in the over-the-hill native area, a 100-acre property worth between £3,000 and £4,000 in Governor's Harbour with two big houses. Within a week of their marriage, they visited Sir Harry and Lady Oakes in Bar Harbour. The whole family was friendly towards him. In July he and Nancy went to Mexico, where she became ill with typhoid fever. Before they left Mexico, she became pregnant. De Marigny also disclosed that Sir Harry had offered him and Nancy a 1,000-acre estate for agricultural purposes, along with a house known as the Jones property, which stood alongside. They declined the offer.

It was after Nancy had an abortion that Sir Harry's attitude towards de Marigny turned hostile. At the Oakes' Palm Beach home "his attitude was very peculiar – he wouldn't talk to me or answer me. He was unfriendly and extremely rude." De Marigny consulted the family lawyer, Walter Foskett, to get to the bottom of the problem, but Foskett was "disagreeable and hostile" and told him it was his own business. When de Marigny went into hospital for a tonsilectomy, he installed himself in the room next to Nancy, triggering Sir Harry's subsequent outburst: "Get the hell out of that room. If you don't get out I'll come and kick you out."

Two weeks later, however, they were back in Nassau on friendly terms. Sir Harry again raised the subject of the Jones property, but de Marigny said they were not going to accept it. "He told me that if I found any of his other land that would be suitable, he would be glad to lease it to me."

Chief Justice Daly interjected: "You were quite friendly then."

"Very friendly," said de Marigny.

Earlier, the witness said Sir Harry could be "very impulsive and moody" and would be friendly one day and not the next. On 29 March, 1943, de Marigny's 33rd birthday, he and Nancy held a party at their home. Nancy's brother Sydney stayed over. At about 4am, there was a "terrible pounding" on the front door, with somebody shouting: "Open the door or I'm going to break it down." When he opened the door, Sir Harry strode in and demanded to know where Sydney was. Shown to the guest room, Sir Harry grabbed the boy by the foot and said: "Get your clothes and get the hell out of this house."

De Marigny told the court: "Since that morning, the 30th of March, I never spoke to Sir Harry again."

On 7 July, he took some chickens to his farm and phoned Harold Christie about obtaining a permit. He also asked him to dinner, but Christie declined, saying he was staying with Sir Harry that night. At 11am, de Marigny went to Godfrey Higgs's office to pay the last instalment on his farm. In the afternoon, he went racing (sailing) and then, after another visit to the farm, he shaved, bathed and dressed for the candlelit dinner party. While lighting candles in hurricane shades, he burnt his hand. When the party broke up at about 12.30am, he drove two guests home to Hubbard Cottages out west. After dropping them, he went straight back home and retired to bed. At 3am, his dog and a cat belonging to his friend, Georges de Visdelou, were fighting. The cat entered his room, jumped between the venetian blind and window, and woke him up. He waited for Georges to return from driving home his friend, Betty Roberts, and called for him to collect the cat, which he did. At 6.30am he rose, had breakfast, and then went into town, where he learnt of Sir Harry's death from an acquaintance, Mr J H Anderson, who was unable to offer any details. De Marigny drove home, informed his friend Georges and, after some discussion about which of several Oakes homes Sir Harry might have stayed, drove to Westbourne. There he met Christie, who was on the telephone and very upset. Later, during the afternoon, he and Anderson returned to Westbourne, arriving a few minutes before Sir Harry's body was removed. He again saw Christie, and had a conversation, during which Christie described how he found Sir Harry burned with a wound in his head. Later still, de Marigny returned to Westbourne again – this time after being summoned by the police chief, Erskine-Lindop. It was then he met Melchen and Barker, who asked if he would subject himself to questions and physical examination. He agreed to do so.

The officers then asked if he would mind having Lieut Douglas as his guest for the night. The following morning, they went to

Westbourne, with Douglas complaining about having to give up his night to stay with him.

"What boils me," said Douglas, "is that they're making all this fuss over Sir Harry because he has plenty of money. If it was some poor coloured fellow in Grants Town I just would be asked to go and take information about it and that's all there would be to it."

De Marigny denied ever saying "That guy Sir Harry, the old bastard, should have been killed anyway." He added: "I never used the word 'guy' or 'bastard' at all. I remember this expression being used by Douglas. He seemed to be dissatisfied."

At Westbourne, they went on to the beach. He asked Douglas if he knew what had been used to kill Sir Harry – "if he had been shot or stabbed or something like that." He didn't know. De Marigny then asked if a weapon had been found. He didn't know that, either.

Afterwards, he asked Douglas: "If they can't find the weapon, how can they carry on with the case? Can they proceed with the case?"

Douglas said: "Yes, certainly."

At about 11am or 11.15am, de Marigny and Melchen went upstairs. The officer asked for information. He wanted to know if Christie was indebted to Sir Harry or had a grievance against him. "I told him Mr Christie was one of my best friends and Sir Harry's best friend and he could get the information from Mr Christie himself."

There was some chat about his childhood in Mauritius, then Melchen pointed his finger and asked: "Are you sure you did not come to Westbourne last night? Didn't you want to get quits with Sir Harry and came here to see him and had an argument with him and hit him?"

De Marigny said he told the officer if he had wanted to talk to Sir Harry, it would have been during the day, not in the middle of the night. Melchen told him he had been seen entering Westbourne, to which he replied: "I defy you or anybody in Nassau to say any such thing."

At that point Melchen invited him to pour them both a glass of water from a pitcher on a small table, and he did so.

Barker put his head in the door and said, "Is everything okay?"

Melchen replied: "Yes."

De Marigny's evidence generated tremendous press interest. The Telecommunications Department transmitted a record 18,750 words from correspondents that day. Meanwhile, the jurymen were taken out for a walk. "They appeared to be in good spirits – they whistled and hummed snatches of popular airs and they walked leisurely along the streets," reported *The Tribune*.

On Guy Fawkes Day, 5 November, de Marigny came face-to-face in court with the hated Eric Hallinan, the Attorney General who he felt had made it his personal ambition to crucify him. The questioning revolved around his finances, his relationship with his former wife, and the elopement with Nancy Oakes, who he had married two days after she became of legal age. Hallinan also honed in on the fact that Nancy became pregnant when she was ill with teeth problems, which were poisoning her system. This had been one of the Oakes' main bones of contention. Having set the scene, he then turned to the antipathy which had apparently developed between the two couples. He referred to the hospital incident, when Sir Harry threatened to eject him, and the hauling of young Sydney out of de Marigny's house in Victoria Avenue, asking if these incidents left him feeling humiliated.

De Marigny said: "No. I knew Sir Harry was a moody man and had a violent temper. He would lose his temper for nothing and might forget the whole thing the next day."

Hallinan asked: "Did he call you a sex maniac?"

De Marigny: "Quite possibly. But when he was angry he said things he didn't mean. I did not resent it."

Hallinan's cross-examination made little impression on de Marigny's composure. The accused denied calling Sir Harry a bastard, or threatening to crack his head. In what *The Tribune* called his "French flavoured voice" he replied to every question with firm, unruffled authority. If Hallinan's objective had been to trick him into indiscretion, he failed. Observers noted that, in the contest of the advocates, Higgs had scored a resounding victory.

The most intriguing and controversial evidence to emerge from the defence was that of Captain Edward Sears, the police traffic chief who swore he saw Harold Christie in a station wagon at around midnight on 7 July. His car and the vehicle passed under a street light in George Street in downtown Nassau. Although the night was wet - there was a drizzle at the time – he was "quite satisfied I saw Mr Christie in that wagon." The vehicles were doing between fifteen and twenty miles per hour at the time.

This evidence was important for one reason. If correct – and no-one apart from Christie ever doubted it – it proved that Christie had lied to the court when he said he spent the entire night at Westbourne. Interestingly, this point – though presented by the defence – was never exploited by them. In trying to free de Marigny, the defence was careful not to suggest an alternative killer. It is baffling, therefore, that they bothered to expose this point at all, other than to achieve a morale-booster at a time when they badly needed one.

The other telling defence evidence came from Captain Maurice O'Neil, supervisor of the New Orleans investigation bureau, who said the now famous exhibit J – the print of de Marigny's right little finger – did not come from the screen in Sir Harry's bedroom, but an object with circular patterns on it. He also said he had never heard of a lifted print being accepted as evidence, unless it was photographed in its original position beforehand.

For the most part, the defence case went well. The one heart-stopping moment came when Georges de Visdelou, a jittery, confused and excitable witness, changed his evidence about collecting his cat from de Marigny's room. Having first said he didn't, and then that he did, the Marquis appeared like a man who had fluffed his script, trying desperately to concoct an alibi for de Marigny after effectively depriving him of one. Later, de Marigny was to recall feeling panic at that moment. He felt his friend's error and subsequent bemused state could send him to the gallows.

The final witness brought moments of high drama. The court was bristling with anticipation as nineteen-year-old heiress, Nancy de Marigny, walked to the witness-box in her black dress and flat white beret. De Marigny, leaning forward in his cage, watched her intently as she took the oath in an almost inaudible voice. Jurors strained to hear her as Higgs began his questioning. He asked her to speak up. At one point, when recalling being told her husband was the guilty man, she swayed slightly. Hallinan suggested she sit down. The jury foreman slipped a stool under her. After a ten-minute adjournment, she opted to stand and remained standing until she was released from the box at 1.25pm. Throughout her testimony, de Marigny did not take his eyes off her.

Her evidence largely concerned family relationships, but also covered Barker's graphic account of the murder, an account which spared no-one's feelings, least of all those of the distraught Lady

Oakes. Barker and Melchen, she said, claimed the assailant had gone into the garage, picked up a stick from a pile of balustrades, climbed the outside stairs to her father's room and struck Sir Harry. Then insecticide was poured over him and his bed before the bed was set on fire. Sir Harry, who had momentarily lost consciousness, was revived by the flames and tried to fight his attacker. Barker said Oakes had been in great agony and was finally overcome, after which the fire was started a second time. During the struggle, the screen had fallen over but was put upright again to shield sight of the flames from the road. They told her that her husband's handprints had been found, and were emphatic in blaming him for the crime.

Higgs: "Have you ever heard your husband use any expression of hatred towards your father?"

"Never," she said.

Nancy told the court of her rejection of £2,000 in war bonds from her parents, and of a letter she wrote to her mother saying she must accept and trust her husband or risk losing her.

"That's a pretty hard letter for a girl to write to her mother, don't you think?" asked Hallinan.

"You might think so because you were not mixed up in it," she replied.

When she stepped from the box, Higgs said: "That is the case for the defence."

So now only the final speeches of the attorneys, and the judge's summing-up, stood between de Marigny and his fate. Nassau, usually so placid, was in a state of high tension. The trial was the only point for discussion in the bars and stores of Bay Street, and in the shanty communities over the hill. Barbers' shops were abuzz with nothing else.

In classic Bahamian fashion, everyone had a view and expressed it volubly. There was a strong belief de Marigny would hang, but not everyone was comfortable with the fact. Many of those in the ruling class were content with such an outcome. "Everyone wanted rid of him," a white Bahamian said years later. Among the workers, though, there was much sympathy for the accused. Although a so-called "gentleman", and evidently proud of it, he was also an outsider – and, in the context of this case, an underdog. There was also a streak of humanity and compassion they liked, not to mention his rebellious streak. De Marigny was a maverick, an individualist.

Higgs opened his address by saying that, never before in the history of the Bahamas, had there been a crime of more sensational nature. It was a brutal and dastardly affair and it fell to the jury to decide whether de Marigny committed "the shocking deed." Never, he said, had a jury been faced with greater responsibility. All over the world, people had been waiting for the verdict. Higgs described the defence's job as a frightful responsibility because a man's life was at stake. He personally had felt it heavily. He hoped he and Mr Callender had done nothing to jeopardise their client's cause. But, he said, great as the defence's responsibility was, it was nothing alongside that of the jury, who would decide whether de Marigny should walk free or be hanged by the neck until dead. Higgs praised jurymen for their patience, and castigated the prosecution for bringing what he regarded as at least twice as many witnesses as they needed to, thus prolonging the proceedings unnecessarily. He said although the prosecution had brought twenty-five witnesses, not one of them, other than Melchen and Barker, had given evidence to support the charge against de Marigny.

Then came an extraordinary concession. Referring to his long cross-examination of Christie, Higgs said this was no easy task for him "because Christie was well-known to all of them." The next sentence was so mind-boggling that some foreign reporters in court were aghast.

Higgs said: "There was nothing to suggest or imply that Mr Christie was in any way involved in the murder of Sir Harry Oakes." But, he said, it was his job to subject him to a thorough examination "because his story was implausible." Yet he was able to say in the next breath: "Not for one moment did the defence desire to suggest that Mr Christie had been implicated in any way in the death of Sir Harry."

Much of the rest of Higgs' address spotlighted deficiencies in the prosecution evidence. He asked if anyone who had really killed Sir Harry would be stupid enough to make some of the indiscreet remarks attributed to the accused. And he focused on Lady Oakes' statement that de Marigny had never shown ill-will towards Sir Harry. "At no time did she say he tried to get pecuniary benefit. On the contrary, she said that after receiving her daughter's letter, she came to the conclusion that they didn't want any more help from her."

Higgs then came to the crux of his case. Having dismissed most of the prosecution evidence as irrelevant, he said the Crown's case would stand or fall on the reliability of Melchen and Barker. He said their evidence addressed three key points: the fingerprint of de Marigny allegedly found on the screen, the burnt hairs on the accused's body and de Marigny's alleged inability to find the shirt and tie he wore on the night of the 7th July. Higgs recognised that the case would ultimately hang on one issue: the print and the dispute over its origins.

He accused Melchen of deliberately taking de Marigny to the upstairs room at Westbourne to obtain his print from another object. There was some doubt about the time this happened, and the police officers all changed their evidence, to make it tie in with that of Lieut Douglas. "At first they wanted to convey to the jury that the print was taken off the screen before the accused went upstairs, because they were afraid the defence would claim that he had touched the screen. But Lieut Douglas told the truth and they had to change their times." By exploiting the blatant perjury of the police on this crucial point, Higgs had effectively delivered the knockout blow. The prosecution case, he said, was composed of irrelevant evidence and the deliberate falsehoods of policemen on whom citizens depended for protection. It would be an unhappy day for Nassau when a man could be convicted on such evidence. He reminded the jury of Nancy de Marigny's claims about Melchen and Barker's graphic account of the murder to Lady Oakes and their subsequent denial. He recalled how Barker told Lady Oakes of the vital print, even though it was not identified until later.

Higgs' duty as defence attorney was to establish reasonable doubt in the jury's mind. In this he had succeeded. Nothing that the Attorney General said subsequently would over-ride that doubt.

In summing up, the Chief Justice referred to the murder as "most foul and most unnatural – a crime surpassing anything in the annals of this colony." But the case against de Marigny was, he said, purely circumstantial. There was nothing to show what weapon was used, how the killer entered the house, or how he committed the crime. The judge was merciless in his treatment of Barker, who was criticised for not bringing proper photographic equipment to the Bahamas, for not producing the contested print on the object on which it was found, and for changing his story when he realised his original testimony about the print and its location given at the preliminary hearing could not have been true.

"This was a very grievous error," said the judge.

He honed in on Barker's extraordinary blunders in relation to the lifting and identification of the print, the long delay (ten days) between lifting it and identifying it, and the change of mind over the marking of the screen.

"Did this indicate that he was a gentleman who jumped to hasty conclusions?"

He said he found Barker's methods "incomprehensible." After five hours, the judge concluded his summation and expressed the hope that the jury would reach a unanimous verdict. The jury retired at 5.25pm and returned at 7.20pm. They had reached their conclusion after less than two hours.

De Marigny, who had been chatting animatedly with policemen during the interim, pacing the floor and smiling nervously, was called back into court. Nancy, who had been waiting tensely on the second floor of the nearby Central Police Station, took her seat. "Her face was pale, her lips quivering," reported *The Tribune*.

Then the jury trooped in, their faces sombre but inscrutable.

When the judge had taken his seat, the court registrar asked the jury if they had agreed on a verdict. Foreman Sands said: "Yes, we have,"

The registrar said: "How say you, is the prisoner guilty or not guilty of the offence with which he is charged?"

"Not guilty," said Sands, and those two words sparked tumultuous scenes, with women spectators springing to their feet and cheering. Police shouted "Order!" but there was no controlling the mayhem. The judge discharged de Marigny, who left the dock to embrace his wife. They had already walked out into the crowded square, where crowds cheered and jostled, without hearing the jury's rider – that he be deported from the colony immediately. The de Marignys breasted their way through excited well-wishers as flashbulbs popped. The only comment de Marigny made to waiting reporters was "The judge is a fair man."

The highly unorthodox action of the jury in acquitting de Marigny, but then seeking his deportation, was later explained by a juror who said the deportation was agreed to secure a vote for acquittal from one man who took strong exception to de Marigny on religious and moral grounds. By agreeing to the rider, the jury was able to return the nine-to-three vote acceptable for a not guilty verdict. A conviction needed to be unanimous. De Marigny escaped the noose, but his troubles were not over, not by a long way. But one of the most famous trials of the twentieth century was over, and it would be talked and written about for decades to come.

The Tribune, in a postscript to the trial, said: "Today Bahamians are looking around for someone to scalp for the unsolved murder of Sir Harry Oakes. In this 'Tragedy of Errors', the question for the public to decide is who made the first and biggest error that led to the greatest fiasco in a criminal trial in this colony?"

In writing that comment, the editor must have had only one person in mind. But the Duke of Windsor, so typically, was socialising with his friends in the United States on the evening that de Marigny was set free. However, his spite was not yet exhausted. Having failed to hang de Marigny, he would now set out to persecute him.

Godfrey Higgs and his wife played hosts to the de Marignys that memorable night. A throng of reporters and well-wishers had gathered outside the young couple's home in Victoria Avenue. Rather than brave the crowd, the couple accepted the lawyer's offer of refuge, and the evening passed in a spirit of relief and jubilation. They drove to the home of friends, the Trolles, where a small reception was held in de Marigny's honour. His friends embraced him in his moment of triumph. He paid special tribute to his friend George Thompson who, he said, stood faithfully by him throughout his ordeal. It was a heady night, with de Marigny and his wife in high spirits.

The prisoner's release brought an unexpected explosion of joy from the public, and especially the blacks, who carried him to his car outside the court. Hallinan had ordered the police to stand by with fire-hoses, expecting that conviction would spark riotous hostility towards de Marigny. But, as the Attorney General and Fred Adderley vanished quietly into the night, the holiday mood spread through Nassau, the bars filled with revellers celebrating the count's victory, over the establishment forces who were out to hang him.

For Higgs, the acquittal was a triumph which, in terms of the international publicity it attracted, would never be equalled during the rest of his long, successful career at the Bar. In every capital throughout the empire, lawyers were talking of the young barrister whose cross-examination of Barker destroyed the prosecution case. The victory enhanced his reputation far beyond the shores of the Bahamas and conferred on him the status of legal celebrity. His exposure of Barker's dishonesty had been the decisive factor: no jury could safely convict de Marigny when it was clear that a significant prosecution witness, and some police officers, were lying in court.

However, Higgs' glory, well-deserved though it was, has cloaked disturbing holes in the defence's approach which, had the verdict gone the other way, would have been subjected to close critical scrutiny by legal experts of the day. When a murder suspect is acquitted, the question immediately arises: so who did it? In working to get de Marigny off the hook, Higgs and Callender did nothing to suggest an alternative suspect, a tactic which could have proved extremely hazardous to the prisoner's cause.

It would be quite wrong to suggest that Higgs and Callender were aware of the Duke of Windsor's manoeuvreings behind the scenes, but they were undoubtedly open to question in trying so hard to remove Harold Christie from the frame. Aside from the more fanciful and outrageous theories about the culprit(s) in the Oakes murder, there was really only one other true suspect. That was Christie. Yet at no point was he treated as such by the prosecution or, indeed, by the defence. And that was in spite of his extraordinary performance in the witness-box and his own admission that his story was implausible.

In fact, the prosecution was so intent on protecting Christie's interests that they allowed him to hold press briefings during court proceedings, even though he was a key witness. This was unprecedented and wholly contrary to the rules governing the judicial process in a British court. Whatever their motives, the defence helped the prosecution in this highly questionable approach by declaring, without reservation or qualification, that Christie was in no way implicated in the crime, even though he had not been properly investigated. In fact, the hiring of Melchen and Barker was evidently intended to expedite the conviction of de Marigny at all costs, with the parallel objective of keeping Christie out of harm's way. To that extent, the defence must be held accountable for putting their client's life at risk, by deliberately ignoring the most obvious alternative suspect in the whole sorry affair.

Consider this: although Christie's whereabouts at around midnight on July 7th were the subject of a spirited dispute, the defence did nothing to exploit Christie's disturbingly shaky account of his activities that night. In fact, Higgs described his story as "implausible" in his final address, yet had made no attempt during cross-examination, or subsequently, to probe his implausibility on de Marigny's behalf. Captain Sears' evidence that he saw Christie shortly before midnight, though uncorroborated at the time, was never seriously questioned by anyone who knew the man. Remember, there was no doubt or equivocation in Sears' evidence. He said he was satisfied that it was Christie he saw that night and no-one else.

Sears' integrity as a police officer was beyond question. In fact, he was so good at his job that, in spite of his bold defiance of Christie's account (something that might easily have jeopardised his career, given the realtor's enormous influence in high places), he went on to become the Bahamas police commissioner in later years. An officer who served under Sears some years after the trial told me: "There is no question that Sears was right. The man's integrity as an officer was unshakeable. If he said he saw him, he saw him." Subsequently, Sears' account was supported by a woman friend who was in his car that night. She said Harold Christie was in the truck's passenger seat. His brother Frank was driving. So Harold was lying. Of that there can be no doubt.

But why was he lying? If you believe the accounts of some quite distinguished investigators, he was on his way to the dock to pick up a hitman, who would be taken back to Westbourne to carry out the murder of Sir Harry Oakes. If you believe the over-active Nassau gossip round, he was being driven by Frank to the home of Mrs Dulcibelle Henneage in Eastern Road, where he was proposing to pursue their passionate affair. She had been at Sir Harry's small dinner party that night. Was the assignation agreed upon there, with an exchange of nods and winks and coy smiles? Probably.

Christie's demeanour in the witness-box was itself a revelation. Perspiration was oozing from him in such profusion during his testimony that it couldn't be attributed to heat alone. The man was almost a caricature of the stressed-out witness, mopping his face repeatedly as swathes of sweat seeped through his suit. It is, of course, beyond doubt that extreme nervousness activates the sweat glands. The lie-detector responds to physical impulses prompted by stress. The more dishonest the witness, the greater the physical reaction.

Two distinguished authors, Erle Stanley Gardner and James Leasor, were in court for Christie's extraordinary performance in the witness-box. Both remarked on two points: the witness's tight grip on the rail in front of him – the white-knuckle grip of a frightened man – and the amount of perspiration seeping from him. Had this taken place in another court in another land, and had de Marigny been represented by a seasoned campaigner from the, say, British Bar, Christie would have been systematically dismantled. He displayed all the classic symptoms of a lying witness, yet Higgs did little to expose him.

This was most evident in relation to the most implausible aspect of Christie's account: his attempt to revive Sir Harry Oakes by lifting his head and pouring water down his throat. Medical evidence suggested Sir Harry had been dead for several hours when he was examined at around 7.45am. The prosecution was suggesting the murder could have been committed as early as 1.20am when, according to witnesses, de Marigny was near Westbourne. Dr Fitzmaurice believed the latest possible time of the murder was shortly after 5am, though the general impression was that it was earlier than that. Police photographs, taken soon after the discovery of the body, show not a freshly dead man but a corpse that was decidedly dead. Evidence suggested that rigor mortis had set in, meaning that proteins had already begun coagulating in the muscles, causing a marked stiffening of the limbs and torso. If this were so, it seems inconceivable that anyone would attempt to revive him, or indeed would be able to lift the head, or pour water down the throat, as indicated by Christie. Although there are no immutable rules relating to rigor mortis, the cooler the conditions the longer it takes to set in. July 7th was a sultry summer night. The fan in Sir Harry's room would have moved the air around, but made little difference to the overall temperature. The face is generally the first part of the body to show signs of rigor mortis.

There was another small, but significant, point in Christie's evidence that put his account in doubt. He could not remember whether Sir Harry's eyes were open or shut. Is it really possible that one could find oneself in such circumstances, lifting his head and pouring water down his throat, without recalling such a thing, especially when it was his close friend he was trying to revive?

Because the defence's strategy was focused so intently on exhibit J – the print – and the dishonest man who claimed to have found it, Barker, there was very little intense discussion of other elements in the case. It is interesting, for instance, that we have no idea, even after sixty years, what weapon was used to kill Sir Harry. Dr Fitzmaurice's suggestion that it was a blunt instrument with a sharp edge itself raises more questions than answers. There was no evidence of chopping, or cutting, or slicing of Sir Harry's head. Nothing was disclosed in court that pointed to a sharp edge of any kind. The wounds in Sir Harry's head were punctures, holes, which supposedly penetrated to varying depths and at varying angles. Were these punctures caused by a single blow, or several blows? No-one knows, yet even the most rudimentary forensic investigation ought to have cast light on this highly significant point.

The theory that Sir Harry died from being "bludgeoned", probably by an opportunist intruder, gained credence in the years following his death. Although there was something not quite right about it, the public tended to suspend disbelief for the greater good. The possibility that he might have been shot at a time when only a privileged few, including Sir Harry himself, owned guns in the Bahamas would have prompted unseemly speculation. It would have meant one of two things: either that he had been killed by one of Nassau society's more prominent figures, or that he was assassinated by a trained hitman.

It was left to de Marigny himself to raise the shooting theory. He discovered a witness, years after his trial, who told him he heard four shots on the night of the murder. The witness claimed to have seen men dashing up the outer staircase of Westbourne, then heard gunfire, then seen flames in the bedroom which rose and died down quickly. The man driving the waiting vehicle was, he said, Frank Christie.

If the shooting theory were correct, Harold Christie's evidence would suffer another damaging hit. For Christie told the court that, apart from his short spell of mosquito-swatting, he slept through the night at Westbourne until he awoke to a bright morning, and the gruesome discovery in Sir Harry's bedroom. Is it possible he could have slept through four gunshots, given that bedroom walls at Westbourne, according to de Marigny, did not extend right to the ceilings so that air could circulate more freely? Very doubtful, I would say.

De Marigny's story is supported by what I consider to be one of the most significant aspects of the case. First, the indecent haste with which Sir Harry's body was flown out of the Bahamas on its way to Maine. Second, the highly suspicious decision to turn the plane around so that, according to the official explanation, Sir Harry's prints could be taken. In the tropics quick burials are common for all the obvious reasons: in a hot climate, corpses deteriorate fast. But this corpse was at the centre of a major murder investigation, and it seemed any autopsy performed on it was at best cursory, at worst downright inadequate. Dr Quackenbush, the first to inspect the body, was ready to declare Sir Harry a suicide case. He had detected only one hole in the skull, into which he famously inserted his index finger. He missed the other three because they were covered by blood. Dr Fitzmaurice, who had lifted the skullcap in a subsequent examination, testified that skull fractures were the cause of death. Bullets were never mentioned.

But de Marigny was convinced that small calibre bullets had been fired into Sir Harry's brain by a hitman hired by Christie. It is a theory that cannot easily be dismissed. When Sir Harry's body was diverted back to Nassau, it was rushed to Nassau Hospital, where a room had been set aside for further examination. Armed guards stood outside while the corpse was subjected to further intense scrutiny. Only Barker, Melchen, Hallinan and Quackenbush were allowed into the room. The extraordinary lengths taken to keep whatever happened in there secret, were enough to arouse suspicion even more. If the purpose had simply been to secure Sir Harry's prints, why the tight security? And is it conceivable that even Barker, the Stan Laurel of crime detection, was so inept that he allowed Sir Harry's body to be flown off without securing prints for elimination purposes? De Marigny, not surprisingly, dismissed this version of events out of hand. Indeed, it is barely credible.

If Oakes had been shot, tangible evidence would have been buried inside his head. While such evidence existed, and a body available to be exhumed for further investigation, the true perpetrators of this horrendous crime would never be able to rest easily. Far better, therefore, to bring the corpse back to Nassau, clean out the skull, remove the bullets, and send it back to Maine for the sombre ceremonials.

In the black arts of advocacy, it is easy to argue that the end justifies the means. Higgs secured de Marigny's acquittal, which is what he was employed to do. But in concentrating so intently on Barker, to great effect, he failed to pursue other blatant weaknesses in the prosecution case, which would have strengthened the foundations of de Marigny's innocence and directed blame elsewhere. Had Mrs Henneage, for instance, been subjected to intense cross-examination (her testimony was confined to a brief description of the July 7th dinner party during the preliminary hearing) by Higgs or Callender, what goodies might have been unearthed? On oath, she would have been under severe pressure to tell the truth and the truth might well have left Christie's version of events in fragments. Was he in bed with her when Sir Harry was being murdered? If not, where was he, in light of Captain Sears' copper-bottomed testimony? She was in a position to help smooth the course of justice, and save an innocent man from the gallows, but she was never called.

The strong impression persists that the defence, in trying to save de Marigny, was deliberately avoiding whole areas of potentially decisive evidence to save other people's skins. Their eagerness to protect Christie, and openly declare him innocent in court with absolutely no justification for doing so, was alarming. Their failure to call Mrs Henneage, well-known and liked among the wealthy white Bahamians on Eastern Road, could only be explained in one way: they did not wish to subject this married mother of two to the embarrassment of exposure. All this would have been understandable, laudable even, had de Marigny been charged with careless driving, or riding a bicycle without lights. But he was charged with murder, and the hanging rope was already lying in a Nassau warehouse, ready for use when he made the morning walk to his doom.

There are two other deeply disturbing factors in the Oakes case which the defence failed to pursue. The most bewildering was the absence of Col R A Erskine-Lindop, the police commissioner. This man, whose integrity was beyond question, was in Nassau for the opening of the Oakes inquiry, but was soon afterwards transferred to Trinidad. It was, on the face of it, a routine promotion, but subsequent disclosures were to prove otherwise. Erskine-Lindop had been held responsible for policing deficiencies during the labour riots of 1942. For many months before Sir Harry's death, he was known to be depressed about the blame being heaped upon his shoulders. However, the murder – by far the biggest case of his career – would have been enough to revive the fortunes of any conscientious police officer. It was the equivalent of a journalist landing his biggest story, or a lawyer winning his biggest case. This was his chance of glory, of redemption. Typically, he approached it with his usual dedication and commitment. Even though he and his force were effectively sidelined by the Duke's decision to call in Melchen and Barker, he went about his business with characteristic thoroughness. Given the kind of man he was, Erskine-Lindop would not have been party to any shenanigans behind the scenes. Years later, he told a Bahamian friend, on the only occasion he is known to have discussed the case, that he had his chief suspect on the brink of a tearful confession, just before he was despatched to Trinidad. What's more, he lamented the fact that the killer, in his view, was still free to mix in Nassau society. Who was he talking about? The imagination need not be taxed in pursuing an answer. Yet Erskine-Lindop was never called to testify. His absence was even remarked upon during the trial, when he was declared "unavailable." Why did the defence accede to this disgraceful state of affairs? Good question.

The second disturbing absence was that of Dr Ricky Oberwarth, the Nassau hospital consultant who took exception to Hallinan's strictures, about committing no medical evidence in the Oakes case to paper. He was unhappy about this instruction, and no wonder. It stank of conspiracy, or perversion of justice. Just four days after the murder, *The Tribune* published the following paragraphs:

Dr Ulrich Ernest Oberwarth of the BG Hospital staff, who has been in charge of medical work at Nassau Prison, has been taken off this assignment, and Dr Huggins has been placed on prison work.

Asked why he had been transferred, Dr Oberwarth told a Tribune representative that he didn't quite know. Asked whether he thought the action had any connection with the de Marigny case, he replied that he knew de Marigny socially and had been his dinner guest on several occasions, but he could not say whether this was the reason for the transfer.

In publishing this story, it seemed *The Tribune* was itself concerned about apparent intrigue. Unable to come right out and air its suspicions, the newspaper appeared to be skirting round the perimeter of the problem so that its readers could draw their own conclusions. Dr Oberwarth's replies were circumspect, and could hardly have been otherwise, but they left everyone who read them feeling uneasy. Exactly what was going on?

With the benefit of hindsight, and the various disclosures made about the Duke and his financial dealings over the years, it is now possible to draw much clearer conclusions. Like everyone else in the Bahamas, the Tribune's editor would have known little about the real goings-on at Government House in 1943. But it now seems certain that Dr Oberwarth's withdrawal from the case was associated with Erskine-Lindop's banishment to Trinidad. They were both incorruptible, and therefore problematical.

As the Duke mobilised his forces in the planned destruction of de Marigny, he was intent on removing all obstacles. The unwavering rectitude of Erskine-Lindop was one obstacle. The obstinacy of Dr Oberwarth was another. Any really proficient defence team would have probed these transfers assiduously, with the objective of exposing the Crown's determination to manipulate the evidence for their own ends. But Higgs and Callender didn't. One can only speculate on the reasons, but an educated guess would lean towards the by now familiar territory. They didn't want to do anything that would upset the Nassau establishment and especially the Duke. Instead of exposing the flagrant abuse of the judicial process instigated by the Duke, and supported at least tacitly by Hallinan, they were content to rely on Barker and his fingerprint evidence as de Marigny's escape route. By playing fast and loose with the accused's life, the defence secured acquittal by only a two-thirds majority and then only because one bigoted waverer was swayed by the decision to deport the prisoner and his friend, the Marquis. It was a highly hazardous tactic, and indefensible when considered coolly at this distance in time.

The most glaring defect of all in the defence's approach to the case emerged in a two-line exchange between the embattled Barker and attorney Higgs. This, in my view, went right to the root of the issue.

"Did not His Royal Highness visit you at Westbourne and come to Sir Harry's room at the time you were processing for fingerprints?"

"Yes, he came up to see the crime scene."

De Marigny was expecting Higgs to exploit this disclosure. He gripped the dock rail in anticipation of what this line of questioning might expose. Instead, Higgs said politely: "I do not think it would be proper for me to inquire as to why he came up, or what was said."

This comment, in the context of a high-profile murder trial, was staggering. But it indicated beyond reasonable doubt that Higgs was only prepared to go so far in protecting de Marigny's life. A conventional gentleman of the old school, even though he was only thirty-six years old, Higgs had been educated in the ways of polite society. Deference was automatically accorded those of royal rank, whatever the circumstances, and he evidently felt inhibited in pursuing the point. Yet Barker, being the man he was, a dishonest scoundrel of limited intelligence, could have been subjected to intense pressure on this issue. There had to be some overpowering reason why he was prepared to fabricate evidence to secure a man's conviction. It must have been more than pure ego. It wasn't, as far as we know, money. So why put his career on the line, why be exposed as a bungling fool – or worse, an evil liar – unless the inducements were irresistible? Barker would have been flattered, and overawed, by the Duke's presence. Here he was, working on the greatest murder mystery of the age, in the presence of one of the world's most famous figures. It was heady stuff for a motor-cycle cop from Miami. Whatever the Duke said to him would have made a resounding impression. A hint, a suggestion, even an inflection, would have sent all the signals the Duke needed to convey. Barker could have been relied upon to absorb whatever impression the Duke wished to leave. Whatever passed between them, Barker secured his print, more or less determining de Marigny's fate in the process. In walking away from the questions he needed to ask, Higgs was again laying de Marigny's life on the line.

Chapter Nine

PERSECUTION

De Marigny escaped the noose, but it was by no means the end of his ordeal. Lest he doubted the seriousness of those who wished to see him hanged, and he didn't, firm proof of their intentions was to be found in the business premises of his old friend, R T Symonette, who twenty years later would become the first Premier of the Bahamas. When de Marigny called to say farewell, Symonette pointed to a pile of hemp in one corner and said it was the hangman's rope, ordered specially for him. De Marigny took a piece of it as a keepsake and regarded it wryly for the rest of his life as a kind of talisman, a symbol of his resilience in the face of adversity.

Meanwhile, the Duke, having been thwarted in his framing of de Marigny, set about making his life a misery, using all the international connections he could muster to drive him into exile and isolate him from society. He became almost manic in his desire to do him harm.

The day after his acquittal, de Marigny announced that he would resist deportation. Theoretically, he had good grounds for doing so, because under British law a man declared innocent should be treated as such. A seemingly arbitrary deportation order bore all the hallmarks of victimisation. Whatever the behind-the-scenes machinations in the jury room, there must have been strong legal grounds for his being allowed to stay. The judge made it clear at the end of the trial that he had no power to enforce the jury's request. However, de Marigny's case was not helped by his conviction on a much lesser charge – that of illegally possessing four drums of gasoline at a time when fuel was strictly rationed. De Marigny and the Marquis were fined £100 and Magistrate Field told them that, if they were not being deported, he would send them to prison. By this time, it was clear the tide of events was running against the count and his friend, and they realised their future in the Bahamas was a lost cause. Together, they appeared a disreputable alliance, sleazy foreigners with an eye to the main chance.

De Marigny said he would appeal, but didn't. Nor did he resist the deportation order once the magistrate's warning was issued. Suddenly, his resolve evaporated. However, leaving the Bahamas caused immense difficulties for him. There was to be no seamless transition. His departure marked the beginning of years of uncomfortable exile. He was rejected by the United States, the most obvious haven, because of his wife's connections there, and he was not inclined to return to the relative isolation of Mauritius. Eventually, he was invited to Cuba, where the sailing fraternity was eager to enlist his skills as a Star class racer.

At Nassau Yacht Club, de Marigny was entertained to dinner by friends and well-wishers. He was awarded the trophies he had won the previous season. Amid the conviviality, there was a certain sadness and plenty of mixed feelings. Whatever the problems he had encountered, de Marigny had enjoyed his Nassau sojourn and to leave so hurriedly left him feeling dejected. Not surprisingly, he was appalled at the injustice of his predicament. On 6 December, 1943, he and Nancy sailed out of Nassau harbour with a final wave to friends and arrived at Havana the following day. For the count, the breach with the Bahamas was almost total. It would be many, many years before he saw the islands again.

The Bahamas government's insistence on de Marigny's departure was highly irregular, and indefensible in law, but it was fuelled by the Duke's vindictiveness, and his instincts for self-preservation. It emerged years later, when official documents were declassified, that Hallinan and Christie had provided daily accounts of the trial to the Duke while he and the Duchess visited friends in the eastern United States. On 19 November, the Duke had cabled London to support the deportation order and asked that a military aircraft or vessel be provided for the purpose. It is easy to imagine the effect this request had among the Whitehall mandarins, who were grappling with the complexities and traumas of a world war. It was another example of the Duke's failure to grasp reality, and that wartime priorities would not permit such an exercise. London turned him down.

For the Duke, de Marigny's presence in Nassau was an acute embarrassment. Worse, it was a potentially explosive hazard. The longer he stayed around, the more people would be reminded of the highly irregular nature of the Oakes inquiry and its outcome. De Marigny, being the outspoken character he was, couldn't be relied upon to accept meekly the plot to frame him, and the indignity heaped upon him in Nassau Prison. He would have insisted on having answers that no-one would be prepared to give. In the Duke's eyes, his banishment was therefore imperative.

When a suspect is acquitted of murder, the question of who really did it automatically arises. If the suspect is the only possible killer, the prosecution accepts defeat and announces that no-one else is being pursued. In this case, it was impossible to do that because Christie was a more plausible suspect than de Marigny on grounds of motive and proximity alone. During the trial, Barker's clumsy fabrication of fingerprint evidence was the only thing to indicate de Marigny's presence inside Westbourne in the early hours of 8 July. The prosecution was able to establish he was on the road passing the house at that time, but unable to show that he traversed the hundred yards or more, of driveway and gardens, from the gateway to the house. There were no footprints or tyre tracks recorded, even though the damp conditions would have helped in the detection of such movements. As far as is known, no attempt was made by Barker, Melchen or anyone else to secure such evidence. Christie, by his own admission, was in the house at the relevant times, even though contrary evidence suggested he was somewhere else, for at least part of the night. As we shall see later, he also had powerful motives to dispose of Sir Harry. Yet he and Hallinan were actually relaying reports of de Marigny's trial to the Duke. It would be difficult to imagine more potent proof of complicity.

During the post-trial furore, the Duke became disturbingly obsessive about de Marigny. He called London, Washington and the colonies, declaring de Marigny and his friend the Marquis "undesirables", claiming de Marigny's matrimonial history showed him to be an unscrupulous adventurer. There was a certain irony in this, as the Duke was himself married to a woman whose matrimonial history showed her to be the most unscrupulous adventuress of the age. This would not have been lost on London at the time. But the besotted, doe-eyed Duke was unable to see how farcical his protestations were.

In his missive to London, the Duke also said de Marigny had an "evil reputation for immoral conduct with young girls." He was characterised as a gambler and spendthrift, a suspected drug addict and violator of immigration laws, probably a reference to the help he gave the Devil's Island refugees and his rental of apartments to American Jews.

During the trial, when de Marigny questioned some of Higgs' tactics, especially in relation to the powder-puff approach to Christie, he was told: "My job is to get you acquitted, not to convict Christie. And besides, you need to live here when this is all over." In other words, to rile Christie was tantamount to ensuring an uneasy and possibly precarious future in the Bahamas. He had been warned.

On considering his options, de Marigny felt, after all, that departure was advisable. His friend the Marquis left for Haiti, where his marked Frenchness would be less incongruous, while he and Nancy made preparations and packed their belongings. Before leaving for Cuba, de Marigny called on James Sands, the grocer who had been jury foreman. Sands explained that four jurymen were Plymouth Brethren who disliked de Marigny for several reasons, none of them linked with the murder of Sir Harry Oakes. Firstly, they resented that he broke God's laws by sailing on a Sunday. Secondly, they were appalled at his reputation around town, especially as a seducer of younger women. Thirdly, he was considered exotic and therefore suspect. Good Christians that they were, they voted for an innocent man to hang, on no firmer basis than their own religious indignation. Sands managed to change the mind of one of them, only by adding the deportation rider, thus avoiding a hung jury and a retrial.

Given that Christie himself was feeding reports of the trial to the Duke, it can be safely assumed that a degree of intimacy existed between these two. The Duke would, of course, have been able to follow quite extensive reporting of the case in the American press, but Christie's accounts were presumably of a different nature. If the pair of them were engaged in a conspiracy to hang de Marigny, there would be specific reference to their special interests, and an assessment of how well they were doing. Christie was an important figure in the Bahamas. Indeed, he was already identified as the key component in the colony's economic development. It is natural, therefore, that the Duke would seek to foster friendly relations with him. Equally, Christie would, on business grounds alone, want to be on good terms with the colony's Governor, whoever it happened to be. This friendship, and the Duke's extreme eagerness to let the Oakes case die away, explains his refusal to pursue other lines of inquiry. No attempt was made, following de Marigny's acquittal, to seek the true killer.

There were, however, other reasons why the Duke wanted the whole thing hushed up, and this partly explains his extraordinary response to the murder in the early stages. His two-day clampdown on information was, almost certainly, an expedient to buy time and thwart any temptation on London's part to send a team of Scotland Yard detectives to investigate the crime. The last thing he wanted was a team of expert sleuths prying into government affairs and his own dubious activities.

Let's recall the tight Nassau social milieu in which the Duke found himself in the 1940s. Apart from Sir Harry Oakes, the so-called "uncrowned King of the Bahamas", there was the pompous Swede Axel Wenner-Gren, and Harold Christie, the rising realtor. Together, they formed a powerful group backed by two of the western world's biggest fortunes, the Oakes mining interests and Wenner-Gren's industrial empire. Outside this influential foursome, there were the governing white Bahamian merchants, whose avarice and self-interest were egregious, even for the Duke's tastes. In their company, the Duke was uneasy, and several times during his governorship he was to find himself at odds with them. These disagreements were usually to do with the strategy for dealing with the colony's various ills. The Duke, following his belief that the masses should be kept in a state of well-fed compliance, constantly came up against the intransigence of a class of people who were interested only in themselves, and regarded the black masses merely as a labour pool which served their many needs. Christie was different in at least two respects: he had a more expansive, international outlook and was infinitely preferable as a companion. The Duke and Wenner-Gren were particularly close. This can be attributed in part to their strong ethnic and ideological similarities. They also shared a less welcome characteristic: both were under close watch by the FBI. The Windsors' many indiscretions in

Europe, and Wenner-Gren's tiresome and self-important meddling in political affairs, made them natural targets of the intelligence services, for they had left distinct impressions among the Allies that they were actively sympathetic to the Nazi cause. They also had close contact with an odious Irish-American, James Mooney of General Motors, whose Fenian nationalism had spawned extreme anti-British sentiments. There was nothing Mooney would not do to discredit Britain, which he saw as the root cause of most of the world's wrongs. This right-wing triumvirate generated so much fury and concern, in Washington and London, that they came under almost constant watch. Meanwhile, the Duchess, ostensibly absorbed in her work for the Bahamas Red Cross, was suspected by the United States of sending "treasonous correspondence" to the enemy.

Whenever they had the chance, the Windsors left Nassau to visit their friends in the United States. This in itself attracted critical attention from the FBI. It was felt strongly in Washington that these excursions were not entirely social. It's interesting that the friends were largely hewn from the same timber; they were an assortment of appeasers and isolationists, people in favour of an accommodation with Hitler. By 1941, the FBI had created a dauntingly large file on the Windsors. Little recorded therein was favourable. The bureau's carefully documented intelligence was accompanied by State Department papers and OSS data. In the US government's higher echelons, the official view of the Windsors was clear: they were Nazi collaborators, people whose loyalty could not in any circumstances be relied upon. Running parallel with these views were the bureau's deep suspicions about Wenner-Gren, whose alleged Nazi links in Berlin and Vienna were also under intense scrutiny. Interestingly, the Duchess was rated more culpable than the Duke, with some papers in the file referring to her, without inhibition, as a Nazi spy.

When Japan bombed Pearl Harbour in 1941, the appeasers and isolationists in America were dealt a devastating blow. It meant that, like it or not, their country was at war and their own cause was lost. Those who favoured a 'wait and see' approach to the European war, saw their opinions go up in the black smoke billowing from America's stricken fleet. Within a week, following frantic lobbying from Washington, Wenner-Gren was blacklisted. Embarrassingly for the Duke he, as Governor, was required to sign the blacklisting order against his friend, who, many times, had hosted the Windsors aboard his yacht, as it meandered through the Bahama isles. At the time, the Swede was Mexico-bound on the Southern Cross. He remained for most of the war at his retreat at Cuernavaca, where he smouldered at the indignity and humiliation heaped upon him by the authorities. The blacklisting was accompanied by a freezing of his considerable assets and the closure of his Bahamas operations. Among companies in which Wenner-Gren was involved was the Bank of the Bahamas, which included the Duke and Duchess among its shareholders. Other businesses in the Swede's portfolio had marked Nazi connections, according to US intelligence. President Roosevelt, and two senior US government officials, including Under-Secretary of State Sumner Welles, were directly responsible for this order, along with Assistant Secretary of State Adolf Berle, whose own assiduous research, via an international network of agents, led him to conclude, without reservation, that the couple were involved in a close and dangerous liaison with Nazism.

British intelligence was focusing on the company H A Brassert, in which Wenner-Gren was a partner. This business had close links with Goering. It was also interesting because, via the Bank of the Bahamas, it was suspected of being a conduit through which Windsor assets, including laundered money, could be moved to the Swede's Banco Continental in Mexico. At this stage of the war, when the outcome was by no means certain, the Duke and Wenner-Gren were preparing for all eventualities. By stockpiling money in Mexico, they would have the means to sustain their lifestyles, however things worked out. A more sinister purpose, according to later disclosures by intelligence agencies, was to safeguard the assets of their Nazi friends who, in the event of defeat, would seek to escape Europe and find refuge among the dictators and juntas of Latin America.

Mexico had been of interest to the Windsors, Christie and Oakes since 1941, when the question of safeguarding assets against any eventuality had become pressing. In March of that year, the Duke had engaged in wholly improper discussions with Maximinio Avila Camacho, governor of the province of Puebla and brother of the Mexican president, during Camacho's stay in the penthouse at Nassau's British Colonial Hotel, as guest of Oakes and Christie. The Duke, as official British representative, had no right to engage in talks with an official of a country which had broken off diplomatic relations with London in 1938. Absence of diplomatic discretion was bad enough, but the purpose of the Duke's conversations with Camacho was actually far more sinister. It was to cement highly dubious relations with Mexico, as a prelude to shifting large amounts of money there, in breach of wartime currency exchange regulations.

The Duke had met Camacho at the instigation of Oakes, Christie and Wenner-Gren to help lubricate the process. In the early war years, the Bahamas was a stagnant economy, with few opportunities to generate money, while Mexico held enticing prospects of oil discovery, something close to the Duke's heart. One of his recurring fantasies was that oil would be discovered on his extensive Canadian ranch: to pursue black gold in a Latin American country veering encouragingly to the right under Camacho's guidance held obvious attractions, especially as Mexico was likely to to be less vulnerable to the outcome of the war than its northern neighbours.

The problem for the Duke and Oakes was that, legally, they were constrained from moving money to Mexico or anywhere else, outside the sterling area. Vast sums generated by Oakes' mining interests were pouring into his Nassau accounts, but he was hamstrung in using it constructively for investment purposes. His known aversion to tax was another constraining factor. Canada, his homeland, was out of the question. Other Commonwealth territories held little appeal. Britain faced massive post-war economic problems, whatever the outcome of the war, so Mexico became ever more alluring as a 'safe' for hidden treasure. The suspicion is that Wenner-Gren's yacht, Southern Cross, was used to transport gold bullion belonging to Oakes, as part of a deal that would eventually see Oakes installed as a substantial stockholder in Banco Continental, the hub of Wenner-Gren's sophisticated financial manoeuvres in that part of the world. The Duke was also deeply embroiled in the Mexican adventure, which probably holds at least part of the key to the Oakes murder.

All this was going on against the backdrop of troubling events in Nassau. Sightings of U-boats in the Bahamas archipelago increased the Windsors' fears, that they might be kidnapped, as part of an exchange deal involving the Fuhrer's deranged deputy, Rudolf Hess, whose madcap peace mission in 1941, when he flew to Scotland in a small plane, brought a touch of light relief to an otherwise sombre period. The Duchess became almost neurotic about it. A detachment of Cameron Highlanders was brought in to guard Government House, where the Duchess remained indoors, fearing a sudden swoop by armed German sub-mariners. If this danger was largely imaginary, other events fermenting in Nassau most definitely were not. While the front windows of the Windsors' residence looked out over the glories of Nassau harbour, with its vivid colours and native bustle, the rear windows rendered a different vista. Beyond the extensive grounds lay a sprawl of shanty slums in which lived the impoverished black masses. Unrest in these slums had been fermenting for some time, worsened by discrepancies in pay between local and imported workers. Rioting broke out that spilled on to Bay Street, the nub of the colony's white wealth. Looters smashed store windows and fled with whatever they could lay hands on. The Cameron Highlanders were enlisted alongside US Marines to restore order, but not before two people died in the melee, with several more injured. The Windsors were off the island at the time, visiting their friends in the United States, so acting Governor Leslie Heape was under pressure to act. It was a worrying time for him and the police commissioner, Erskine-Lindop, who was subsequently criticised by Christie and Oakes for not bringing events under control with the local force. Businesses closed and a curfew was imposed. Although calm was restored to the downtown area, disturbances rumbled on in the native communities, where a police base and fire station were set alight.

The Duke returned immediately to Nassau, leaving the Duchess to shop with friends. Racist though he was, his regal presence had an impact on the blacks, who responded to his call for calm. The Bay Street Boys were, of course, solely concerned with their personal welfare and commercial interests, and wanted to know what the colonial administration was going to do about both. On advice from Attorney General Hallinan, the Duke fell back on a tried and trusted palliative: he set up a commission of inquiry, then broadcast to the people, urging patience and restraint, and firmly asserting that he would not tolerate indiscipline. Somehow, he managed to convince the masses he was on their side. It was, in fact, something of a triumph for colonial authority.

The Duke's diplomatic approach brought positive results, but it didn't satisfy the Bay Street Boys, who demanded no-nonsense reprisals against the looters and fire-raisers. Again the Duke fell back on history in justifying his actions. The French and Russian revolutions were built on the backs of harsh repression by former rulers. To punish and humiliate the masses at this delicate juncture would bring only further trouble. In calming things down, the Duke was not displaying what some construed as liberalism, but hard-headed pragmatism. To have acted otherwise would have placed the colonial government, and probably the lives of himself and his wife, in danger.

As black resentment simmered, and the Duke allowed himself congratulations for a job well done, the intelligence agencies in Washington and London continued to squirrel away incriminating information about the Windsors and Wenner-Gren. A State Department file, dating from the summer of 1942, showed the Swede as having the following sums on deposit: London $50 million, the Bahamas $2.5 million, the United States $32 million, Mexico $2 million and Norway $32 million. The Bahamas deposits were said to have been made at the Duke's request and, partly at least, for his benefit. This file also confirmed what authorities had for some time suspected, that the Duke was breaching wartime currency restrictions and investing in highly dubious business enterprises.

Considering the information being fed to them from international contacts, it is not surprising the State Department took such an uncompromising line, especially against the Duchess, whose missives to Europe were denied exemption from censorship, despite the Duke's pleas for concessions. There were strong suspicions that, certainly during the early years of her Bahamas sojourn, the Duchess was engaged in correspondence with the enemy. Apart from their well-established connections with Wenner-Gren, the Windsors were also in frequent contact with the businessman Charles Bedeaux, whose eagerness to pursue business contacts, on both sides of the wartime divide, landed him in jail for trading with the Germans.

Of the many theories, about the Oakes murder, which circulated in Nassau in the mid-1940s, few cited a black intruder as the culprit. But among the often ludicrous stories offered by those who dared to discuss the crime, were a couple which researchers were to cite later as reasons for the Duke's extraordinary actions in the immediate post-murder period. One was that Oakes was enjoying a sexual relationship with the wife of a black Bahamian, and that the killing was no more than a revenge crime by a crude amateur who tried to set fire to the bed and body to destroy evidence. The other was that Christie employed a black cult hitman from Florida who slaughtered the baronet ritualistically with a fishing spear, then followed other death ceremonials by setting small fires on the carpet. The cult demanded that the man who hired the killer should wear an item of the victim's clothing. Hence, Harold Christie in Sir Harry's pyjamas when he discovered the body the following morning.

Why would such killings influence the Duke's approach to the investigations? Because he was determined to quash any suspicion of a black killer, in light of the colony's highly fragile state. In his eagerness to scotch any suggestion of a black crime, so the story goes, the Duke targeted de Marigny, and engaged two crooked detectives, to fit up the suspect for the noose. There is an appealing simplicity in this approach, but I don't believe it.

Much more likely is that all the Duke's known instincts for self-preservation came into play. It was 10.30am before he summoned Melchen and Barker, and then only after intense discussions with the Duchess, Erskine-Lindop and, extraordinarily, with Christie himself. When the officers left Miami, they would have been aware that only the most rudimentary detection equipment was required. De Marigny was already identified as the man to hang. All other efforts would be directed towards concealing the truth.

For the Duke, this enticingly simple solution, to an extremely troublesome predicament, had a much greater advantage than mere convenience. It would circumvent any talk about enlisting the services of Scotland Yard and the FBI, both of whom were well aware of the suspicions surrounding him. By calling in Melchen and Barker – both, incidentally, strongly suspected by Washington of having strong Mob connections – he was blocking any possibility of expert snoopers prying into his own activities.

As an ex-King with allegedly traitorous inclinations, plus a penchant for money laundering and breaching currency laws, he was disinclined to leave himself exposed. The campaign to save himself and destroy de Marigny was underway.

In February, 1990, de Marigny flew to Nassau to promote his book about the case. In spite of the fact that he blamed Christie for the murder, he felt safe at that stage from reprisals. Most of the major figures of that wartime spectacle were now safely dead and frazzled emotions had calmed down with time. However, during an interview with *The Tribune*, it became clear that the Oakes ordeal had left its mark on him, and that fifty years of reflection had done little to heal the hurt he felt.

It was the first time in twenty years he had spoken to the press, and it was clear that the persecution he suffered, after the trial, was as painful to him as the court proceedings themselves. Repeatedly, he found himself in immigration cells in various parts of the empire as he sought a place to live. Despite his innocence, he felt like a fugitive as the case came back to haunt him.

"I was a man without a country because I think the authorities had arranged to tell all the British countries wherever I would go that I was a dangerous man," said de Marigny in that "French-flavoured voice" *The Tribune* had noted at his trial.

After his spell in Cuba, and six months spent in Santo Domingo awaiting US entry documents, he headed for New York City, where he accepted a random succession of jobs. At one point he walked dogs for the wealthy. At another he was engaged as a strike breaker. Although he had once been flamboyant and extrovert, he was by now keeping a low profile, seeking anonymity in a big country. But he was unable to shake off the reputation he gained from all those headlines. Wherever he went, it re-emerged. He was, it seemed, destined to remain "the man tried for the murder of Sir Harry Oakes." Sometimes this became, among the ignorant, "the man who killed Sir Harry Oakes". He grew increasingly resentful of the burden he was obliged to bear.

In the dead of night, said de Marigny, he was still tormented by images from those distant days. He had recurrent dreams about the filthy cell in Nassau, the native music in the night that kept him sane, the bucket in the corner that was changed only twice a week, the choking odours from his own waste, the injustice of his plight, and the "pack of lies" emanating from the prosecution as they built their case against him. He endured four months and two days of torment while awaiting trial.

Though ejected as undesirable in 1943, de Marigny was treated as a celebrity on his return to Nassau in 1990. Time had softened the negative feelings of old, and friends who always believed in his innocence were able to renew acquaintances and reminisce. At the Island Bookshop in Bay Street, he signed copies of his book and shook hands with well-wishers. For old-time Nassauvians, his presence was a potent reminder of the trial and the dark days of war. The Windsor years are still seen as among the most colourful, and eventful, in Bahamas history.

While in town, he drove along Victoria Avenue, now barely recognisable from his day. His old home had long gone. Car parks now occupied plots where colonial-style homes once stood, and the avenue had lost much of its traditional elegance. Only the royal palms on either side recalled its grander days. Mary, his wife of thirty-eight years, accompanied him on his Bahamas trip, but only after reassurance from trusted friends Lewis Williams and Dr Matthew Rose, who said there was no longer a need to fear sinister influences in Nassau. There was something poignant in what she had to say, for it became clear during her talk with a reporter that Nassau had meant a lot to de Marigny over the years. During his seven years on the island, he had evidently formed a tremendous attachment to the place and its people. "He's the happiest man in the world," she said, "He's back on the island he loves."

During his stay, he enjoyed reunions with Sir Durward Knowles, the Olympic gold medallist sailor who had been a keen yachting companion in the war years, and Ernest Callender, the junior defence counsel at his trial. Regrettably, senior counsel Godfrey Higgs was already dead and de Marigny, almost eighty himself at the time, gave credit for his own longevity to his family's "good genes." He said: "We normally live to be 100 in my family." In fact, he did live on into the twenty-first century.

Reflecting on the trial, he said: "They did everything they could to break my spirit. It taught me humility." Referring to his early success in business, he said: "Everything I did turned good and I'm afraid I became arrogant. If you're successful very young in life you have a tendency to be very cocky." He believed that arrogance was, in part, a reason for his persecution.

His egalitarian approach to life had puzzled Nassau society, he recalled. He was always on the side of "the beaten people" and this earned him many enemies. "I believe in a classless society," he said, and recalled delivering chickens from his farm to society homes where, later in the day, he might be a guest at dinner. Nassau's elite found this baffling.

Mary chimed in: "He believes what's in their hearts and heads," confirming his belief in substance rather than superficiality. He had come a long from his youth, when he chased twittering society fillies at Ascot and Henley.

With his entrepreneurial flair, de Marigny rebuilt his business life, with a printing company in Cuba, a plastics firm in Mexico and, finally, a real estate enterprise in Houston, Texas, where he spent most of his later years. Though no longer a competitive sailor, he became an accomplished bridge player and keen tennis fan, remaining active in the game well into his seventies. With two artificial knees and five discs removed from his back, he confined competition to men of similar age. "The mind was willing but the body had to be dragged," he said. "I play tennis with other old men and we talk about what to do to suffer less."

The movie *Passion in Paradise*, which depicted de Marigny in the Oakes murder trial, thrust celebrity status upon him at a time when he least wanted it. He had been content to live quietly in Houston, but when the film hit the television screens his telephone began to ring, with many calls from old contacts in the Bahamas. This led to his return for a brief vacation, for which he had to seek permission because of that old deportation order. Government officials, he said, were very friendly towards him. "They seemed to like me," he declared.

Of his book, de Marigny said: "I just want to tell the world the truth. I don't want my children and grandchildren believing the rumours and lies that have been written about me while I have the opportunity to tell them and the world the truth."

One point he made forcefully was that his many woes of the post-war era, his tough struggle to rebuild his life from nothing, and his lifelong fight to clear his name, were all exacerbated in some way by the pernicious influence of the Duke of Windsor, whose spite seemed to know no limits.

Chapter Ten

PRIME SUSPECT

To this day, Harold Christie remains the prime suspect in the murder of Sir Harry Oakes, not so much because of what happened before the event, but for the extraordinary cover-up that occurred afterwards. Though now long dead, he was never in his lifetime able to dampen down the speculation which, though invariably whispered behind hands, never went away. In later years, he allowed friends to explain his lies in the witness-box about his whereabouts on the night of 7-8 July, 1943, by saying he was protecting a married woman's reputation. When challenged directly by the newspaper magnate Lord Beaverbrook, who said "Come on Harold, tell us how you killed Sir Harry Oakes," Christie smiled inscrutably and said the murder was committed by a betrayed husband. There the matter rested.

The Duke of Windsor rejected de Marigny's call for a reopening of investigations once the jury's verdict was known. The police, none of whom believed de Marigny to be the killer, left the matter on file. It was an unsatisfactory outcome and no-one in the Bahamas has ever felt entirely comfortable about it.

It has to be said that the Christie theory is not the only one out there. There are several quite fanciful stories still being advanced by criminologists, authors and others about the person or people responsible for Sir Harry's death, some of them doubtless circulated as camouflage manoeuvres to keep investigators away from the truth.

The main one concerns the Mafia boss Meyer Lansky, who was pursuing a casino licence in the Bahamas during the early 1940s and came to see Sir Harry as an obstacle. That theory can be considered later. For now, we'll review the case against Christie, which is by far the most interesting and plausible.

Christie was a man on the make in the 1940s. Although almost self-effacingly mild-mannered, he was actually quite a shrewd operator in his field and won the respect of fellow businessmen for his prowess in oiling wheels and cutting deals. He was the ambitious son of an impractical poet of a father and a strong, no-nonsense mother who provided the drive to keep her large family afloat during quite tough times. Henry Christie was more a shirker than a worker and spent much of his time ambling around aimlessly, charming his equally feckless friends with his harmless versifying and idle chatter. Like many others in the Bahamas, he was also a preacher, venturing off on week-long journeys round the islands to spread the Word. He was rarely in touch with reality and shunned the harsh practicalities of life as he carried the gospel to far-flung settlements. It was left to his long-suffering wife Margaret to square up to the onerous responsibility of raising eight children, and she did so with distinction, doubling as a straw vendor and real estate saleswoman. There is no doubt she became Harold's role model, and the inspiration for his future success. He thought the world of her.

As a teenager, Harold left Nassau for New York to seek work. Later, he moved to Canada, where he was briefly enlisted in the Royal Canadian Air Force. Then, in his mid-twenties, he returned home to launch the enterprise that would become his life's work. Fortunately for young Harold, he inherited his mother's dynamic traits, and they were to serve him well. After his spell abroad, where he acquired a more expansive outlook than most of his fellow whites in the Bahamas, he was able to view his country's potential more objectively. Land sales became his passion and he proved a master of his trade. If there was one characteristic he did inherit from his ineffectual father, it was an evangelistic streak. It was to prove very useful.

The company he founded, H G Christie, survives in the family to this day, having been launched by Harold in 1922, and is one of the many agencies now profitably engaged in property sales throughout the island chain. When it began, however, real estate dealings were in their infancy, and Christie was a pioneer.

Though the Bahamas' reputation as a tourism resort and tax haven for the wealthy was later attributed to the lawyer, Stafford Sands, and the developer, E P Taylor, who created the famous enclave for the rich called Lyford Cay, it was really Christie who spawned the Bahamas boom, tirelessly promoting the colony's near perfect climate, its magnificent beaches and emerald seas. Though born into a poor home, where the ways of the wealthy were alien, Christie quickly developed an amiable manner that endeared him to those of greater resources, whose business he pursued. It was said of him by Godfrey Higgs, the lawyer who defended de Marigny, that he could sniff a commission from a thousand miles away, and it's true that he travelled widely to secure land sales among the super-rich in Europe and America. Christie was the first man – and long before Taylor and Sands got involved – to capitalise on the Bahamas' few natural resources; namely, the almost ever-present sun, the incomparable sea, and virtually endless strands of pinkish, powder-like sand. For the jaded plutocrats of Europe and North America, who lived much of their business lives in chilly climes under low grey cloud, the warmth and vivid hues of the Bahamas were to become nigh irresistible, thanks to Christie's promotional skills. In his travels, he offered tracts of virgin land (mainly scrub-covered rock, actually) fringed by vast beaches and lapping surf. In Nassau and the Out Islands of the Bahamas, Christie was ultimately to amass a considerable fortune, by selling off beach lots at vast profit to foreigners seeking not only a place in the sun, but a shelter from the attentions of the taxman.

During the 1930s, only a decade after he had established his real estate business, Christie encountered by far his best prospect to date. He was visiting Palm Beach, Florida, when he met the squat, square-faced former prospector Harry Oakes. At first, Christie was taken aback by Oakes' coarse demeanour, which was markedly at odds with his own quiet, rather diffident, manner. Here was a man whose aggressive ways had been burnished by disappointment, humiliation and relentless adversity in the harsh environs of the Yukon. Oakes was brusque, prickly and intimidatingly outspoken, but beneath the tough veneer lay a magnanimous and quite compassionate spirit.

For Christie, Oakes' appeal was not his manner, but his money. Since his involvement with Lake Shore Mines in Canada, then the second biggest gold producer in the world, Oakes' assets had burgeoned impressively. From being a near penniless prospector, trawling for mineral wealth in both hemispheres, Oakes had become the richest man in the British Empire, with an estimated two hundred million dollars, at a time when most people were earning only a few hundred dollars a year. The other aspect of Oakes, that appealed to the realtor in Christie, was his deep-felt resentment of the Canadian government and its tax policies. Oakes felt, with justification, that the Bennett government of the day was determined to target him for taxes far beyond his obligations. As Canada's richest man (and he was substantially richer than any of his fellow countrymen), Oakes was seen as a soft touch for the revenue collectors, who set about persecuting him quite shamelessly and with relish. When he met Christie, Oakes was fit to be hog-tied, so angry was he with his adopted homeland (though American-born, Oakes was a Canadian citizen) and its seemingly punitive tax system.

Salesmen are taught to identify and exploit a prospective customer's vulnerability, and it took little time for Christie to find Oakes' T-spot. Tax was Oakes' obsession. It bedevilled his days and ruined his nights, leaving him smouldering at the injustice of it all. Unlike those who inherit wealth, or come by it easily, Oakes felt keenly the sacrifices he had to make to secure his financial future. He didn't want politicians, probably fired by prejudice and envy, chiselling into the fortune he had, almost literally, been forced to scratch from the soil.

Christie drew for Oakes some tempting impressions of life in the Bahamas. He emphasised its physical beauty, its long golden days, its pristine seas - and, most tellingly, the great investment potential in its land. But most enticingly of all, he impressed upon him the delights of a tax-free environment, where a man was allowed to keep everything he earned. Oakes was smitten. He quickly arranged to move his fortune to the Bahamas.

For Christie, by now an urbane bachelor in his forties, with much influence among the Bahamas' ruling elite, the "capture" of Oakes was his biggest business coup to date. He saw him as much more than an investor. Oakes was a potent symbol of a prosperous future, not just for Christie, but for the Bahamas as a playground for the rich. Once a man of Oakes' wealth was happily ensconced in the off-shore colony, other investors would be sure to follow. By transferring his money to Nassau, Oakes would effectively be endorsing Nassau as a tax haven, and that was to prove to be a large part of its future.

There is little doubt that a genuine friendship developed between the two. It may have been an attraction of opposites, for it's hard to imagine two characters more different. Oakes was combative and confrontational, Christie gentle to a fault. "He would go miles to avoid unpleasantness," said a Nassau friend.

However, Christie was instinctively a wheeler-dealer who could not resist a good business proposition. Also, he was born and brought up in a society almost wholly lacking a sound moral framework, where illicit deals, of one kind or another, had featured prominently in the survival of the local economy, such as it was. Oakes was, by all accounts, a straight shooter, with little time for under-handedness. Christie was more inclined to deviousness. This fundamental difference in approach to life caused what may have been the decisive fracture in their friendship. It wasn't a total breakdown, but it created suspicion where none had been. It was to have appalling consequences.

Having been attracted to Nassau by Christie's blandishments, Oakes set about acquiring land and influence in this sun-blessed haven. One of his early purchases was a large tract of land at the western extremity of New Providence, some of which, years later, would become Lyford Cay, the luxurious gated refuge of some of the world's wealthiest people. During Oakes' tenure, however, it was a scrub-covered seaside plot with a rocky promontory. Right up to his death, Oakes was looking for land with investment potential and Christie, as the island's most prominent realtor, was his eager middleman.

In the spring of 1942, Oakes was negotiating to buy a tract of land adjacent to Oakes Field, the airport he created in his personal crusade to open up the Bahamas to the outside world. The idea was that the land would then be sold eventually to the British government for an RAF base. Though almost obscenely rich, Oakes never lost his taste for securing a good deal. At the point where it seemed he had the land in the bag, Oakes began quibbling over the price. Christie, according to Nassau sources, responded by selling it behind his back to a syndicate. Oakes was left feeling he had been double-crossed. If this was the prime source of friction between them, it was by no means the only one. There is a strong suggestion that Christie owed Oakes quite substantial sums of money. Through much of his early life, Christie was considered "land rich, cash poor," and the nature of his business was such that cash flow problems were a recurrent hazard. If Oakes advanced substantial sums to buy land, and if that land subsequently proved hard to sell, the Christie business was left floating on Oakes' money. The survival of H G Christie, realtors, was therefore very much in Sir Harry's big, square hands in more ways than one. He was, in fact, by far Christie's biggest client. Symbolically, he also represented the future.

It is now thought almost certain that Oakes was, along with the Duke, involved in illicit schemes to move money into Wenner-Gren's Mexican bank. It was a time when, in spite of America's intervention in the war, the outcome was far from certain. In the event of a German victory, all those living on Britsih territory, even four thousand miles away from London, would be in a vulnerable position. Like Wenner-Gren himself, the Duke and Oakes were keen to ensure their money was relatively safe and, in the event of a Nazi triumph, accessible for future use. As Wenner-Gren was suspected by the Allies of hoarding Nazi money, it is tempting to assume that the Mexican bank was as safe a place as any to stockpile funds. That, in any event, appears to be how the Duke was thinking.

Oakes, as an ex-prospector and a hard-headed realist, was also fully aware of the changing fortunes of currencies in wartime, and the enduring value of gold. Remember, it was the glint of gold that drove him to unimaginable extremes of endurance to secure his fortune. And it was gold that became an obsession with him, along with the Canadian tax authorities he despised.

In June, 2003, I wrote a story in *The Tribune* that focused on Oakes' fixation with gold. It concerned the sale of Oak House in Sussex, England, which had once been one of several Oakes properties around the world. A sombre Victorian mansion that once stood on eight hundred acres, it was said to contain one of Sir Harry's many hoards of bullion, though none of the owners who had bought the property in the post-war era had ever been able to find it.

When Sir Harry acquired the house between the wars, he had the family motto inscribed over the fireplace, in the main hall. He also installed a tight security system, partly to protect his priceless art collection – which included an original Rembrandt – and to stave off the many people who hassled him for money after the Wall Street Crash in 1929. However, other society sources believe his obsession with security was more likely the result of his gold-hoarding fixation, which was protection against the vagaries of the Stock Market and the rise and fall of currency values. The man selling Oak House in 2003, Mark Sullivan, told reporters that he had looked everywhere on what remained of the old estate – fifty-two acres of land were being offered with the house – but had found nothing of Sir Harry's fortune. He had discovered a strongroom in the cellar but, alas, no gold. However, well-placed sources in Nassau have told me that gold is the key to the Oakes murder mystery, and that Sir Harry's movement of gold to Mexico was at the root of the entire affair.

With the Duke, Sir Harry and Wenner-Gren all locked in a plot to shift money to Mexico, it's not difficult to imagine what might have transpired in Nassau, given the Bahamas' dependence on Oakes' fortune. As things stood then, leakage of the Oakes money to another country was tantamount to dispersing the colony's economic future. It also had enormous, and barely tolerable, ramifications for Christie himself.

As one of Nassau's "inner circle" of the day, Christie would have been privy to these arrangements, though there is no reason to suspect that either he or Sir Harry was aware of the Nazi connection. Oakes, notoriously protective of his fortune, in spite of his generosity, would have been deeply aware of the consequences of a German victory, and the impact it would have on his own resources. For Christie, however, Oakes' Mexican links had more worrying implications, for it became clear early in 1943 that the baronet was considering moving his home, family and fortune to Mexico, which he considered a safer option, whoever won the war. Had this happened, it is not difficult to predict the outcome for Christie's soaring ambitions. Not only would he have lost the most potent symbol of the Bahamas' investment potential – Sir Harry Oakes himself – he would also have lost his number one client and, most worrying, the man to whom he owed considerable sums of money. If Sir Harry, irked by the land deal double-cross, called in his loans prior to departure, Christie would have found himself in a mudslide up to his ears.

Elimination of Sir Harry would not, on the face of it, help Christie's cause. But it would slow up, or halt, the departure of Oakes' capital, probably tie up his land holdings for years and, most importantly, forestall repayment of the loans, which were probably offered on a handshake. All of these factors add up to a much more powerful motive for murder than anything they could pin on de

Marigny and, if all these points are true, they would explain Christie's extraordinary demeanour in court. Even Hallinan, the Attorney General de Marigny claimed was trying to "crucify" him, was to admit in later years that Christie's performance, which did nothing to support the prosecution's case, suggested he had something to hide.

The one possible motive never seriously considered for the murder of Sir Harry Oakes is outright, straightforward theft. Yet the gold-hoarding stories which now abound about Oakes make it hard to discount. Was Sir Harry storing gold at Westbourne or on one of his vast tracts of land? Was he moving it out to Mexico on Wenner-Gren's yacht? Was there a plot to dispose of Oakes and steal his gold? These theories gain credence during chats with some of the few sources left in Nassau who, in younger days, would have been in a position to absorb the theories of Oakes' contemporaries.

One told me: "There has always been disquiet among Oakes' friends, and some members of his family, about the fate of the family fortune. When the estate was revealed, it was significantly less than imagined and there have always been strong suspicions that the bulk of the fortune went astray. I have never heard a theory on its whereabouts, or whether the Duke, Wenner-Gren or indeed Christie were somehow involved, but there has always been deep concern about the lost money. Those who have been close to the nub of the matter over the years have always believed that gold was the key to it all. Gold was a powerful hedge against the war and whatever it might bring. It was a rock solid asset and in great demand. I believe the motive for the Oakes murder was greed, pure and simple. Whoever killed him did so for the gold."

If Christie remains the prime suspect, the shrewd Mafia figure Meyer Lansky, then based in Florida, was a distant runner-up. This ruthless killer was an incongruity in the Sicilian brotherhood, mainly because he was a Jew. But he had all the attributes a capo needed, including unbridled avarice and a contemptuous disregard for human life. In addition, his intelligence and ingenuity were treasured in an organisation fast establishing itself as a key fixture in American life, and his Jewishness was not seen as a handicap, in a fraternity dedicated to the pursuit and acquisition of money.

Lansky had met both the Duke and Christie, and had business connections with the then thirty-two-year-old lawyer Stafford Sands.

His kind flourished off the hustlers, chancers and conmen that abounded in the Florida and Bahamas of the day. In the Bay Street Boys, and specifically figures like Stafford Sands, Lansky was able to detect the unbridled avarice of kindred spirits. Their methods were different, but their motives were identical. Self-enrichment, at whatever cost to others, was the thread of amorality linking the Florida gangsters with the movers and shakers of Nassau society. If there was one major difference, it could be ascribed to the huge cultural gulf between 1940s America and the British-controlled island chain. In America, sinister elements still considered themselves frontiersmen and carried guns. Rivals were blown away. In the Bahamas, the British aversion to firearms was evident, and differences were settled by subtler means. If Meyer Lansky's involvement in the murder of Sir Harry Oakes is to be believed, these two cultures collided violently in the summer of 1943.

Lansky, it seems, wanted to establish casino gambling in the Bahamas. With one eye on a projected tourism boom after the war, most of the prospective visitors being wealthy Floridians, he began lobbying his contacts in Nassau, with a view to setting up an extremely convenient off-shore base. An island gambling headquarters less than two hundred miles from Miami, with all the trappings of a tropical paradise, would be a perfect tonic for rich Americans wearied by war in search of stimulating recreation. The Mob in New York and Florida needed new revenue streams to replace the fruits of the Prohibition era boom, and casino gambling seemed the way forward. In addition to offering guaranteed profits, and very handsome ones at that, the casinos would provide a credible means of laundering ill-gotten gains from the mainland. The attractions of casinos were obvious: all gamblers are mugs, of course, and the odds are stacked massively in favour of the house. For casino owners there are no risks. Their biggest hurdle is to get the punters to the tables. Once that had been achieved, the money fell into their laps like rice at a wedding.

Lansky told his New York bosses that Nassau was ripe for the taking. With the Duke seen as weak, impressionable and avaricious, and the likes of Sands and Christie as egregriously acquisitive predators, it would be easy to secure clearance for an off-shore operation, with all the additional advantages of big tax breaks and tariff concessions. Lansky travelled to Nassau to meet Sands and Christie. They talked of building new hotels with Mafia money, but Lansky's conditions were clear: no casinos, no investment.

For Christie and Sands, the prospect of all that incoming investment was too tempting to resist. The fact that it was crooked money, Mob money, did not deter them. With no moral impediment, they were free to consider the much more daunting obstacle of legality, for casino gambling was against Bahamas law. In itself, this need not have pr.esented too much difficulty in the climate of the times. The Duke, at least nominally in charge of Bahamian affairs, was himself ambivalent in matters of right and wrong, finding it difficult to discern the often fine line between the two. The fortunes of most Bay Street Boys had been founded, for the most part, on highly questionable activities. And as Christie was one of the main men in the governmental process, it did not seem inconceivable that he might overcome, or eliminate entirely, the pettifogging regulations that forbade what was, after all, a recreational pursuit.

For this reason, Christie and Sands were persuaded by Lansky to set in motion the procedural mechanism required to achieve the desired result. He was in no great hurry, for the war itself was an obstacle to progress. It was the post-war era that interested him. In the event, it would be the astute legal mind of Sands that would address the statutory obstructions. He was appointed the government's legal affairs adviser and set about seeking amendments to the penal code.

The Bahamas' objections to casino gambling were easy to understand. There was a strong religious lobby in Nassau which saw games of chance as sinful and potentially devastating in a social sense. Church leaders, and many more, thought any form of legalised gambling, open to locals, would spell ruination for Bahamian family life. Sands and Christie were not, however, interested in opening gambling to Bahamians, black or white. As blacks were excluded from other areas of Nassau life, including downtown theatres and hotels, there was no reason to include them in casinos. In fact, their presence would be counter-productive, deterring the white high-rollers who were the principal targets of the Sands-Christie initiative. Lansky's prospective clientele was well-defined. The native population of the Bahamas was considered irrelevant.

With Sands set to benefit from a personal "sweetener" if the anti-gambling legislation could be changed, Lansky must have felt that his plans were on the high road to success. But he reckoned without Sir Harry Oakes, who was said to have resisted casino gambling for several reasons. The first was that it did not fit the image he cherished of his sunny fiefdom. Casinos attracted a certain type, and it was a type Oakes disliked. He felt the Bahamas could find itself besieged by a particularly obnoxious breed: noisy, flashy, vulgar and shallow people in riotous pursuit of instant riches. The puritanical aspect of his character – the hard man of toil who despised shysters and double-dealers – came through strongly on this point. He was the Bahamas' most influential man and he was dead against it. Oakes was also conscious of the radical power shift that could occur if the Mafia were allowed to establish a foothold in the Bahamas. Lansky was not the kind of man to play the triangle or Chinese block in any orchestra. He and his boys would conduct the show, and Oakes would not entertain such a prospect. A third and most potent reason for his opposition was the social impact Lansky's presence would make on the Bahamas, and the political influence he would wield, in changing the nature of the islands. Oakes had a clear vision of the Bahamas' future. He wanted development for sure; he also wanted a fair deal for the people. What he didn't want was an economic base for the colony founded on criminality. Though the islands' moral antecedents were dubious, they had at least escaped the direct taint of organised crime, even though the Mob were part of the rum-running schemes of the Prohibition era.

Lansky and his boss, Lucky Luciano, were not men to tolerate undue interference with their plans. When obstacles appeared, their response was to the point: remove them. Oakes was reported to be the man in the way. He had to go.

How Oakes was killed has prompted as much speculation over the years as the "Whodunnit" aspect of the mystery. The consensus is that Christie, acting for reasons of his own, and possibly urged on by his brother Frank, or in concert with Lansky, had Oakes killed for one or all the reasons listed above. The competing theories, that he was despatched by a cuckolded voodoo priest or casual intruder looking for money, have generally been discarded. On one point, though, all the Christie-Lansky theories agree: neither man was involved personally in the brutal, bloody act itself. The bludgeoning or shooting of Sir Harry was the work of one or more hitmen. And it's possible they didn't even know or care who they were killing. Speculation over how Oakes was killed has taken on fanciful, even grotesque, dimensions over the years. The destruction of real evidence at the scene, at the Duke's prompting, has enabled fantasy and hyperbole free rein.

Perhaps the most extreme theory of all is that Oakes died at the hands of a black cult practitioner, who ritualistically jabbed his head with a fishing spear four times, in accordance with ancient African traditions. This theory suggests that Christie was involved inasmuch as he laced Oakes' nightcap with a powerful sedative (remember the dark liquid found in his body at autopsy?), crept into the darkness, climbed into his car, which had been parked away from the house, and drove through the stormy night into Nassau. It is speculated that he met the hitman, a member of the Brujeria sect of south Florida, at his Bay Street offices, then had the hired killer, or another person, drive him by truck to his girlfriend's house on Eastern Road, before returning to Westbourne to perform the killing.

In despatching Sir Harry, the killer followed the precise ritual of a Palo Mayombe murder, ensuring that only sufficient damage was caused to the head to achieve death. Then, using small quantities of gunpowder, he set small fires on the floor and spread feathers on the corpse, again all part of a ceremony with roots deep in African, and specifically Congo, history. Spattered with blood, and staggering round the unfamiliar room, the killer then unintentionally left smudged palm prints on the walls, tried to clean himself with towels, and made his getaway in the waiting truck. Throughout this gruesome sequence of events, Christie was supposedly seeking solace from the accommodating Mrs Henneage dressed in Sir Harry's pyjamas, a vital requirement of the Palo Mayombe ritual. If all this sounds ludicrous, it was not regarded as such by some quite serious students of the case. Their belief is that the killer punctured Sir Harry's skull four times, the point of the triangular-shaped spear penetrating just enough to prove lethal. Then the corpse was sprayed with insecticide and set alight, after feathers from Sir Harry's pillow were scattered in accordance with Congolese tradition. The truck returned to Eastern Road, took Christie back to his car, dropped off the hitman at the waterfront, and then returned to its base, wherever that might be. By the time Christie 'discovered' the body and raised the alarm, the spearman was on his way by motor-launch back to the United States mainland. Credible? Barely, but there are theorists who are convinced this is the way it happened.

The other principal version of events is that Christie drove with Sir Harry to a waiting launch that night, to meet Mob representatives of Meyer Lansky. The Mob delegation's mission was to change Sir Harry's mind, by force if necessary, on the casino gambling issue. During this meeting, things got heated and Sir Harry, typically, began displaying some of the coarseness of the Klondike by telling the hoodlums where to go. One of them allowed his thuggish instincts to take over, struck Oakes with a grappling hook, or winch, which happened to be lying on the deck, killing him instantly. The corpse was then loaded on to the truck, probably face down, and returned to Westbourne, where it was dragged upstairs and dumped on the bed. The fire and feathers ritual, in these circumstances, would have followed to suggest a black crime. Christie, a helpless witness to the entire episode on the boat, was panic-stricken and genuinely distressed. If this theory is correct, his intention was not to harm Oakes, but merely to expose him to Lansky's persuasive henchmen. Again, a barely credible tale, but certainly more likely than the Palo Mayombe scenario.

The third theory, and this was put forward by de Marigny, was that Christie and his brother Frank drove a hitman to Westbourne, where the baronet was slain more conventionally with a small calibre weapon aimed, execution-style, behind the left ear. The secret "operation," in a heavily-guarded room at Nassau Hospital, after Sir Harry's body was diverted back to the Bahamas while en route to Maine, was – in de Marigny's view – to clear the skull of evidence, because any suggestion of gunfire would have blown apart Christie's testimony, that he slept through the night apart from a couple of mosquito-swatting diversions in the dark hours.

An intriguing theory, and one that cannot be dismissed out of hand, comes from Nassau publisher Paul Bower, who was a young naval officer at the time of the murder, but settled in the Bahamas some years later. He relayed it, via e-mail, to an old friend of his, Dorothy Lindsley, who knew Nassau well in the 1930s and 1940s and frequently dined with the Oakes family at Westbourne.

In the message, Bower said: "We may never know whodunnit – but I think I know whatdunnit. I think whoever did it clobbered him with the spire of a conch shell, of which there were plenty hanging around everyone's house in those days. A conch shell would explain those odd-shaped holes in his left temple as he lay in bed. (I've seen the police photographs of his body lying on his right side in the bed with blood trickling down from the holes). The conch shell theory was suggested to me by Richard Rose, professor of archaeology at Rochester University, New York, who was visiting the Bahamas at the time of the quincentennial and gave a lecture at the seminar that Edward St George gave at Freeport, to mark the event. I also gave a brief opinion on what island, out of many, best fitted the description of the landing point in Columbus's log – San Sal (San Salvador) of course. So after the talks ended, Rose asked me to join him for lunch."

"Rose had just been digging on Sal Salvador and told me that when you dug down to pre-Columbian levels the conch shells all had irregular holes, which were made by the Arawaks with the spire of another conch shell – the hardest tool or weapon they had. Later, after the arrival of the white man, conch shells were all marked by horizontal slashes from a machete to break the vacuum and allow the animal to be pulled out, which is what Bahamians use today.

"Rose had just been reading the latest book on the Oakes murder - the Mafia one, if memory serves me right – and asked me what I thought of it. I told him that I thought it was a lot of nonsense, as 1943 was the height of the Battle of the Atlantic, and British and US naval patrols were all over the area, hunting U-boats and all sea traffic was closely monitored. A Mafia yacht would never have got clearance to cross to the Bahamas. So we turned to other theories and I remember telling him about the CID photos I had seen of the four irregular holes in Oakes' left temple, similar to the holes made by pre-Columbian Arawaks with the spires of their conch shells and then, almost as if a voice had whispered in our ears, and looking back on his lecture of the morning, we both simultaneously hit on the conch shell theory of Oakes' death. I pointed out to him that at Westbourne, right on the beach, there would be no shortage of conch shells about the house, as these were used as doorstops and ornaments and, to this day good large ones are often seen on occasional tables to give a Bahamian touch to people's houses.

"All this, to our minds, indicated that it was probably a local Bahamian black who did the job – probably who had a grudge against Sir Harry. (Stan Moir, the former police chief here, once told me that before there were so many guns around, the police called conch shells 'Bahamian bullets'. The theory would also explain why the weapon was never found. The clobberer just walked out of the house, which was right on the beach, and tossed the blood-stained shell into the sea."

In a letter to the author, Paul Bower offered a final fascinating twist. "When a right-handed person holds a conch shell, the spire points upwards, which makes it very difficult to bash the spire on anyone in a downwards direction (though a right-hander could inflict considerable damage with the smaller protrusions on the side of the spire). Whether blows with these side protrusions would have been deep enough to enable the clobberer to hit with sufficient force to penetrate the skull-bones, however, is doubtful, as the full strength of his arm could not so easily be brought to bear. If that's the case, the murderer would have had to have been left-handed. This rules out de Marigny, Harold Christie and any of the usual suspects."

Bower believes the conch shell theory is the likeliest explanation of Sir Harry's death. "Sir Harry, not the most even-tempered of men, had made quite a bunch of enemies in the Bahamas over the years and a lot of locals bear grudges. At any rate, the conch shell theory is a much more likely theory than the Mafia theory involving Meyer Lansky's yacht. As I have said, at the height of World War Two, with an RAF base at Windsor Field and British and American patrols hunting U-boats all around the Atlantic, it's most unlikely that Lansky's yacht could have made the trip to Nassau undetected."

My own theory, for what it's worth, is that Oakes was shot in his bed in a classic execution by a hitman, and that Christie was implicated in the crime, possibly for one or all the reasons mentioned earlier in this chapter. Because the crime scene was virtually destroyed for detection purposes in the immediate aftermath of the murder, the case against Christie has to rest on what happened in the days and weeks following the crime. His highly questionable performance in court, his "authorized" press briefings during proceedings, his feeding of trial reports to the Duke in the United States, and his shameless perjury, all point to complicity. And that's not to mention the powerful motives outlined earlier. The Oakes' family, though they have maintained a dignified silence for six decades, were deeply disturbed by the fact that this case was never properly investigated – and that Christie was never subjected to proper scrutiny. One must also consider the role of the Palm Beach lawyer, Walter Foskett, and the fact that his name later cropped up among Florida socialites as being party to the crime. If he was, it would go a long way towards explaining his off-hand attitude to de Marigny when he sought his support in patching up family differences. Establishing antipathy between the Oakes and de Marignys would undoubtedly help his cause if he were working on a plot to dispose of Sir Harry. Were Christie and Foskett working in unison? And was the over-riding motive gold? Those questions have yet to find answers, but there are strong suspicions among high society figures who wonder where the Oakes fortune went.

I support de Marigny's contention that the evidence was cleared from Sir Harry's skull during that secret operation at Nassau Hospital as part of a wider conspiracy to frame de Marigny and keep Christie clear of suspicion at all costs. There are no further firm clues to support this claim, save the circumstantial evidence cited throughout this book. It is by far the most credible explanation.

For those who find the shooting theory unbelievable, I would say this: small calibre bullets can be "adjusted" in a way which makes them less powerful and less noisy. It is, therefore, conceivable that the bullets could be fired from close quarters without emerging from the other side of Sir Harry's head. There have been cases in the past where small calibre bullets have entered the skull and traced the contours of the inner shell, coming to rest in the brain or other soft tissue. It was a theory cited in the 1999 killing of the British television personality Jill Dando, who died after being shot once behind the left ear at close quarters, outside her London home. Such interference with the bullets could also explain the irregular shapes of the holes.

There is another reason for supporting the gunshot theory: the position of the wounds was exactly the one favoured by skilled professional killers. Bullets fired into the head behind the left ear achieve instant death. Jill Dando suffered that fate along with a very long line of "execution" victims before her. It is a position guaranteed to get the right result with no hope of recovery.

Implicating Harold Christie is, of course, nothing new. But my belief is that there was no involvement of "outsiders", either in the conspiracy itself or the execution of the deed. Though well-informed in the evil arts of assassination, the hitman was almost certainly local. It is extremely unlikely that Mafia killers would have made a night-time voyage from Florida in wartime, when the straits between the Bahamas and the US mainland were alive with Allied patrols. It is possible that the reported landing of a launch at Lyford Cay was a diversionary tactic, with the Meyer Lansky theory a convenient smokescreen.

None of those who have pointed fingers at Christie in the past have suggested he committed the murder himself. But it is probable that the entire enterprise – the plot and its implementation – was centred on New Providence itself, involving local people. The fire, far from being a ritualistic adjunct to murder, was intended to destroy evidence, nothing more. However, pure panic left the job unfinished.

It is only fair to say that everyone I have spoken to who knew Harold Christie personally disagrees with this conclusion. They believe he was too easy-going, too timid, too sensitive and too non-confrontational to ever become involved in such a foul deed, directly or indirectly. They believe his blatant lies in court were to protect the honour of a married woman, and that his nervousness was simply in line with his retiring nature and not a sign of guilt. All I would say to that is that when men get desperate – and Christie was undoubtedly desperate – they can act out of character, even to the point of killing a close friend. The annals of crime are full of such cases.

If the killer, and his method, remain in doubt, there is one aspect of the Oakes affair that need no longer be subject to conjecture. That the Duke of Windsor was involved in a wicked conspiracy to hang an innocent man and keep his friend Harold Christie in the clear is now pretty well beyond doubt. To apply any other theory to the extraordinary series of events before, during and after the trial would be stretching credibility to breaking point. Both de Marigny and the private eye, Raymond Schindler, asked the Duke to reopen the case while he was still Governor of the Bahamas. In Schindler's case, the request was based on what he claimed was new evidence not available at the trial. For de Marigny, his acquittal left many questions unanswered. These requests were rejected out of hand, with the Duke declaring firmly: "The case is closed." This was not the response of someone eager to clear up a disturbing mystery, but of a conspirator with something to hide. The Bahamas badly needed closure on the Oakes affair, but has never to this day achieved it. This lack of a conclusion to a case which shook the colony to the core has left a bitter taste.

If this alone is not sufficient to convince the doubters, consider again the major points indicating a cover-up:

The Bahamas police chief, Col R A Erskine- Lindop, was never called to testify at the trial of Alfred de Marigny. Instead, he was transferred to Trinidad, ostensibly on promotion, but in truth to get him out of the way. In spite of Melchen and Barker's involvement in the investigation within hours of Sir Harry's death, Erskine-Lindop was later to reveal that he, personally, had taken a suspect to the brink of a tearful confession before he was summarily withdrawn from the case. This suspect was not de Marigny. Furthermore, Erskine-Lindop told his friend Sir Etienne Dupuch, the publisher of *The Tribune*, that he was shocked that the killer was still mixing freely in Nassau society. This was several years after the murder.

Apologists suggest that Erskine-Lindop's transfer was planned in advance, and prompted at least partly by the events of the previous year, when Oakes and Christie had been extremely critical of his handling of the labour riots in Nassau. It is barely credible that the local police chief would be removed from his post, just as his force was embarking on its biggest-ever case. It is beyond reasonable doubt that Erskine-Lindop knew too much, and was too insistent on pursuing the truth, to be allowed to stay in the Bahamas. His presence was an obstacle to the Duke's conspiracy. For the rest of his life – and he lived into his nineties – Erskine-Lindop maintained a dogged silence, even in the face of questioning from his own family. The only time he dropped his guard, so far as is known, was when Sir Etienne Dupuch asked him bluntly for his theories about the case. Alas, Erskine-Lindop's secrets went with him to the grave. Why was he silent? Almost certainly because he was an officer of the old school. There were niceties of protocol to be observed, and a Royal Governor could not be defied. He would also have been acutely aware that those who knew too much about the Oakes affair, and were inclined to talk, usually met a tragic end. The Duke would have been directly involved in the decision to move him on.

Dr Ricky Oberwarth, who refused to comply with Hallinan's strictures about written medical evidence, was transferred to another post. Hallinan insisted he abandon all normal procedures and commit nothing to paper about Oakes and the way he died. The request made him uneasy. He suspected behind-the-scenes shenanigans and was justified in doing so.

The decision to call in Melchen and Barker has been characterised as a blunder by a known blunderer, but it wasn't. The Duke, I believe, summoned these men because, having met Melchen previously, he would have known them to be sufficiently dishonest to comply with his evil scheme. The wilful destruction of all evidence at Westbourne that did not implicate de Marigny, and the two officers' clumsily contrived plot to fabricate fingerprint evidence point fairly conclusively to a classic fit-up. Barker's admission that the Duke and he were alone at the crime scene as he tested for prints lent support to the belief that the Duke was briefing him, explicitly or implicitly, on the expected outcome. From that point on, Barker's concocted evidence was inevitable.

Christie's press briefings during the trial were highly prejudicial to proceedings and designed to discourage suspicions against himself. He admitted that he had sought, and apparently received, clearance from Hallinan before giving these briefings. We can be sure that Hallinan would have made the Duke aware of the briefings, and the Governor did nothing to stop them. The only official expression of disquiet came from the trial judge, Sir Oscar Daly, but this was strangely muted, considering the seriousness of the situation. Again, this leaves the distinct impression that the Duke, Christie and Hallinan were in cahoots.

Police sources have disclosed to me that, when investigations began on 8 July, 1943, there was only one true suspect: Harold Christie. Not a single member of the force, they said, believed de Marigny had anything to do with it. Despite this, the force was not allowed to pursue its suspicions. Instead, local officers were sidelined by the Duke, who allowed the Miami detectives to lead inquiries. The only function of local officers was to clear up all those prints and smudges at the murder scene that would confuse the issue and blight the prosecution's case.

When de Marigny was acquitted by a nine-to-three margin, the Duke was obsessive in his desire to implement the jury's recommendations of deportation. He clearly saw de Marigny's continued presence in the Bahamas as extremely hazardous, especially to his own interests. De Marigny was a headstrong, outspoken and frequently tactless man, whose silence could not be depended upon. Having been cleared after a four-month ordeal in a filthy cell, he would not have rested easily without trying to unveil the true killer. As de Marigny believed Christie to be implicated, this would have created deep tensions in local society. Like Erskine-Lindop, he had to go.

. In spite of Captain Sears' explicit, unequivocal evidence against Christie, when he exposed him as a liar, there was no attempt by police to trace or examine the truck in which Christie had been spotted around midnight on 7 July. Such an examination would have revealed all the evidence required, either to support, or destroy, the various theories about the Oakes murder. It would have contained fingerprints, not only of Christie, but also the driver (later identified as Frank Christie) and possibly the hitman, if indeed there was one. If the Palo Mayombe version of events has any credibility, it would also contain bloodstains. A proper forensic inspection of that truck would have cleared up the issue either way. But it didn't happen, and all because of the Duke's extraordinary behaviour in the aftermath of Sir Harry's death.

For those who still doubt complicity, consider this: the Duke's sustained persecution of de Marigny, even after he had left the Bahamas, was unconscionably malign. He sought military transport to fly or ship him out of Nassau, a request that was, predictably, rejected. Over a period of weeks, the Duke tried to find de Marigny a domicile, without success. All the time he lost no opportunity to besmirch his name. On 25 November, 1943, he cabled the Colonial Office in

London, saying he was contacting the Governor of Mauritius, to see if a place could be found for him there. His urgent priority was to get him out of Nassau.

"De Marigny has made inquiries as to the chances of his getting to Haiti but must point out that, unless the government has the means to transport him compulsorily, de Marigny may remain in this colony, as the only inducement for him to leave of his own volition is the threat that he may be sent to Mauritius. I, therefore, very greatly regret your decision that transport by Royal Air Force cannot be justified and I very strongly urge that Air Marshal Bowhill be given an opportunity to consider my request, and that copies of all telegrams which have passed between us to be sent to him for consideration. I am sure that you will meet me thus far. Although I would be loath to worry the Prime Minister at this time, I feel so strongly on this question that I would not hesitate, as a last resort, to approach him direct because I am convinced that unless the Bahamas Government is armed with the power to move both deportees, the British colonial administration will be subject to derision in the United States, and the relations of the Government with the local people strained to a breaking point."

By any standard, this was an extraordinary plea by the Duke. There was no evidence to suggest de Marigny's continued presence in Nassau would strain relations with local people to breaking point. Indeed, de Marigny's acquittal had been cause for jubilation among local blacks. So the 'local people' the Duke was referring to were, presumably, the same self-serving white group, who were hell-bent on protecting Harold Christie at all costs. More pressing than their interests, though, were those of the Duke himself. The longer de Marigny was in the Bahamas, the more likely the Duke's exposure as a treacherous felon. Little wonder that his messages to London betrayed a note of urgency and anxiety.

There was no precedent, no authority, under British colonial law for de Marigny to be deported, considering he had been acquitted of murder without qualification or reservation. Yet the Duke, who had the power to veto the jury's recommendation, instead pursued it with disturbing relish. Requesting air transport at the height of the war was so typical of the man; he wanted all other considerations cast aside to serve his own devious ends. That he should threaten to go over the Colonial Secretary's head in pursuing his vendetta was also typical. He had, throughout his over-indulged life, been used to exploiting his high-level connections in pursuit of his own interests. All the worst Windsor traits were emerging in the aftermath of the de Marigny trial because things had not gone as he planned. Having been thwarted in his primary aim, to have the suspect hanged, he was now hell-bent on achieving the next best result: banishment that would lead de Marigny into many years of restless exile. During this uneasy period, de Marigny claimed that more than one attempt was made on his life. Bullets were fired into his bed. He maintained that the Duke was an accessory to these murder attempts, and that he was trying to achieve, through hired assassins, what the court would not allow - the elimination of Alfred de Marigny. While his friend the Marquis found refuge in Haiti, and later Britain, de Marigny repeatedly ran into obstacles, as he travelled the world in pursuit of stability and happiness. In Canada and South America, he tried in vain to secure status and residency. And all the while he believed his troubles were prompted by ducal meddling. This, he claimed, went on until the Duke's death nearly thirty years after the case, when he eventually settled in the United States, married the daughter of a Roosevelt aide and raised a family.

In making the case for conspiracy against the Duke, there is little by way of documentary evidence to support the charge conclusively. But the circumstantial evidence is heavily weighted against him. If the test of civil law were to be applied, based on probability, there is little doubt he would lose the case. If the test of criminal law were invoked, with the burden on the prosecution to prove the matter beyond reasonable doubt, he would also have a formidable task on his hands.

There is no doubt that the conspiracy to murder case against the Duke – and that is what it amounts to – is much stronger than was the murder case against de Marigny. There were no fingerprints, bogus or otherwise, to be considered, but the circumstantial evidence was powerful and the motives clear.

To make a case for the Duke's innocence, you would have to set aside the Erskine-Lindop and Dr Oberwarth issues, accept there was no reason for even a rudimentary investigation of Christie, acknowledge there were sound legal reasons for the Duke's fevered determination to deport de Marigny, and see Melchen and Barker as legitimate choices to conduct the investigation. All are well beyond the bounds of credibility. You would also have to overlook the Duke's own deceit in hiding money in Mexico and continuing his pro-Nazi activities. One author dismissed the evidence against the Duke as "unsubstantiated gossip", but it goes far beyond that. To protect himself, his friend Christie, and his future career prospects, he deliberately bypassed the expertise of Scotland Yard and the FBI. He feared exposure and he was ready to sacrifice de Marigny in preventing it.

There are a couple of postscripts to this unfortunate affair that deserve to be recorded. In 1950 a New York docker called Edward Majava said, while drunk, that he knew the killer of Sir Harry Oakes. He claimed the name had been passed on to him by a society portrait painter in Florida who was well-acquainted with the Oakes family's Palm Beach friends. Majava was vacationing in California at the time of his disclosure and local police decided to act. They called in the Nassau police chief Augustus Robinson, who travelled to California to interview the man. When Majava revealed the name of the killer as Harold Christie, Robinson reportedly confirmed he was correct, but failed to disclose why no action was being taken.

A few days later, a Canadian woman told the FBI that Christie was implicated and had plotted Sir Harry's death with a powerful accomplice. Declassified FBI files later revealed that accomplice to be Walter Foskett, the trusted family lawyer who had done his best to assist in the destruction of Alfred de Marigny. We have already examined Christie's possible motives for disposing of Oakes, but Foskett's are less obvious unless – having become an indispensable retainer – he had somehow engineered Oakes' will to include legacies to himself. As Foskett was an ambitious, avaricious and quite unscrupulous lawyer, money or Sir Harry's gold would almost certainly have been at the root of this particularly evil act. And it is conceivable that he alone outside the family – with the possible exception of Christie – would know the whereabouts of any hoard of gold Sir Harry might have stored in Florida and the Bahamas. It is also likely that he would know of any movement of money or gold between Nassau and Mexico.

In 1959, the flamboyant Bahamian journalist-politician Cyril Stevenson made an indirect accusation against Harold Christie in the House of Assembly. He told fellow members that he could point to the man who had killed Sir Harry Oakes. Christie said nothing. Stevenson went further and demanded a full inquiry by Scotland Yard. Both houses of the legislature supported him. Publisher Paul Bower recalls the occasion well. He told me: "In 1959, after Cyril Stevenson had tabled his famous motion to have the Oakes case reopened, Harold Christie (who was a member for Cat Island) sought my opinion, as Editor of *The (Nassau) Guardian,* as to whether the UBP should pass the motion. 'Why not?' I said, 'You're innocent, aren't you?' Harold didn't bat an eyelid, and at the next meeting the motion was passed. Scotland Yard came out and after several months' investigation reported that they had found no new evidence. That was the end of that but the publicity eventually gave rise to several books and scads of newspaper articles. Christie, incidentally, voted in favour of the Yard inquiry. He could hardly do otherwise."

Chapter Eleven

AFTERMATH

The murder of Sir Harry Oakes brought to an end a truly remarkable life, and one of the great zero-to-hero stories of the twentieth century. He started out poor and ended up spectacularly wealthy, and it was the wealth he had sought so desperately throughout his early life that was to bring it to a premature end. His demise had tragic consequences for many people, especially his family. And it casts a shadow in Nassau, even to this day.

The baronet's death devastated his wife, Eunice, and their children. The widow's shattered countenance in the courtroom during the de Marigny trial was an accurate reflection of its effect on her. She was inconsolable, and her distress was keenly felt by her sons and daughters, who were all to suffer in their own way from the consequences of their father's death. It is not an overstatement to suggest that the Oakes family seemed blighted from 1943 onwards.

For all his faults, Sir Harry was a towering figure in their lives. At five feet six inches tall, he was hardly a commanding figure physically, but the sheer force of his personality gave him a dominating presence, and he used it to effect in running his household and his diverse business interests. There was also something slightly comical about him, especially to those in the upper reaches of society, who recoiled somewhat from his coarse manner and brusquely expressed views. He was, undoubtedly, a "character" in an age of characters, who had so imprinted his presence upon the British Empire that his death made headlines round the world, even at the height of the Second World War.

As a young man, Oakes had overcome desperate feelings of inferiority to create a fortune by hard toil, and eventually, to secure an hereditary honour from the King. He had become the wealthiest man in the British Empire, and acquired the status accorded very rich men, but never lost the uneven temper, the sometimes piggish irascibility, that he had acquired in the harsh environs of the world's goldfields. Study the Oakes countenance and it is all there: the doggedness, the bloody-mindedness, the deep imprint of thwarted dreams. There is no serenity in his face. Even today, Oakes is remembered for his temper. One Nassau professional man who, as a boy, met him frequently told me: "He was among the most ill-tempered men I ever encountered. He was quite obstinate and often downright irrational."

Alongside his temper sat almost boundless magnanimity. He went out of his way to help those less fortunate than himself. He gave generously to charities and possessed real compassion. He identified with life's strugglers because had been a struggler himself. At no time in his life did he feel entirely at ease with those whose status was based on privilege and preferment.

The Tribune's Centenary Edition of November 21, 2003, carried the following:

"Whatever happened that thundery night, one thing is certain. The Sir Harry Oakes case is now regarded as one of the great celebrity murder mysteries of all time and is even listed on a crime website alongside the deaths of Marilyn Monroe, actor Sal Mineo and pop star Brian Jones, plus famous defendants like O J Simpson, Claus von Bulow and Fatty Arbuckle.

His demise brought to an end one of the most incredible success stories of his era. Born in 1874 in Maine, he arrived in northern Ontario to seek his fortune with just $2.65 in his pocket. That was in 1912 when he and four partners staked claims which became the first operating mines in the area. He later sold that enterprise to finance the Lake Shore Mines, which became one of the richest gold producers in the world. By the time he arrived in the Bahamas as a Canadian citizen in 1935, his fortune was reckoned by some to be as high as $200 million.

The baronetcy awarded by King George VI in 1939 was due partly to his many philanthropic contributions, especially in Britain itself. The title was considered unusual because heritary honours were rarely bestowed outside the rarefied upper reaches of British society. Humbler lifetime honours were more usual for colonial dignitaries.

The title, however, did nothing to soften the tough veneer Oakes acquired during his long years of frustration before finding his fortune.

Disappointment had been the prime feature of his life as he prowled the world in a seemingly forlorn search for mineral riches. Hardship congealed into hatred, and grudges were stockpiled for future reference.

Oakes was unfailingly generous to those who were loyal, but totally ruthless to his detractors. He toiled in blisteringly hot and paralysingly cold climates in both hemispheres in pursuit of what he knew to be his goal, a fortune built on mineral wealth which would bestow riches on his family forever. And the experiences he endured along the way left an abrasiveness many people found hard to handle.

The Klondike, Death Valley, Dawson City, Australia, New Zealand...all featured on the Oakes itinerary in his quest for the ultimate bonanza. In spite of many setbacks, his ambition never wavered. He was resolute even beyond exhaustion and despair. He eventually discovered his destiny, but he paid an enormous price. Years of adversity left a core of stone in his soul.

The author Geoffrey Bocca wrote of him: 'He did not forget a single injustice, real or imagined, that he had suffered. Everyone who had laughed at him or refused to believe in him he regarded with deadly detestation.'

One such man was a storeman in Canada named Jimmy Doige, who made him look a fool when he tried to order overalls on credit. After striking it rich, Oakes forbade any of his men to buy anything from Doige, who was eventually forced to leave town a ruined man.

Oakes watched him go with pleasure, suffering no pangs of conscience. But when he learned some years later that Doige was on his last legs, he said: 'Tell my secretary to send him a cheque for $10,000.'

That strange mixture of magnanimity and malice was typical of Oakes, whose years of toil left him bitter, resentful, disagreeable and sometimes downright detestable. But one always sensed that, beneath it all, was a basically good and decent man whose mind had been bent and beaten on the anvil of fate.

All the principal characters in the Oakes affair were deeply affected by the baronet's death. De Marigny's associates believe to this day that the fall-out from the trial blighted his marriage to Nancy. The unsatisfactory stay in Cuba, the restless time in Canada, the continued problems arising from the Duke's poisonous escapades behind the scenes, imposed stresses and strains upon their relationship which were decisive. The marriage cooled and was finally annulled.

De Marigny admitted years later that doubts about their marriage set in soon after the trial. At root, he was a mature man, she little more than a schoolgirl. She had endured the trial and all the peripheral pressures that went with it but, according to her husband, quite enjoyed the notoriety, too. When de Marigny's arrival in Cuba attracted widespread publicity, she savoured the attention, as most girls of her age would. But de Marigny found her response irritating. It seemed to highlight the gulf between them. While Nancy was being portrayed as a young, faithful heroine – a source of strength for her imprisoned husband – he had to endure continuing suspicion as "the man accused of the murder of Sir Harry Oakes." For the rest of his life, he bore that burden of suspicion.

Nancy's apparent disregard for his predicament irked him. He had been left dejected by his experience, but she seemed to relish the attention the trial brought. There was tension, too, over Sir Harry's will which, when probated six months after his death, dislodged the main plank of the prosecution's case against de Marigny. The estate was valued at just under $12 million, most of it land, with half bequeathed to Lady Eunice. The rest was divided between the five children, each receiving $12,000 a year until the youngest, Harry Jnr., reached the age of thirty. De Marigny said his own income at the time of the murder was twice the children's combined annual inheritance, yet he had been forced to endure public portrayal as a mercenary predator. The point that annoyed de Marigny was that Hallinan had asked the trustees to delay probate until after the trial, to be fair to the accused, but in truth had done so to preserve one of the main thrusts of the prosecution case. Throughout, de Marigny had been the victim of quite extraordinary ruthlessness, from men who were apparently eager to see him die. Nancy went on to marry again, living for a time in Mexico, then in Europe, where she died in early 2005.

Sydney Oakes, who inherited Sir Harry's title, and had featured in the trial as the schoolboy hauled from de Marigny's home by his furious father, grew into a handsome pillar of Nassau society. He was frequently pictured in *The Tribune* at various black-tie social occasions. Like many sons of rich men, he had grown up with a taste for the finer things in life, and especially luxurious high-performance cars. He was a skilled driver who liked the exhilaration of high-speed on open roads. New Providence offered few opportunities for such a man. Apart from the obvious restrictions of living on an island only twenty-one miles long and seven miles wide, his motoring instincts were thwarted by the condition of local highways. There were few straight stretches of any length and road surfaces were generally dire. Even today, Nassau's road system is potholed. But the airport road in those days was the straightest and smoothest on the island and offered a huge temptation to speed fans. It was this taste for acceleration that brought his life to a premature end.

In the late summer of 1966, Sir Sydney died tragically at the wheel of his sports car, which left the road at high speed and struck a utility pole. So great was the impact that the impression of the car's registration plate was clearly embedded in the wood. The crash was viewed as an accident at the time, but the higher reaches of Nassau society continue to buzz quietly with rumours, suggesting that this tragedy was, in fact, another by-product of the murder twenty-three years before. Sir Sydney had been working on documents relating to the Oakes' land holdings on New Providence. There is talk of a faulty drive-shaft and possible interference with the car. What seems certain to Nassau sources I spoke to is that this was no ordinary crash involving a fast driver who made a mistake. It was death by design, with someone deliberately ensuring the car was unroadworthy, especially at high speed. "Sydney was a very good driver," said a well-placed source, "It is inconceivable that he simply lost control and left the road. No, that's rubbish. The car was tampered with. It developed a severe mechanical problem on an open road along which Sydney could be relied upon to put his foot down. The car crashed because something happened mechanically – I believe the drive-shaft fell apart or something. That's the truth of it."

Sir Sydney's sister, Shirley Oakes Butler, was also the victim of a car crash, which happened on the same road fifteen years later. This incident, too, is cloaked in suspicion because she was said to have been working on a will at the time. In society circles in the Bahamas, the talk to this day is of conspiracy and shenanigans, with Mrs Oakes Butler characterised as a target for plotters with something to lose. Although she did not die in the crash, she never recovered from her injuries and was in the Cedars of Lebanon Hospital in Miami when her mother, Lady Eunice Oakes, passed away in June, 1981. After Sir Harry's murder, Lady Eunice retained her connections with Nassau and died at her home, Dale House on Prospect Ridge, after a long illness at the age of eighty-seven. Unhappily for this seemingly jinxed family, neither Shirley nor Nancy was able to attend her memorial service at Christ Church Cathedral in Nassau, the former because of her severe crash injuries and Nancy – by this time Baroness von Hoyningen-Huene – as a result of what doctors described as a "delicate health situation." She was unable to travel from her London home.

Lady Oakes, an Australian, met and married Sir Harry in 1923, and was always considered the softening presence alongside her abrasive spouse. His murder shattered her, but she pressed on doggedly with life for the sake of the children and expanding family, which at the time of her death included six grandsons and four grand-daughters.

At the memorial service on 13 June, 1981, Eugene Dupuch QC, whose book on the de Marigny trial remains the most complete record of proceedings, paid tribute to Lady Eunice and the husband whose influence in the Bahamas could never be forgotten.

Recalling Sir Harry's arrival at a time of chronic poverty, Mr Dupuch said: "Sir Harry's advent in this time of distress appeared to be a miracle. He provided succour that even the government of the day could not afford. His gracious wife was always by his side. Workers of that generation, given employment in their time of need, have never forgotten the benevolence of the Oakes family."

He added: "Today, almost half a century later, this country enjoys a degree of prosperity never envisioned in the 1930s and the Oakes name has become a part of the history of our nation's progress."

Lady Oakes was cremated and her ashes returned to Bar Harbour, Maine, where they were laid in the family burial plot alongside the remains of Sir Harry. It was tragic that, for all her wealth, Lady Eunice's life had been marred by a succession of losses. Two of her three sons – Sydney and Pitt – predeceased her and, at the time of her death, she was tormented by the plight of Shirley, who was lying desperately ill in a Florida hospital. Money did not buy her everlasting peace. On the contrary, it might be said that money had triggered the appalling succession of events, which began that summer night in 1943. It seemed that nothing, absolutely nothing, went right from then on. The pall cast by Sir Harry's murder, the loss of her sons, and the injuries suffered by her daughter darkened her twilight years. And she was saddened, too, by the hurtful fracture in family life caused by Nancy's marriage to de Marigny, whose "irresponsibility" – her word – brought such strife and recrimination.

The death of Pitt Oakes was itself a tragic postscript to the events of 1943. He was obsessed by his father's murder and developed paranoia to the extent that he carried a small revolver, believing "they" were out to get him, too. With a generous allowance from his father's estate, Pitt had no difficulty funding a growing drink habit, which provided respite from his demons. The prevailing wisdom of the time was that alcohol finally killed him, just a few years before his brother Sydney's car collided with that utility pole, snapping it in two. But even that is now a point for conjecture, especially among Nassau's wealthy white elite. In Lyford Cay and among the villas of Cable Beach, the talk is of conspiracy and dark deeds, with Pitt supposedly succumbing to poison injected by a nurse working on some plotter's behalf. "He didn't die from drink," a source told me, "He was inclined to talk a lot about his father's murder. He couldn't keep quiet about it. There were embarrassing scenes. Someone felt the need to silence him forever."

A former acquaintance of Pitt Oakes told me: "He was a pleasant man, but somewhat haunted by the family's past. Oddly, in a society which discouraged such things at the time, he seemed to prefer the company of blacks. Maybe this was because he felt uncomfortable among the wealthy whites who he felt had deprived him of his father. In any event, he was convinced that Christie was the killer. That became something of an obsession with him."

Pitt Oakes mixed not just with blacks, but poor blacks, as if he was consciously repudiating both his race and social circle. He spent many hours every week at the Conch Shell Club on Blue Hill Road, in Nassau's over-the-hill shanty communities. He enjoyed chatting with locals and seemed to identify closely with them, even though ethnically and financially they were far apart.

Although racial divisions during the 1950s and 1960s were still marked, Pitt Oakes found solace among the deprived, and rejected the prejudice so prevalent among his fellow whites. He felt safer with the blacks, and the bar owner Forrester Bowe was a close friend and confidante. Among the white die-hards, Pitt's over-the-hill preferences reinforced a view that the Oakes family were unusually close to the native community. It was a trait which gained little approval on the Eastern Road.

So the move to the Bahamas in the 1930s, which Sir Harry Oakes felt crucial to the survival of his fortune, proved calamitous for a family that, by the mid-1930s, seemed to have it all. He was obsessed with holding on to his wealth, and financially empowering his children, but the greed of others might well have been his undoing. There is talk in the more salubrious salons of Nassau today that the demise of Sir Harry Oakes coincided with the disappearance of a large portion of his fortune. Those who knew the family well find it hard to believe the two are not connected.

Other leading figures in the Oakes affair were subject to mixed fortunes in the immediate post-war era. De Marigny and his friend the Marquis, once the Jack-the-Lads of Nassau society, went their own ways after the trial. As de Marigny began his rootless wandering, the Marquis left Nassau alone on 10 December, 1943, bound for Haiti, that mysterious black republic to the south of the Bahamas. With its potent mix of French and African culture, its voodoo rituals, staunch Catholicism and colourful art, the old colony from whose shores Napoleon's army was hounded in disgrace in 1804, seemed a fitting refuge for such an exotic figure. However, his deportation brought heartache, for his Bahamian girlfriend, Betty Roberts, declined to follow her Mauritian beau into exile. When The Tribune's book of the de Marigny trial was published in 1959, it reported that the Marquis had "disappeared completely" except for an unconfirmed report that "someone might have seen him in London a few years ago." Betty Roberts, it said, went to New York "where it was reported that she was to marry a Russian count."

James Barker, the lying detective whose false evidence effectively destroyed the prosecution case against de Marigny, lived out his final years under suspicion of having close Mob connections. He and his colleague, Melchen, were suspected of being in the pay of Meyer Lansky, the Florida godfather. At the time, the Miami police force was regarded, rightly or wrongly, as the most corrupt in the United States, mainly because of the powerful Mafia presence on Miami Beach and the willingness of people like Barker to accept Mob money. There were stories at the time that he even tried to enlist police colleagues to fall in with Lansky and his henchmen.

Soon after the Oakes case, Barker's fingerprinting techniques were closely scrutinised by police authorities. He was asked to review his methods by the International Association of Fingerprinting in Detroit. Out of regional loyalty, the *Miami Herald* supported him, recognising that civic honour was at stake. But Barker was never able to live down the disgrace of being so ruthlessly exposed in such a high-profile case. The pressures on him grew. Attention was focused on his rapid climb through the ranks and the possible influences that might have propelled that rise. Was Mob influence behind it? Did the Mafia want to see "one of their own" in a position of power? The questions remained unanswered, but Barker was eased out of the Miami force on sick leave, and sank into obscurity, apparently finding solace in heroin addiction. However, on 26 December, 1952, the Christmas holiday turned sour for Barker and his family. The ex-cop, acting under pressures we can only guess at, went berserk, turning the festive season into one of tragedy. He was shot dead by his own son, James Duane Barker, with the service revolver Barker had used during his police days. A coroner's jury later returned a verdict of "justifiable homicide."

Captain Melchen was still an officer in the Miami force when he died of a heart attack on 5 July, 1948. Again, he never quite lived down the ignominy of the Oakes case. The lingering suspicion, that he had conspired with Barker to trick de Marigny into leaving his print on a drinking glass, was to haunt him to his dying day.

The barrister, Alfred Adderley, whose legal skills in the prosecution team were rightly feared by de Marigny, also met a tragic end. He had flown from Nassau to London in 1953 to attend the Coronation of Queen Elizabeth II, but died on the return flight. To this day he is revered as a pioneer of black achievement in the Bahamas, attaining a high level of professional success at a time when blacks were still subject to appalling discrimination. Alas, his death came only three years before race barriers were outlawed by the Bahamas House of Assembly. It was the first major step towards black self-determination in a land which had for two centuries been under the stranglehold of a self-serving white oligarchy.

Interestingly, when *The Tribune* – in a special Millennium supplement – listed the ten most influential Bahamians of the twentieth century, Fred Adderley was the only one to gain a place whose life had ended before the political upheavals of the 1960s. Tribune readers voted for him in large numbers, even though only those of advanced middle age would have been able to remember him.

The Chief Justice, Sir Oscar Daly, returned to Ireland when his days as a colonial judge were over and died there. Meanwhile, that fellow product of the Irish Bar, Sir Eric Hallinan, who led the prosecution case against de Marigny, achieved the promotion he desired and ended his colonial service career as Chief Justice of the old West Indies Federation. When questioned about the Oakes case in later years, Hallinan always seemed somewhat embarrassed by it and was reluctant to discuss it. He even told one researcher that he had all but forgotten it, a most unlikely story given its global exposure and the involvement of the Duke of Windsor. It was incomparably the biggest trial of Hallinan's career but, naturally, advocates are more inclined to forget their defeats than their victories. The de Marigny affair had been an embarrassing failure for him, made more irksome by his unshakeable belief in the Mauritian count's guilt and his determination to see him hang. He and the Duke appeared to share that view – but no-one else, apart from the distraught Lady Oakes, believed it for a second, and nor do I. Hallinan lived to be eighty-four, dying in County Cork, Ireland.

Lieut Col R A Erskine-Lindop, whose rapid transfer to Trinidad in the early days of the investigation raised many eyebrows, especially as he was never called to give evidence at de Marigny's trial, lived into his nineties. The Tribune's publisher, Sir Etienne Dupuch, always maintained that the former police chief was the only man who knew for sure who killed Sir Harry Oakes, but said he would never discuss it. It was during a conversation in Trinidad some time afterwards that Erskine-Lindop revealed that he had a suspect on the verge of a tearful confession at the time of his transfer and expressed dismay that the killer was still mixing in Nassau society.

Captain Edward Sears, the man who saw Harold Christie in the station-wagon in George Street on the night of the murder, rose to become the Bahamas police commissioner. This was surprising, given that his evidence – on which he never wavered – exposed the colony's most influential politician as a brazen liar. Such integrity was rarely rewarded in the Bahamas of the time, for his unshifting position caused severe embarrassment for the colony's ruling elite. His subsequent elevation must have been the result of outstanding ability, or fear that victimisation of Sears would deepen suspicion still more about Christie's role in the affair.

One of Sir Harry's three guests on the night of his murder – Charles Hubbard – became another road crash victim. His car struck a casuarina tree in West Bay Street, killing him instantly. There was no suggestion of foul play, but inevitably talk of jinxes and coincidences.

There is also a question mark over the fate of Assistant Superintendent Bernard J Nottage Snr., the senior detective in the de Marigny affair. During the 1950s, he died from massive bleeding after having his teeth pulled by a Nassau dentist. It was always thought that Superintendent Nottage knew far more than he let on, and that he was among the select few privy to the whole truth about the Oakes murder. Superintendent Nottage was a remarkable man, the first black to reach such heights in the Bahamas force and well-regarded by colleagues of all shades. His appointment with the dentist was a routine matter which had tragic consequences. He was a healthy, active man and his death shook the Nassau community. It came at a time when suspicion was growing about Oakes-related conspiracies, and it was inevitable that his demise was seen as one more example of evil scheming.

A relative of Superintendent Nottage told me: "He was a nice, warm person who – to my knowledge – never spoke of the Oakes and de Marigny affair. But there is no doubt that he knew everything there was to be known, and that knowledge possibly cost him his life. The feeling now is that he fell victim to powerful forces in Nassau at the time, and that his death was no accident."

Superintendent Nottage's death added to the conspiratorial brew, and was one of several incidents during the 1950s which eventually led to a parliamentary showdown, when the House of Assembly was urged to reopen investigations into the Oakes case.

Over the years, one figure kept resurfacing as speculation about the case spluttered on. The private eye, Raymond Schindler, who had proved such poor value for money in the 1940s, spent most of the 1950s insisting he knew the killer and asking for the opportunity to reopen investigations. In newspapers, on radio, in magazine articles and on television he dropped hints by the score, suggesting a gigantic government cover-up in Nassau was protecting an influential local citizen. Everyone knew who he was referring to, but no-one was really listening anymore.

Meanwhile, Harold Christie prospered. The financial foundations laid by his association with Sir Harry Oakes, in the late 1930s and early 1940s, were to support a growing real estate enterprise. Christie became the name for foreign investors to seek out when they looked to the Bahamas for exciting real estate opportunities. As the colony's prosperity took root in the late 1950s and bloomed impressively during the 1960s, Christie's status grew, too. He retained a key role in the colony's political life and was firmly entrenched among the white elite, who so assiduously protected his name in the years following the Oakes affair. With the glow of mounting success came the inevitable honours. First, he was appointed Commander of the Most Excellent Order of the British Empire by Queen Elizabeth II, and later Knight Bachelor, enabling him to attach 'Sir' to his name.

Thus, the murder suspect became a fully-fledged Establishment figure who, bolstered by his burgeoning wealth, travelled the world promoting his homeland and mixing in the higher reaches of European society. There was hardly a titled or ennobled personage there who did not know about the ubiquitous Christie and his persuasive sales talk.

Christie was always regarded by his friends and associates as a confirmed bachelor, though he never lost his taste for female companionship. There was something quietly, almost sensitively, enigmatic about him. Naturally, women found him appealing, though looks were not his strong point. He has been referred to by some writers as leathery and reptilian, but his gentle manner and growing fortune were enough to make him the most eligible man in town.

However, it was 1959, sixteen years after the Oakes affair, before Christie married. His wife was Mrs Virginia Johnson, a Miami friend, and they celebrated their union with an extended honeymoon which took them to Europe, Great Britain, the United States and Canada. The marriage was a success and they enjoyed a blissful middle age, with Lady Christie describing him as a gentle, agreeable companion with a genuine love for the Bahamas and its culture.

They lived in a beautiful colonial-style house in the centre of Nassau. Their front entrance was, in fact, only a few yards from the bustle of Bay Street, Nassau's premier shopping thoroughfare, but behind their garden walls were two acres of scented tropical gardens, in which they nurtured rare plants and trees. The house, Cascadilla, was a cool oasis, with ceiling fans wafting the warm tropical air from elegant, lofty rooms, and an assortment of balconies and verandahs. His library contained possibly the most comprehensive collection of Bahamian books, covering everything from the flora and fauna of the islands to their earliest history, beginning with the Lucayan Indians, then the age of Christopher Columbus, through to the colonial settlement and the slave plantations of the seventeenth and eighteenth centuries.

The Christies hosted genteel soirees at their home and those favoured with invitations recall, even today, the cultivated charm of the couple, as they fussed over their guests. Apart from Nassau friends, they entertained quite illustrious figures from the wider world, Lord Mountbatten among them, along with newly-rich entrepreneurs like Sir Billy Butlin, the holiday camp king. One Nassau resident who attended Christie gatherings told me: "There was nothing ostentatiously grand about them. The occasions were quite relaxed and informal, though servants were always on hand, moving quietly through Cascadilla's elegant rooms. Though one was aware of their gentility, there was nothing stuffy or overbearing about them. Conversation was always lively and sometimes quite provocative. Sir Harold especially liked local history."

There was, of course, one facet of Nassau's recent history that remained off-limits. On the odd occasion when the Oakes affair was raised in Lady Christie's company, she said it was long before she met her husband, and it was never discussed between them.

Sir Harold remained active into old age, and never gave up the work he loved. In fact, it was during a real estate promotional trip in 1973 that he died suddenly of a heart attack in Germany. Right up to the end, he was extolling the virtues of his beautiful Bahamas, and seeking to extend his business connections among wealthy Europeans. The business he established continues to flourish today, its offices alongside the now crumbling Cascadilla, which fell into a derelict state in later years, with creepers and tree roots undermining the floors once trod by Royalty and the famous. As I write, this charming relic of Nassau's past – it was built in the 1840s, soon after the abolition of slavery in the British Empire – is being left to rot, its louvres cracking in the sun, its ceilings in a state of collapse. Lady Christie, who left Cascadilla soon after her husband's death, lived on into the twenty-first century, dying in 2002.

Sir Etienne Dupuch, who broke the Oakes story to the world that summer morning in 1943, continued as publisher-editor of *The Tribune* until 1972, becoming the longest-serving newspaper editor in the world and earning a place in the Guinness Book of Records. Even after handing over the reins of the business to his daughter, Eileen Dupuch Carron, he remained contributing editor until his tragic death in 1991, when a garden accident ended his long and fruitful life. Besides his journalism, for which he earned several international honours, Sir Etienne enjoyed prominence in Bahamian politics and was the key figure in breaking down racial discrimination in public places in 1956. His beloved widow, Lady Dupuch, lives on in Nassau to this day, and is now in her late nineties.

Interestingly, neither Sir Etienne nor his younger brother Eugene, who reported the de Marigny trial for *The Tribune* and died in 1984 after a long, distinguished career at the Bahamas Bar, believed Harold Christie to be guilty of complicity in the Oakes murder. They, along with others who knew Christie personally, believed him incapable of such an act.

Levi Gibson, the driver-retainer who delivered Christie's car to Westbourne on the eve of the murder, and later maintained that it remained in the same spot throughout the night (he said the ground under the car was dry, in spite of heavy rain) also supported his former employer's cause long after Christie's death. He told the *London Daily Express* during the 1980s, that his ex-boss was "a gentleman and great friend of Sir Harry", who would have neither the temperament nor motive for a murder plot. Gibson, who still lives in Nassau, was helped by Sir Harold in later years to become a successful businessman in his own right.

The Oakes and Christie families remain firmly rooted in the Bahamas to this day. Sir Harry's younger son, Harry Jnr., remained a prominent name in Nassau business circles and continued to own for many years the British Colonial Hotel in downtown Nassau, which his father had acquired in his early years in the Bahamas. Interestingly, he too discounts Christie as a suspect.

The scene of the murder is unrecognisable today. Not long after I attended a party there in the late 1960s, the bulldozers moved in on Westbourne, clearing space for the new Sonesta Beach Hotel, which was itself superseded in later years by further beachfront development. The site is now occupied by SuperClubs Breezes, an all-inclusive resort for young vacationers. A photograph in *The Tribune* of 24 August, 1970, shows the old mansion buckling under the exertions of the demolition gangs. Every trace of the 20th century's most enduring murder mystery vanished amid the dust and rubble.

The Duke and Duchess of Windsor never recovered fully from either their Nazi associations or the Oakes affair during the rest of their lives. Although the Duke disliked his Bahamas posting, and made clear his belief that its duties and status were beneath him, he felt a job well done in Nassau would convince his detractors in London that he was worthy of more significant work. He felt his prestige as an ex-monarch, and his soaring abilities, were more fitted to senior ambassadorial roles. Washington was among his ambitions, and Viceroy status in one of the great dominions was undoubtedly another, but neither came to pass, and the couple were left to live out the rest of their lives quite worthlessly among vacuous socialities in various ports of call around the world.

Of course, disclosures in more recent times, with the opening of various intelligence files, indicate clearly why the Windsors could never be considered for serious diplomatic work. Her affairs with the handsome German ambassador to London, Jaoquim von Ribbentrop (later Hitler's foreign minister) during the mid-1930s, and the Ford motor salesman Guy Trimble at the time when the Duke was about to abandon his throne for her, alerted intelligence services to the true nature of this woman long before the couple wed. She was subjected to close surveillance from the moment it became clear that she was important to him, and what the sleuths unearthed was far from encouraging. For a time Ribbentrop sent her nineteen red roses a day, symbolic of the nineteen times they slept together, and long after their affair ended, she maintained contact with him, even after he attained Cabinet rank in Hitler's evil government. The Oakes affair and its aftermath could be considered small beer alongside such considerations, but the Duke's mishandling of the investigation would go down as just one more reason why he should be denied the kind of role he craved.

Although the Duke remained slavishly devoted to his Duchess until his death in 1972, there are serious doubts about her devotion to him. True, she maintained an almost maternal solicitude towards him, showing concern in old age at his various frailties, but there was a strong suspicion among those who knew them best that she had grown bored and irritated long before by his almost servile dependence upon her. The Duchess, for all her faults, was an intelligent, witty and quite demanding woman. For all that, she was not drawn to strong men. The Duke, weak-willed and disconcertingly effete, was a classic product of his class. He was not only sexually ambivalent, but slightly masochistic with it. In the 1970s and 1980s, a London bordello queen described a brand of upper-class Englishman whose public school background – and notably the sodomy and flagellation common in those often oppressive institutions – induced quite extreme masochistic tendencies. She told of prominent barristers turning up at her door, with briefcases jammed with short pants and schoolboy cap, begging to be thrashed for imagined wrong-doing. Her leather-clad whores were trained to demand. 'Who's been a naughty boy, then?' before belabouring these sad souls with bull-whips. There is no evidence to suggest the Duke was into such practices, but he clearly relished the dominatrix the Duchess turned out to be, and the oriental sexual skills she picked up in Shanghai in her youth, which she discussed quite openly with friends. The Duke's allegedly low sex drive was frequently jump-started by these unspecified practices, which helped establish the total control she had over him for the rest of his life.

In the early 1950s, some years after their Bahamas sojourn ended, the Windsors were joined by their celebrated homosexual socialite friend Jimmy Donahue, whose wealth sustained them for some years. The exact nature of the relationship between the Duchess and Donahue is not documented, though it developed a closeness that caused the Duke distress. There was a time when it seemed the Windsors relationship was irreparably undermined, with society friends even contemplating the horrors of possible divorce, but it survived, with the Duke the patsy in a rather distasteful menage a trois, the feisty Duchess and her egregiously promiscuous beau frolicking around Europe with him in tow.

The odd threesome was the talk of international society. Gossip among the toffs was all about the Duchess and her peculiar devotion to the execrable Donahue, who was horrendously amoral, even by their standards. The Duke was under additional strain because society sources suggest he, too, was attracted to Donahue. Torn by the prospect of losing the woman he loved, and surrendered his Throne for, to a younger beau he actually fancied himself, the Duke was in turmoil. The astringent wit of the playwright Noel Coward, himself a noted homosexual of his day, found a target in the Duke's unusual predicament. The Duchess, he said, had "a royal queen to sleep with, and a rich one to hump." The Donahue episode ended with an argument. The Duke, asserting himself on an all-too-rare occasion, threw the playboy out after an unseemly incident at dinner, when Donahue kicked the Duchess in a rage. A little over a decade later, Donahue's over-indulged body succumbed to drink and drugs.

At their chateau in Paris, the Windsors maintained a rather pitiable Ruritanian regality, with the Duke insisting on her being called Your Royal Highness· by guests, in defiance of Buckingham Palace strictures to the contrary. Portraits of the Duchess gazed down from all the walls, some showing her in queenly gowns and spangled tiaras. There was something infinitely sad about this absurd play-acting but it was obviously important to them. When seating plans were drawn up for dinner parties, "His Royal Highness" and "Her Royal Highness" were marked in capital letters at the two extremities, with a guest list generally featuring other equally pretentious titled folk, many of them remnants of deposed royal lines and obscure European dynasties. These black-tie affairs, with the women decked out in their long dresses and best jewellery, often featured disgruntled right-wingers whose dreams dissolved along with the Nazi regime in 1945.

Among their friends were the preposterous Oswald 'Tom' Mosley, the discredited British fascist, and his wife Diana (nee Mitford) who married in Germany in 1936 with Hitler and Goebbels as witnesses. Diana Mosley, a noted beauty of her day, became the Duchess's closest friend, sharing her devotion to the Nazi leaders, whose brutal regime brought such misery to Europe, and most of whom perished on the hangman's rope after the Nuremberg Trials, among them Ribbentrop, the Duchess's erstwhile lover.

Even long after their cause was lost, this peculiar foursome continued to fantasise about what might have been. Mosley readied himself in France for Britain's frantic call, imagining that post-war austerity would force the British people to reconsider their position and summon him as their saviour. It was a forlorn hope. What he and many like him overlooked in the British was their dogged conservatism and unshakeable patriotism, neither of which translated easily into the evil doctrine promoted by Mosley and his bull-necked blackshirts. The more rigid, humourless German mentality was susceptible to the blandishments of fascism, but the self-mocking British regarded Mosley as no more than a comic opera character, a ranting lunatic whose antics were seen as more suited to the music hall than the election hustings. He could never come to terms with the indignity of it all. His hero Hitler was seen in a similar light. With his absurd brush of a moustache, his sharply parted hair and ridiculous salute, the Fuhrer was never anything more than a buffoon in the eyes of the British. A sinister and evil buffoon, but a buffoon nonetheless, and the image of him that pleased them most was of the waistless Fuhrer in lederhosen showing off fat, dimpled knees.

Until his death, the Duke displayed the rigidity and almost suffocating formality instilled by his family and reinforced by the German in him. His ramrod regimentation and stultifying German stuffiness were among the many irritations which ultimately turned the Duchess's head. In Nassau on one occasion, a journalist witnessed the Duke drilling young Bahamians, trying to get them to march like soldiers. He was insistent in imposing an unbending disciplinary regime upon them. His heavy handedness caused the journalist to remark what an "absolute shit" he was, and to record how he came to dislike him thoroughly from that day on.

There is an interesting illustration of this in Karl Pfeiffer's portrait of the writer Somerset Maugham, published in 1959. Maugham's home in the South of France, the Villa Mauresque, was one of the many high society hideaways, around the world, visited by the Windsors during the last twenty-five years of the Duke's life. But Maugham discovered that entertaining them was a demanding and exhausting business. The Duke always insisted on knowing in advance who would be his fellow dinner guests. Worse still, he remained a stickler for protocol by making such requests through "proper channels." This involved Maugham's butler phoning the Duke's butler to run down the list of guests, offering reassurance that all had been properly screened. Once the Duke had consented to accept, his butler would then phone Maugham's butler to confirm the arrangement. The event itself would invariably be stuffily formal, with everyone clinging to everything the Duke said, however banal. On one occasion when Maugham's long-time companion Gerald Haxton made a light and inoffensive joke about the court cards during a game of bridge, the Duke, like his illustrious great grandmother, Queen Victoria, before him, was not amused. He deeply resented familiarity from commoners and was insistent that people should know their place. To have royal status mocked was unacceptable. It was at such a party that the Duchess dropped her famous bon mot when Maugham declared a hand of kings. "What good are kings?" she said, "they always abdicate."

This witty indiscretion sent all the society women at the party twittering to the bathroom, or seemingly so, but Pfeiffer was convinced they were on the phone, reporting the Duchess's comment to their friends along the Cote d'Azur.

From time to time, the Windsors revisited Nassau to stay with their friends, the Earl and Countess of Dudley at Graycliff, their elegant colonial home across the road from Government House. In addition to pursuing old friendships, the Duke was interested in the Bahamas' investment potential. Apart from his partying, the Duke thought of little but money and golf, and now his former domain was becoming the world's predominant playground for the rich. Despite the sometimes turbulent nature of their relationship, the Windsors stuck together, and on visits to Nassau he would leave her to her socializing, to investigate land deal opportunities with his old friend Harold Christie. It is interesting to speculate how often Sir Harry Oakes' name came up in conversation.

These returns to Nassau could not have rekindled happy memories, for the Bahamas governorship was not a high point of the Duke's life. In fact, he was rated quite a good governor based on his everyday duties. He took the job seriously and made one or two significant dents in the intransigence of the Bay Street Boys. But the Oakes debacle overshadowed everything else. The wisdom of the day suggested he bungled it. Now we suspect far, far worse of him.

Looking back, Bahamians whose lives overlapped with the Windsor governorship see it as symbolic of an age long gone. Throughout the Empire at the time there was a fawning deference to authority, and especially royal authority. Even the press, the least servile of institutions, was spaniel-like in its reporting of royal matters, lapping at the boots of their betters and saying nothing to undermine Britain's unshakeable edifice of privilege. The Duke and Duchess were very much products of their times, regarding such deference as theirs by right, and in Nassau they were not denied it. If anything, Britain's colonial subjects were even more abject than the people of the United Kingdom itself. Today, more than thirty years after independence, things are different, but there was a long tradition in the islands of almost slavish devotion to London's rule, certainly among the lower orders.

However, there was an incident, only recently recalled in *The Tribune*, which cast light on the Windsors and the way they lived. It centred on an incident in the early 1940s, before Axel Wenner-Gren was banished ignominiously from the Bahamas because of his suspected Nazi dealings. The Windsors were aboard Wenner-Gren's yacht, the Southern Cross, and were cruising between Eleuthera and Abaco in the north-eastern Bahamas.

Unfortunately, the captain managed to get the yacht stuck fast on a sandbank between the islands, and the Windsors were evacuated to the nearby settlement of Cherokee Sound, to await the rising tide. While the Duke accepted the inconvenience with good grace, and spent his time visiting local schoolchildren, the Duchess was visibly annoyed, barely concealing her impatience. At one point an islander, seeing the couple's pet dogs were hungry, brought out tin plates for them to eat off. The indignant Duchess would have none of it. Her dogs could eat only off china crockery, she insisted, and more plates were made available to her, so that the mutts could chomp their food in the style to which they were accustomed.

The story sounds apocryphal, but isn't. The simple folk of Abaco, though both astonished and delighted to find the Royal Governor and his Duchess on their doorsteps, were left to ponder the enormous social chasm which lay between themselves and the couple at Government House, whose dogs were accorded privileges they could only imagine. This simple incident illustrates quite graphically the couple's severe detachment from reality. It was a shortcoming destined to remain with them for life.

Chapter Twelve

MEYER LANSKY

APART from Harold Christie, there was only one other popularly touted suspect in the Oakes murder. Meyer Lansky was a Jewish incongruity in the Mob, but his Sicilian colleagues did not hold that against him. He was ruthless and financially astute, both cherished qualities in the Florida underworld, where opportunities were constantly being sought for generating new revenue and laundering money extorted on the mainland.

Lansky's attention turned to Nassau in the 1940s, when he first explored the opportunities afforded by the possibility of casino gambling in the islands. Having made contacts in the Bahamas during the Prohibition era, when bootleggers had generated massive revenues from their illicit rum-running voyages to the US mainland, he devised plans to exploit the colony's moral slackness by looking up old friends. It was during this period, soon after the Windsors' arrival in Nassau, that Lansky and Christie met by chance in Miami. From that meeting there were several important developments, ultimately involving the Duke, but initially confined to Christie and his attorney friend, Stafford Sands. Lansky travelled to Nassau for a meeting with the two men at Sands' office, and there a deal was hatched which had far-reaching consequences. The thrust of this arrangement was that Lansky would funnel Mafia earnings into the Bahamas for property and resort development, but that casino gambling was a crucial proviso. The Mob saw Nassau as a convenient off-shore haven for ill-gotten revenues in the US, with casinos not only catering for an anticipated post-war influx of high-rollers, but also providing laundering facilities for hot money.

There was one major obstacle to Lansky's plan: casino gambling was against Bahamas law and new legislation was essential if the scheme was to go ahead. Sands was offered a sizeable sum if he could secure a change in the law, but he was thwarted by one man – Sir Harry Oakes. There were several reasons why Oakes would have resisted such a scheme, but foremost among them was his integrity. Though not spotless when it came to financial dealings, especially in the matter of protecting his fortune, Oakes retained a basic, instinctive rectitude when it came to moral and ethical issues. The French writer Balzac wrote that behind every great fortune is a great crime, but in Oakes' case that was far from the truth. Few of the twentieth century's wealthiest men had made their fortunes like Oakes, by clawing it from the ground. Many were ideas men, sharp entrepreneurs with original minds. Oakes was a frenzied, driven member of the toiling classes who took a long time to achieve his objectives. But having made it, he was almost puritanically proud that his vast holdings were not at the expense of others, and that he had never cheated his way to the top. He had a deep-seated dislike of shysters. He would, therefore, have resisted the Lansky plan on moral grounds alone, quite apart from other considerations. Not only would casino gambling destroy his idealistic notions for Bahamas development, under which the colony's British quaintness and relatively civilised social mores would be preserved, it would introduce the taint of gangsterism, with disreputable hoodlums running loose.

According to those who believe in Mob involvement in the Oakes murder, Lansky responded to the intransigence of Sir Harry in time-honoured Mafia fashion. Obstacles were candidates for elimination, so Oakes had to go. The theory is that Lansky despatched a team of hoodlums from Miami to Nassau aboard a launch used twenty years earlier for rum running. Their mission was not murder, but persuasion Mafia-style. Christie drove Oakes to Nassau waterfront where "negotiations" were to take place aboard the launch. The suggestion is that Christie was not involved in any plot to harm his friend, only to ensure he heard what Lansky's men had to say. When discussions got heated, and Oakes was felled by a thug who struck him with a winch, Christie became a terrified onlooker, caught up in a sequence of events, culminating in his friend's body being driven back to Westbourne and hauled up the stairs to the bedroom, where it was dumped on the bed. This, the theorists say, is how blood came to flow across his face rather than vertically straight on to the bed.

The Lansky theory is implausible for many reasons. Christie knew his friend well enough to be sure that no amount of talking from mobsters would change his mind on anything. If there is one thing on which all agree about Oakes, it is that he was very much his own man; a man who answered to nobody. The whole pattern of his life had supported this thesis. He was one of life's supreme individualists, a dynamo with very clear convictions. It is unlikely, therefore, that he would have agreed to a meeting with Lansky's thugs in the first place.

If one accepts that the meeting did take place, is it likely the Mafia would have reacted the way they supposedly did? Killing Oakes achieved nothing, and it's unlikely a calculating thug in charge of such a mission would have blown it by succumbing to raw fury in this way. Such an outcome would have upset Lansky, who wouldn't have wanted to jeopardise his casino scheme still further by disposing of the colony's most important citizen in such a brutal fashion. The theory that Oakes died at the hands of a winch-swinging hoodlum does not hold up. Whatever their deficiencies, Mafia mobsters were professionals when it came to dealing with opponents. If elimination had been seen at some future date as the solution, the job would have been done subtly, probably by "accident" or more clinically while Oakes was away from Nassau. Killing Oakes brutally, on his own territory, was not the Mafia way. It would have aroused the suspicion of the colonial administration in the long term and would have been a poor foundation for their operation in the Bahamas, where official co-operation was imperative for their future success. What has to be remembered about such colonies at the time is that they were still subject to quite tight British control. Not only were governors appointed by London to oversee local political affairs, all senior civil servants and police were British appointees, who saw their jobs as upholding standards along UK lines. There was, therefore, a governmental structure in place which could not allow itself to be undermined by Mob rule.

It is true that the Bahamas was sometimes considered to be less controllable than most British territories of similar size. The dominant whites had always been mulish in defence of their rights, but the basic colonial template was nonetheless in place. If need be, London could exercise its powers, and sometimes did.

There is a suggestion that the Duke and Duchess might themselves have feared Mafia reprisals, and were compliant to Lansky's demands because of possible investment benefits. Though the Duke is generally credited with little by way of personal probity at this difficult time of his life, it is extremely unlikely that he allowed himself to fall this far. A Mob-ruled Bahamas is not a legacy he would have wished to bequeath to Britain or the colony's people. Most telling of all, though, was the medical evidence. Some of the blisters on Sir Harry's body were ante-mortem injuries. Had he been dead when dumped on the bed, these would not have appeared when the fire was started.

In any event, casino gambling did not arrive in the Bahamas during the immediate post-war era, so Lansky did not get his way. Twenty years elapsed before the Bahamas became a casino centre, and that was prompted to a large extent by the closure of Cuba as a recreational hotspot in 1959, when Mafia interests had to skip town. Is it conceivable that Lansky would dispose of Oakes without pressing home his demands? When local resistance to casinos was broken down in the 1960s, Sands was the prime mover, and the breakthrough came in an autonomous enclave on Grand Bahama island, where foreign interests had been allowed to establish a free port area outside of central government control.

There is no doubt that the Cuban communist leader, Fidel Castro, was unwittingly a moving force in the Bahamas' involvement in casino gambling. His descent from the hills in battle fatigues in 1959 with his band of rebels meant expulsion for, not only the Batista regime, but also the Mafia barons who feasted off Havana's reputation as the vice capital of the Caribbean. Banished from Cuba, hassled in the US, the Mob wanted an environmentally friendly refuge and found it in Grand Bahama, a straggling strip of bush-strewn limestone in the northern Bahamas which, at its westernmost point, was only eighty miles off the Florida coast. West Palm Beach is almost due west of the settlement of West End.

It is an interesting though discomfiting fact that the Bahamas tourism boom (from well under a million visitors in the mid-1960s to more than four million today) has been built on the back of Cuba's decline as a recreation mecca. When Castro closed down Havana's vice and gambling trade, imposed all the life-sapping constraints of communist puritanism, and made profit an ugly word, he handed the Bahamas a licence to prosper. The modern Bahamas economy, still buoyant after three decades of independence, has been assisted enormously by the Cuban Revolution, and its early impetus was provided by Stafford Sands. This prematurely stout attorney was the archetypal smart-ass fixer, and his shrewdness was to have a lasting impact on Bahamian life. As Minister of Finance and Tourism in the 1960s, he was the undisputed kingpin of the Bahamas, a man who was respected and feared in equal measure. He was a bloated, grasping, one-eyed plutocrat who would have made a perfect villain in a James Bond novel.

In the same year that Castro seized control of Cuba, Sands was elected chairman of the Bahamas Development Board. This fortuitous conjunction of events eased considerably Sands' activities in the next few years, when he spearheaded an extremely fruitful campaign to make the Bahamas a premier tourist destination of the western world. Though considered even by friends a virulent racist with the firm conviction that blacks were incapable of ruling themselves, he was honoured long after his death by those same blacks – now successfully governing themselves – when they recognised his unique contribution to Bahamian prosperity, by printing his head on the country's ten dollar banknotes. It was Sands' rapid thinking which, in 1959, enabled the Bahamas to capitalise on Cuba's closure for business. When the Bahamas adopted Cabinet-style government for the first time in 1964, Sands took on the dual role of Minister of Tourism and Finance, thus controlling the colony's treasure chest and its number one industry. However, when elections brought the young black lawyer Lynden Pindling to power three years later, he could not countenance life under black rule and fled to Europe, living out his remaining years in bitter, unhappy exile. He died, prematurely old at fifty-eight, in his suite at London's Dorchester Hotel in 1972, the year before the Bahamas gained its independence under Pindling's leadership. His demise was the symbolic end of the old order, clearing the way for nationhood.

In 1959, though, black majority rule seemed a distant prospect and Sands was devising schemes to bring new streams of revenue into the islands. Though uplifting the living standards of blacks was not among Sands' prime objectives, there is no doubt that his ingenious schemes benefited every level of Bahamian society. Whatever his critics' reservations about the man himself, there was no doubting his achievements. However, the strategy for Grand Bahama was not to everyone's taste, and for good reasons. Put simply, Sands sought to create on Grand Bahama a "country within a colony" – an autonomous enclave in which wealthy foreign investors would be granted extensive powers, and impressive tax and tariff concessions, to generate untold wealth from gambling and tourism. In the process, local blacks would be engaged as menials or left on the outside looking in, mere bystanders in what would prove to be a spectacular economic surge for the island. The arrangement mirrored perfectly Sands' elitist ideals, and reinforced the discriminatory status quo in the Bahamas of the time. Not surprisingly, it was also anathema to the educated black radicals who sought a different future for the islands.

The project was based loosely on one formulated in the 1940s by the Duke of Windsor and Wenner-Gren, the Swedish tycoon whose Nazi contacts had so tainted his own life and enraged his American detractors. It would involve the purchase of huge tracts of Crown land at nominal prices for transformation into splendid resort facilities. At the centre of the scheme was an old Sands associate, Wallace Groves, a shadowy character who had served time for mail fraud. Together, they were to put together an enterprise from which the new city of Freeport would emerge, with Sands retaining all legal rights. It was a cosy arrangement for the protagonists, with Groves guaranteed generous returns, and Sands on a mighty commission, but the Bahamian people were little more than dispossessed spectators.

Freeport came to symbolise many things, good and bad. It was to become the hub of an unprecedented boom in Grand Bahama which, until the city rose from the pine barrens, was a lifeless collection of depressed settlements. More than a hundred miles north of Nassau, the capital, it was a large but all-but-forgotten outpost of the archipelago. The Groves-Sands initiative certainly created boom times for the island, which was to pioneer the development of casino gambling in the Bahamas, but also attracted undesirable Mob elements jettisoned from Cuba. The virtual autonomy, granted by the Hawksbill Creek Agreement, made Groves the uncrowned king of the Freeport area, echoing Sir Harry Oakes' unique status in the 1940s, though Oakes was never the beneficiary of such a sweet deal. All went well – certainly for Groves and his cohorts, who were generating mountains of money – until Pindling's rise to power in 1967, when he quickly made known his opposition to Freeport's special status. As leader of a black populist government, he could not entertain the prospect of a foreign-ruled enclave in his own land. In what became known as his "bend or be broken" speech, Pindling made it clear that changes were on the way and Freeport, from being the boom city of the 1960s, went into a thirty-year decline from which it has never fully recovered. Foreign investors who had sought to ride on the coat-tails of the Sands-Groves initiative saw their properties drop dramatically in value. Several lost their shirts. The "revolution", though always viewed as a distant prospect, came earlier than expected. It shook the Bay Street Boys and their friends to the core.

Even before Pindling's rise, however, there were gathering misgivings over the kind of people being attracted to Freeport's casinos. The presence of mobsters created disquiet, even among some of the Bay Street Boys themselves, and especially Sir Roland Symonette, the first Premier of the Bahamas, who challenged Stafford Sands about the possible ramifications of Mob influence.

Until the change of government, Freeport was emerging as a cash cow for Groves and Sands, who were prime beneficiaries of an arrangement which, apart from creating a few lowly jobs for blacks, was of little use to the Bahamas or its treasury. Groves imported foreign workers, enjoyed enormous tax concessions and did little to improve the lot of the ordinary people of Grand Bahama, who continued to live in wooden shanties outside the city limits. There were a few gestures, but they were quickly recognised for what they were. Freeport perpetuated, even emphasised, the racial divisions and rampant avarice of the Bay Street Boys era. Back in Nassau, several members of the white government were receiving consultancy fees from Groves, though few were consulted about anything, other than the bank accounts into which they wanted their swag to be directed. These sweeteners had softened many a misgiving about casinos and their possible social impact, and it surprised no-one when gambling was formally legalised by the Executive Council in 1963. Thus, as the 1960s got into their swing, Lansky's associates moved into Freeport and creamed off a third of the profits, occupying several key posts and importing other underworld figures with gambling savvy. Many of them were part of the old Havana crowd. They had discovered a convenient post-revolution bolt-hole and a lucrative outlet for their expertise. One observer of the day expressed surprise when official indignation arose over the Mob presence. "If you want someone to manage a church, you call on priests. If you want someone to manage a casino, you call on hoodlums. People who run gambling enterprises are rarely the goody-two-shoes of life. Casinos are a way of mugging the public without the mess."

For Sir Roland, however, this pat explanation was insufficient. He began to receive troubling reports about the hard men drifting into the Bahamas, in pursuit of easy money. He was concerned enough to raise the matter with his Cabinet colleague, Stafford Sands. Symonette told the minister that police should have been forewarned about the possible influx of questionable characters, and told him to get them out of the colony before he imposed deportation orders. To his credit, Sir Roland also made known his intention to blacklist the gangsters.

The presence of Groves and his disreputable cohorts brought an unpleasant edge to Grand Bahama life. For decades this enormous pine barren had slumbered peacefully in the sun, its simple people subsisting on fish and whatever they could grow on the island's thin, rocky soil. Now, it took on the patina of a police state. Those who contravened the enclave's rules were quickly despatched, hustled away by Groves' heavies and the local immigration department. When restaurant manager Rico Heller was fired after an argument, he was disturbed from his sleep by a pre-dawn visit from the immigration men, who were ensuring he did not hang around. He was given four hours to go, minus his belongings. A black Bahamian cab-driver who fell out of favour was barred from the Port Area. Under the Hawksbill Creek Act, Groves had the absolute right to exclude anyone he chose.

Thus, the Bay Street Boys had effectively granted autonomy to foreigners of dubious repute, in what was potentially the most prosperous section of the colony. Had they stayed in power, Freeport would have become a haven for wealthy whites, offering attractive investment opportunities that would have contributed little, or nothing, to the well-being of Grand Bahama's impoverished blacks. Outside the dazzling new city's perimeter, thousands of blacks lived in dilapidated shanties, with no running water, no waste disposal facilities and no telephones. All the traditional contrasts in wealth were given new emphasis in Freeport, where a form of apartheid was being practised with government approval.

Today, casino gambling is an integral part of the Bahamas' economy, though successive governments have wisely forbidden locals to play the tables. The closure of Cuba tossed unimagined opportunities to the Bahamas and the country continues to prosper from them today, flourishing as an eastern alternative to Las Vegas, an island gaming mecca in the sun, with all the traditional glamour of the tropics.

What would Sir Harry have made of it all? He would no doubt have squirmed inwardly, because casinos were never part of the idealised image he cherished for his adopted homeland. But, being the pragmatist he was, he would ultimately have come to realise the powerful impact gambling made on tourism, which continues to be the foundation of the Bahamas' prosperity. Did he die because he blocked Lansky's plans? There are very few in the Bahamas today who believe that story.

However, the flowering of Freeport did produce some of the horrors he might have envisaged. Groves was not a man Sir Harry would have liked. But he would have liked even less the deal he had managed to concoct for himself, with a ten per cent rake-off from all retail revenues, and a cosy agreement with Sands that gave Nassau's Mr Big of the day a monopoly in legal fees amounting to millions.

It's likely the casino idea had its genesis with Lansky, but it was at a secret meeting called by Groves at Miami Beach's Fontainbleu Hotel on 26 September, 1961, that it really took root. As the new Lucayan Beach Hotel took shape in the winter of 1962-3, a huge room facetiously called The Handball Court became an integral part of the structure. Its shape and layout was being supervised by a Groves associate called Dino Cellini, once a Lansky henchman. Its real function was obvious. It was soon to become the Monte Carlo Casino, facilitated by an 'exemption' from the Bahamas' anti-gambling laws.

Chapter Thirteen

DISQUIET

For sixteen years following the Oakes murder, Nassau was in a state of barely concealed fear. For each of those years, there was an average of one death said to have associations with the case. It represented an alarming upsurge in the homicide rate for a colony which – the 1942 riots aside – was noted for its quiet, easy-going approach to life and lack of serious crime. The brutal murder of Dorothy Macksey, a former Christie secretary who was thought to know too much, sent tremors through Nassau. While the shanty communities were alive with speculation, the grand homes of Eastern Road and Cable Beach maintained a tense silence. As with all deaths linked with the Oakes case, alternative explanations were offered for Mrs Macksey's fate, but these did nothing to quell the furtive murmuring around town.

The high-profile nature of the Oakes mystery kept the ardent self-publicist, Raymond Schindler, involved in developments, or what he imagined to be developments, in the case right into the 1950s. From time to time he would re-emerge with more unfounded claims of a breakthrough. "I know who killed Harry Oakes" was now a familiar cry among drunks, ne'er-do-wells and Walter Mitty figures, who were eager to tap into the case's celebrity potential. However, none of them lived in Nassau, where the general unease surrounding the case fostered wariness and restraint. Even the bar-flies of Bain Town kept their counsel, however high they were on rough rum and bourbon, for fear of dreadful consequences. Loose talk really did cost lives in the Nassau of the day.

Into this couldron of fear and suspicion stepped an intrepid American woman, Betty Renner, who was variously described as an investigative reporter, inquisitive lawyer and FBI agent. Whatever her precise role in life, she was in search of the truth about the death of Sir Harry Oakes. She flew into Nassau from Washington and began to make inquiries among locals. It is possible that Ms Renner under-estimated the feelings aroused by the case in the Bahamas, where intrigue had now seemingly become part of national life. It is even possible that she was working on the wrong premise, imagining that foreigners were behind the murder, and that she was, therefore, relatively safe from reprisals. Whatever the truth of it, she appeared to handle herself in a way that was at best foolhardy, at worst suicidal.

Instead of going undercover, posing as a tourist, Ms Renner made known her objectives. She said she was going to "crack" the Oakes mystery once and for all. For a journalist, or lawyer, or law enforcement agent, such a mission had undoubted appeal. There was the prospect of stardom for anyone producing solid evidence leading to Sir Harry's killer. For a journalist, it was the kind of story Pulitzer Prizes are made of. For a lawyer, it would have enduring allure as a society mystery with an illustrious cast. For a law enforcer, it was a career-builder, a guarantee of advancement. For the unwary, however, it was potentially lethal, and so it proved. Ms Renner's mission never reached fruition, for she was grabbed by an assailant, bludgeoned to death and dumped upside-down in a banana hole, one of the cavities left by rain in the limestone rock of New Providence, which were used to sustain meagre subsistence crops. Ms Renner's death, less than two days after her arrival, encouraged the growing suspicion that the Oakes murder plot was a local affair, and that certain people were intent on keeping the lid on the truth at whatever cost.

The conspiracy of silence made many people uneasy. Nassau took on a sinister air. The suspicion was that certain local people were being protected, or protecting themselves, in an extraordinarily ruthless manner. Since working-class blacks of the day had no power, no status and virtually no say in anything, it's unlikely the plot involved them, except as mere functionaries or enforcers. Only the ruling whites would have the gall, the will, and the wherewithal, to dispose of potential trouble, with such brutal finality.

If, as many believe, Christie was implicated, it is easy to see why he and his associates would go to such lengths to conceal the truth. Had it ever been disclosed that the Bahamas' major investor was killed by local white interests, it would have had a devastating impact on the colony's economy. In fact, it is no exaggeration to suggest that the Bahamas boom of the 1960s might never have happened, had Christie been exposed as the killer. Stafford Sands, the most dominant figure in Bahamas political and legal affairs of the immediate post-war era, would have known all there was to be known of the Oakes affair. He, too, would have been more than usually aware of the ramifications of disclosure. This is not to suggest he had a role in it, but to illustrate the fact that powerful forces would have been directed into a cover-up at all costs. Ms Renner, possibly out of stupidity or naivete, or both, became a victim of these forces, and a warning to anyone else who might try to expose the truth.

When I first arrived in the Bahamas in the late summer of 1966, the fear was still nigh palpable. As a young reporter with crusading instincts, I was immediately warned of the Oakes affair and the long line of tombstones it had created over the last two decades. Colleagues sensed immediately it was my kind of story, but most of the protagonists were still alive, and the implications were obvious.

At the *Nassau Guardian*, the morning paper where I spent two years as a staff reporter, I was told bluntly: "Leave the Oakes thing alone. We don't want you dead." At cocktail parties, speculation was discouraged. Even innocuous asides were preceded by glances all around to ensure no-one was within earshot. The case still had the power to intimidate.

This secrecy was in spite of Cyril Stevenson's exertions in 1959, when he succeeded in getting parliament to call in Scotland Yard. When the detectives arrived, they were unable to produce further evidence. Hardly surprising, really, when the Duke had ordered local police to destroy everything at Westbourne that did not support the case against de Marigny. Stevenson's call was too little too late, for those in a position to throw new light on this affair had already been disposed of. The few who probably knew the truth were resolutely silent. However, Stevenson, a leading figure in the black radical Progressive Liberal Party, and a firebrand journalist of some ability, earned widespread admiration with his clarion call for action. "This whole business has been one big whitewash from start to finish," he cried, "People in high places know who the killer is. It is time the true facts were brought out into the open, so that this nightmare of violence this colony has suffered for sixteen years can be ended." His call created a mixture of relief and disquiet.

Dramatically, Stevenson said the killer was sitting among them, but that he was not proposing to use his parliamentary privilege to name him publicly. There were repercussions from this outburst. Like de Marigny, Stevenson suffered an unnerving attempt on his life as a result of his outcry. The day after his call in the House of Assembly for a full inquiry, a fusillade of bullets was fired into his office. Had he been sitting in his usual chair, he would have been silenced forever. Luckily for him, he was in another room at the time. The thugs who tried to dispose of de Marigny, and who succeeded in killing Betty Renner and others, were now trying to dispose of Stevenson. It was an unnerving period for Nassau. There were some who thought the rule of law in the Bahamas was under threat, with influential forces buying silence with bullets. Their disquiet was deepened by a plaintive cry from Nancy Oakes, who broke her silence in 1960, as speculation about the murder reached a new pitch.

Christie himself was seriously discomfited by Stevenson's allegations, and more especially by the journalistic fall-out in the United States. He felt, with good reason, that the continuing scandal would affect the colony's progress as a centre for tourism and investment. It was an important part of his crusade for foreign business that the Bahamas should be portrayed as a safe, stable and congenial environment. This was a difficult message to convey when venomous speculation was everywhere, not just about the Oakes murder and the motives behind it, but his suspected role in it. Eventually he was stung into action, issuing a statement through his US lawyers, threatening actions for libel and slander, against those who persisted in spreading the "inferential calumny" that had engulfed him since 1943. More important than the harm to himself, he said, was the damage wrought on the Bahamas, his beloved homeland. For one so mellow, the outburst was impassioned and seemingly heartfelt. It was as if years of mounting exasperation had become a lava flow from his soul. For those who wanted to believe him, the threat was seen as at least a temporary poultice for a seeping wound. For those who saw him as the guilty party, it was a tactic to secure silence by intimidation. Here was a rich man ready to turn to litigation in an attempt to lower the heat on himself.

Christie's warning, though seemingly heartfelt, did little to convince the doubters. And it reopened Nancy's wounds. She issued a statement to *The Tribune*, declaring the murder to be "a disgraceful thing to live with for all these years." She said the matter should now be cleared up once and for all, whoever might be affected.

"Count Freddy de Marigny was arrested in an atmosphere of hasty confusion. It should never be forgotten that up to now there has been no true investigation by qualified authorities. The cost to some of us has been appalling, in terms of callous treatment, unnecessarily brutal practical difficulties and endless humiliation of an intensely personal nature. Certain interests have kept alive lies and suspicions down through the years. It appears like a conspiracy, aimed at eternally diverting and confusing public attention, while astutely attempting to justify errors, idiocies and machinations of others.

"Logic would dictate a few basic questions as to why a man in my father's position, with multiple international interests, should die so mysteriously at such a particular time. For the good of the country, and for justice and decency, they should insist on a vigorous effort now being made to clear this up, regardless of who might be affected by the truth."

Nancy Oakes' statement was an agonised cry from someone who had suffered great anguish over many years. As the teenage wife of de Marigny, she had endured the pangs of loss, but it was in her mature years that she had time to reflect on the calamitous reverberations of the murder on her mother and siblings. Now, seventeen years after she had hugged her dearest Freddy on his acquittal, she was calling for closure, for a solution. Alas, it never came.

Examining the statement now, more than forty years on, one is left to imagine the emotional convulsions behind it, and specifically the multitude of suspicions that must have tormented the Oakes children over so many years. The conspiracy she refers to, the idiocies, the errors, the machinations...all are highly emotive words that must have sprung from a deep well of suppressed feelings. And she clearly had someone in mind.

The total and absolute truth about the Oakes affair will now almost certainly never be known, unless there are classified papers in London or Washington that still conceal essential truths. Those still alive who may know slivers of the truth are not talking, and have never talked, except to recite the tired old platitudes about the deep, close friendship between Oakes and Christie, and the unfortunate bungling of the Duke of Windsor and the Miami detectives.

Alfred de Marigny claimed that his life was threatened, even as late as the eighties, when he announced he was proposing to write a book about the affair. He took them seriously enough to suspend his plans for several years. Interestingly, it was only after the deaths of the Duke and Duchess of Windsor (in 1972 and 1986 respectively) that he felt it safe to proceed. His book recalls the story of Edward Majava, mentioned earlier, whose life was also threatened because of information he possessed about the Oakes affair. Majava, an American of Finnish descent, supplied the FBI with a copy of a letter which accused him of having "intimate knowledge" of the murder. When Nassau's police chief, Augustus Robinson, flew to San Francisco to see Majava, he was given wholly plausible information, which had been doing the rounds of Florida high society, citing Christie as the killer. Majava had received the information from Mrs Hildegarde Hamilton, an artist who was well-known to socialites in south Florida. The FBI recorded that Robinson was convinced of the truth of Majava's information, but took no action on his return to the Bahamas. Though Robinson's reasoning is not available to us, it is not difficult to understand the pressures he was under. He was a newly-appointed colonial police commissioner. The arrest of the Bahamas' most prominent and influential citizen, close friend of the Duke of Windsor, inspiration behind the colony's economic resurgence, would not have been a wise career move. And there the matter rested.

Chapter Fourteen

A MEETING

In a dark corner of a Nassau bar during the early months of 1969, I confronted my contact. I knew I was about to be told something significant, but I wasn't sure what. The contact was calm but serious. To further conceal the identity of this person, I am not disclosing gender, but the information imparted had the additional virtue of being current, and concerned a prominent house in Nassau.

A cordon had been set up on the road outside this house, because extensive renovations were underway and debris was being jettisoned from upstairs windows. The street had been closed to traffic as rubbish rained down into the road. Among the mess was a passport and other travel documents belonging to a woman, now dead, who had arrived in the Bahamas some years before to investigate the murder of Sir Harry Oakes. At the time, I was unfamiliar with the name Betty Renner and my contact did not identify her. All references were to "the woman reporter, or investigator, who was murdered." The contact said the discovery had been made that very morning.

I said: "Are you sure?"

"Absolutely sure."

"Where are the documents now?"

"They were handed to a senior police officer. They are now in the hands of the police."

"How do you know?"

"Because I'm in the best possible position to know."

From my personal knowledge of the contact, this was beyond contradiction, yet I had felt the need to ask because I wanted to be doubly certain of everything that was being said to me that day. To be reassured so unequivocally was comforting.

Had this information come from a grade B, C or D source, I would have treated it with due caution, and probably scepticism. It sounded just a little colourful and melodramatic. However, this was a grade A source of impeccable credentials. Furthermore, this person could have no possible motive, other than to expose the truth, for calling the meeting to relay this information. The contact knew that, in the context of the times, the information was unpublishable, but felt I should know the facts for future reference. It was, the contact reasoned, important that such pieces of Bahamian history be made known to the press, so that they would not be lost to posterity. I suppose the fact that I was in my twenties influenced the decision to inform me. One day I would be able to disclose the truth. I have retained this information in my head until now, as I reveal it publicly for the first time.

Of course, the discovery of these documents does not incriminate, conclusively, the occupant of the house in the murder of Sir Harry Oakes, but it does suggest very strongly that he or she was an accessory in the killing of Betty Renner, and possibly in some of the other unexplained Nassau murders as well. It also, for me, confirms what I now firmly believe, that the murder of Sir Harry Oakes was strictly a local affair, plotted and executed in New Providence by people with compelling reasons to dispose of him. I also feel those same people, with so much at stake, not least the entire foundations of their lives, systematically silenced those who knew too much, or were determined to find out more, over a period of years.

The house in question still stands in Nassau, a hollow reminder of that fascinating meeting. My contact, so far as I know, is dead. By telling this story, I feel I have fulfilled an obligation to that honourable person.

Why is the Oakes murder still important today, sixty years on? And why is a new generation of Bahamians so eager to find out more?

Firstly, murder mysteries – and especially those with such a rich cast of characters – are always compelling, especially when they occur more or less in your midst. By providing a few new angles on an old story, I hope to have dispelled some misconceptions and inspired a new generation to look anew at the Oakes affair. In this case, fascination is deepened by the Duke of Windsor's involvement, at such a vitally important time in the history of the western world. The

Oakes case remains probably the greatest murder mystery of the twentieth century, and criminologists continue to debate its many unique features. Secondly, the cover-up which followed the murder, and the callous scheme to frame de Marigny, have left feelings of deep unease in the Bahamas, where for more than half a century, citizens have been forced to live with the painful reality, that certain people are immune from justice, and that innocent men can be sent to their deaths to protect the guilty. Even six decades on, the Oakes story remains deeply relevant to the way Bahamians live their lives.

The selective justice heavily implied by the Oakes affair has a resonance today in Bahamian society, with at least two people currently at large who, because of the protection afforded by powerful connections, will never be called upon to face the judicial process. That is a heavy burden for a young nation to carry, for it compromises all who know the reality, and undermines the rule of law and the fabric of civilised society. Now, as then, there are policemen in the Bahamas who feel frustrated that the system of justice can be so wantonly abused. The Oakes affair provided the Bahamas with a disturbing precedent for this state of affairs, and has for sixty years besmirched all those engaged in the business of law enforcement and the judicial process because no satisfactory conclusion was reached.

In conspiring to hang de Marigny, and in failing to order a proper investigation of the Oakes murder, the Duke of Windsor left a deep scar on Bahamian society and brutally undermined public faith in the system of justice. It is a legacy with which the people of the islands are still obliged to live today. It's a legacy of fear, mistrust, injustice and – for those directly affected by the entire gruesome episode - bitter resignation in knowing that Sir Harry Oakes' life was squandered so recklessly, with no punishment, no penalty, and no apology.

Sir Harry was a complex man with a number of personal demons. There had been too much pain, too much disappointment, in his life to leave him mellow and contented in old age. He was never wholly at ease with himself. In fact, he was often ill-tempered and sometimes obnoxious, yet beneath all that was a core of magnanimity and compassion that occasionally broke through his stormy countenance like sunshine.

As I was close to completing inquiries for this book, a black

Bahamian friend who has known the Oakes family over many years told me: "As a family, they have always been different from other rich whites. For a start, they always liked black people. They were never prejudiced. They have always been nice people, a power for good in the Bahamas. Generous, caring, empathetic, the Oakes family laid a template for the modern Bahamas. The country owes them more than many are prepared to acknowledge."

Fundamentally, Sir Harry was a good, kind and decent family man. He deserved far better than he received at the hands of his killers and those whose job was to find the culprits. So did his family, whose hurt has persisted over so many years and who today are still left to wonder why he died the way he did, in a mad confusion of blood and fire.

AFTERWORD

A fter this book was completed, I was able to conduct two further interviews which added extra dimensions to the story of the Oakes murder. One was with Levi Gibson, the driver who worked for Sir Harold Christie during the war years and later went on to become a successful realtor in his own right. Although he is now in his early nineties, Mr. Gibson remains alert with good recall of the events of those distant times. He still goes to his Nassau office most days, and retains fond memories of his years with Sir Harold, a man he clearly revered. The other interviews were with a retired British journalist, Roy East, who once worked for the International Press Corporation in London, but is now in his eighties and living in Cornwall, England. Mr. East's connections with the Bahamas are scant but significant, having arrived in Nassau firstly as a serviceman during the 1940s, when the Oakes case was still very much a hot topic, and more than 20 years later as a reporter, assigned to cover the historic Bahamas general election of 1967. As you will see, two entirely different perspectives of the Oakes case emerged from my conversations with these men, but they are worth recording as contributions to the continuing saga.

The Gibson interview was particularly significant because the ageing ex-retainer had maintained a dogged silence, for six decades, about a mystery which blighted his former employer's life. In Over-the-Hill communities in Nassau, Mr. Gibson's seemingly eternal silence was interpreted in several ways, most of them unflattering to the man himself. On the odd occasion when Mr. Gibson had been persuaded to say anything, usually by insistent foreign newsmen, he has confined himself to routine denials on Sir Harold's behalf and assurances that his boss was too kind, too gentle and too non-confrontational to ever find himself in the roles of plotter or murderer.

On 8th February 2005,, however, there was a development of a kind to set a journalist's heart a'racing. A contact called me to say that Levi Gibson was talking for the first time about the Oakes case, not to newsmen, you understand, but casual acquaintances who showed an interest. As a result, I called Mr. Gibson and engaged him in a 15-minute telephone conversation, in which he was surprisingly forthcoming. His disclosures were fairly predictable but no less interesting for all that. Anything he said, as one of the last significant surviving figures connected with the Oakes affair, was Bahamian history in the making, and I think it is important to record his views as part of this book.

Initially, I thought Mr. Gibson would be evasive and non-committal. Instead, he stated categorically that Count Alfred de Marigny was the killer of Sir Harry Oakes, and that he was helped in the gruesome task by a friend and a Bahamian associate. Mr. Gibson named the friend and the associate, but I am unsure whether these men are still alive. For legal reasons, therefore, I am not naming them. De Marigny, as already stated, has now been dead for several years.

Mr. Gibson has said many times before that Sir Harold was not the killer, but he has never, to his own knowledge or mine, revealed his own suspicions in print about who the killer was. Indeed, until de Marigny's death it would have been hazardous for him to have done so. I just happened to be the first journalist to speak to him about the case since the count's demise.

Speaking from his Nassau home, Mr. Gibson noted that he was approaching his 91st birthday, yet was still an active realtor, calling into his Nassau office most days to attend to business and check his mail. Of the Oakes case, he said: "There has never been any doubt in my mind that de Marigny and his friend were the killers. I believe they were shown the way to where Sir Harry was sleeping by a Bahamian who knew de Marigny well. I don't want to discuss motives or anything else, but I feel very strongly that this is what happened."

Mr. Gibson offered no evidence for his claims, but said there was no-one else with a reason to kill Oakes. "Sir Harry's butler, Munro, was at the other Oakes home in Maine at the time, but the man who helped de Marigny knew his way about Westbourne," he said.

Of the murder itself, Mr Gibson added: "All I know is that I took Sir Harold's car to Westbourne that night and it was still there in the morning. Although it had been raining, it was still dry underneath, so I feel Sir Harold had been at the house all night. However, he slept very hard. I know that when he called me that morning to tell me about Sir Harry's murder he was very upset. I then went to the airport to pick up the family's lawyer, Walter Foskett."

Mr. Gibson was questioned by the lead investigator, Major Pemberton, shortly after the killing and accused of knowing who was behind it. "He invited me to the police station. They were trying to put it on Sir Harold, but I told them to go to hell. The whole thing was a mess-up. The police department screwed it up."

Mr. Gibson also blamed the Duke for "screwing up" the investigation by calling in the two Miami detectives who, he said, did not know what they were doing. "You must remember," he added, "that Sir Harold had no reason to do it. He was shocked to hell that morning. There is no doubt in my mind that de Marigny and his friend did it, no doubt at all."

Despite six decades of intrigue and suspicion, and the attempt in the House of Assembly to get the case reopened, Mr. Gibson maintained that the Oakes and Christie families remained firm friends. He said he personally had remained on very good terms with all the Oakes children, and knew Nancy Oakes right up to her death in January 2005.

"Whenever I was in London, we would go to dinner together," said Mr. Gibson, "I also knew Sydney and Shirley very well. I used to take them out when they were kids. After the murder, the two families continued to be friends."

He said that, in later years, Sir Harold did not dwell too much on the murder "because he knew he was innocent" in spite of the suspicion flying around. "The fact is that Sir Harold was not the kind of man to hurt anyone. He wouldn't kill a fly." he said.

Roy East's information centred on Sir Strafford Sands, the astute lawyer who was to become the Bahamas Minister of Finance and Tourism, and the Duke of Windsor. It did not throw light on the culprit, but did reinforce the view that the Duke was involved in a conspiracy after the killing.

East first arrived in Nassau in the mid-1940s, when Oakes Field, and later Windsor Field, were used as training bases for Royal Air Force flying crew. He did his first flying as a navigator at Oakes Field on Mitchells, then transferred to Liberators at Windsor Field. He remembers men at the bases being told they should keep their own counsel on the case. "They went out of their way to warn us off any discussion about the Oakes murder."

The warnings were issued in tandem with strictures about the possible temptations laid in young servicemen's paths by Bahamian ladies of the night. "We were told not to go Over-the-Hill in Nassau because of the danger of syphilis." he said. He claimed Nassau was a divided town in those days in a racial and social sense. "The blacks and NCOs like me were not allowed into the British Colonial Hotel. That was the domain of the commissioned officers. If the young servicemen of lower rank wanted a drink, we generally ended up at the Royal Victoria."

Mr. East arrived in Nassau in late 1944 and left early in 1945. He and his colleagues had little interest in the Oakes murder, but senior officers were insistent in warning them away from any discussion of the case when they were out and about in the town.

"I remember it was a quiet town in those days, with horse-drawn carts everywhere. We used to go to what was known as the Town Beach, and sometimes we would get rides on glass-bottom boats to Hog Island, where we would lie on the beach."

In 1967, East returned to the Bahamas as a reporter. He was covering the Bahamas general election of that year, when Lynden Pindling's PLP swept the Bay Street Boys from power, and also investigating Mafia links with Freeport. He was especially keen to establish whether the actor George Raft had Mob links in the Bahamas, and the exact nature of Sir Stafford's legal and financial standing with the new Grand Bahama Port Authority. He was also probing certain land deals in which Sands was involved.

His inquiries led him to the Bay Street office of Sir Stafford, who had been shaken by his party's defeat at the polls and was making plans to leave the Bahamas forever.

Sands was asked where his future lay following his loss of power.

More than any of his political colleagues, Sir Stafford symbolized the old white order, and it was generally believed – with justification – that he would not countenance life in the Bahamas while Pindling and his black government were in charge. Sands had always been regarded by the detractors as a virulent racist because he had, apparently, stated more than once that negroes were incapable of governing themselves. This assessment of his outlook has since been challenged, but the fact remains that he did not hang around once power changed hands. The rest of his life – only five years, as it happened – were spent in miserable exile in Europe, where friends say he pined for the Bahamas and its warm open skies.

During East's brief meeting, Sands expressed disquiet and said some of his political colleagues were fearful for their financial future in the Bahamas, now that Pindling had taken charge. They were fearing the worst, a quick African-style descent into chaos, with politicians plundering the country's wealth and setting it on an inexorable downward spiral.

Sands answered East's probing by declaring that Britain would always take care of him because of an "insurance policy" he had in his possession. This was documentary evidence of the Duke of Windsor's involvement in a cover-up following the Oakes murder. "Sir Stafford told me he and his colleagues were fearful for their financial future now that their party had been deposed. But he then went on to talk about his 'insurance policy' and the fact that the British government would always look after him," said Mr. East.

From his home in Cornwall, he added: "Of course, he never showed me this documentation, nor do I know for sure that he was telling the truth, but he certainly said it and appeared to mean it. He indicated he had everything written down on paper. There is no doubt that Sir Stafford felt the Duke was directly involved, not in the murder itself, but in what happened afterwards."

While in Nassau, Mr. East joined in Pindling's post-election celebrations and subsequently had several conversations with the former prime minister. In one of them, he raised the subject of Sir Stafford and his "insurance policy" regarding the Duke of Windsor. "Pindling was undoubtedly aware that Sir Stafford had information of this kind," said Mr. East, "It was never discussed in detail, but he knew what I was talking about."

Associates of Sir Stafford have, since Mr. East's claims were first published in *The Tribune*, thrown doubt on his version of events, saying Sands was known for never talking to the press. Mr. East, however, recalls clearly how difficult it was to get access to him, and how his accompanying photographer was made to stand outside, while he was granted what was intended to be a ten-minute audience.

Mr. East believes now that only sheer persistence, and a reference to land deals involving an agent called Susan Garth, broke down Sir Stafford's usually implacable stand against press interviews. "I think he wanted to know just exactly how much I knew," he said. "I think his curiosity was aroused."

While with the ex-minister, Mr. East mentioned his wartime service in Nassau as a way of smoothing his way into trickier territory, when he would ask awkward questions about the land deals he was investigating.

It was Sir Stafford who raised the Oakes affair, asking if the young airmen had drawn any conclusions about it at the time. Then came the reference to the Duke which Mr. East insists was made with no hint of levity or jocularity. "He did not smile once the whole time I was there. What he said was deadly serious, though I have no way of knowing if he was telling the truth. He said I must have heard a lot of talk at the time. But there was a strict colour bar, and a strict rank bar, in Nassau when I was there as a twenty-year-old navigator, so there were only certain places we could go. In any case, the Oakes murder meant very little to us. I had read about it, but we were indifferent."

At the time of his interview with Sir Stafford, the Duke was not generally suspected of having any involvement in a conspiracy or cover-up in the Oakes case. Such suspicions emerged much later, as classified documents were released relating to his currency dealings, and Nazi sympathies.

But Mr. East remembers leaving Sir Stafford's office convinced that the ex-minister thought the Duke's involvement was much greater than anyone had previously believed. "I did not pursue him on this matter because I was there to talk to him about something else," said Mr. East. "My fear was that if I started probing what he knew about the Duke, he might not tell me what I wanted to know about the land deals. When I got back to London, I told the office about Sands' remarks and asked if I could investigate further, but the editors thought I was trying to wangle another trip to the Bahamas and nothing came of it."

Doubtless another consideration was the fact that the Duke and Duchess were still alive at the time. To pin a conspiracy claim on the Duke would have been legally hazardous.

In their relatively short meeting, Sir Stafford appeared to Mr. East to be "a very careful lawyer" who was not very forthcoming. "But if I had to put money on it, I would say he was telling me the truth about the Duke. I suppose he could have been bluffing but I don't think so."

If Mr. East's recollections are correct, and I strongly believe they are, they support my contention that the Duke's handling of the Oakes affair can never be construed as pure incompetence. There was something sinister afoot during those late summer months of 1943, and Sands – as a young attorney who knew not only all the principals in the case, but also had an insight into the colony's political dynamics at the time – was in a good position to judge the Duke's manoeuvres at close range. He was also well enough connected to have been able to tap into whatever documentary evidence became available in Nassau, or the United States, when the Duke and Duchess were under suspicion and surveillance. Was Sir Stafford privy to US intelligence material through his Florida associations? That is the likeliest explanation, but we cannot be sure.

At the time of Sir Stafford's disclosure to Mr. East, his options were strictly limited because both the Duke and Sir Harold Christie were still alive. The "insurance policy" was, therefore, likely to remain unredeemed, at least for the time being.

As things turned out, fate had the last laugh, for Sir Stafford and the Duke died in the same year – 1972 – and Sir Harold Christie survived them only into 1973. In the course of a 12-month spell, these three giants of Bahamas history were extinguished, taking who knows how many secrets with them to their graves.

So Mr. Gibson points without equivocation to de Marigny, and Mr. East says Sands had proof of conspiracy. There is no possibility that the Duke would be covering up for de Marigny, a man he loathed, so the inference to be drawn from Sir Stafford's disclosure is that Mr. Gibson is wrong. Whatever his protestations to the contrary, Mr. Gibson has to face the fact that Sir Harold and the Duke remain the likeliest villains in this unfortunate affair, the first as perpetrator, the second as protector. That a hitman or hitmen were hired to do the actual deed is still the best theory in town, and that they were paid off handsomely for their diligence is beyond serious doubt.

When all classified papers on the Windsors and their wartime activities are revealed, we shall be closer to a definitive answer. Until then, the Oakes case will yield its secrets piecemeal, gradually destroying the myths, legends and folklore in the process.

CONCLUSIONS

The now widely-held belief that Harold Christie was involved in a conspiracy to dispose of Sir Harry Oakes was given further credence by official files released in London, in June, 2005. And his suspected accomplice, as revealed in Metropolitan Police papers, was the aforementioned Walter Foskett, the Florida attorney.

Foskett, legal darling of the Palm Beach set was exposed as a swindler in a statement made to the FBI in 1959 by a Maryland art dealer called Fred Maloof. He told agents that an enraged Sir Harry, in the weeks leading up to his murder, had vowed to "straighten him out" after being told that Foskett had cheated him in a deal involving two valuable paintings, one of them a Rembrandt.

It's true there was no love lost between Maloof and Foskett, but Maloof's evidence cannot be discounted. It tied in neatly with the information doing the rounds in Palm Beach, suggesting that the lawyer was, in fact, an opportunistic villain who saw the Oakes fortune as his own personal cookie jar.

Maloof's statement to the Feds, dated 27th May 1959, was given voluntarily at the agency's Washington bureau and referred on to New Scotland Yard, the London police headquarters, so that authorities could, if they wished, reopen inquiries. However, apart from a fairly cursory visit to Nassau by detectives, there was no serious effort to resume investigations into the case. Raymond Schindler and others formed a clear impression that the British were not interested in pursuing the matter.

Maloof, of Lebanese descent, lived in the magnificent Oxon Hill Manor, overlooking the Potomac River in Maryland. He had made serious money dealing in high-priced paintings, including old masters. Sir Harry, having accumulated a substantial fortune from his mining interests, saw art as a hedge against inflation and invested heavily.

Sir Harry and Maloof first met in the mid-1930s when the latter was running an art gallery specializing in the kind of works that appealed to rich collectors. They became friends, Maloof's uncle, "Big Pete" Farrah, having grubstaked Oakes in his early mining days in Canada.

Foskett, said Maloof, had formed a corporation to embrace Sir Harry's many enterprises. In his statement to special agents, Maloof disclosed that he and Oakes agreed on a deal in which Sir Harry was to sell him a Miami Waterfront hotel for $20,000. However, instead of money changing hands, it was decided that Oakes should receive a Rembrandt painting.

Subsequently, Maloof and Oakes had a "falling out" because the then Mrs. (later Lady) Oakes did not care for the art dealer's background and relatives. Maloof claimed Foskett influenced this hostility, setting Sir Harry's wife against him, an echo of the influence he exerted in her antipathy to de Marigny. Later, said Maloof, Foskett invited him to his law office to conclude the art deal, handing over $20,000 for the Rembrandt but insisting that a Gilbert Stuart painting of George Washington also be included. During this encounter, things got heated and Foskett pulled a gun. Maloof claimed he disarmed the attorney and left.

FBI agents reported that Maloof next saw Sir Harry at the Plaza Hotel in New York, a few weeks before the murder. Maloof asked Sir Harry what had become of the Stuart painting, but he disclaimed any knowledge of it and became enraged at the idea that Foskett, acting as his representative, had swindled him. Sir Harry said he was going to see Foskett in Miami or Nassau to "straighten him out" – a threat which may have cost him his life.

Maloof told agents that Foskett was probably swindling Oakes through various legal "shenanigans", and that, when confronted by Oakes, made arrangements to have him killed. Maloof stressed that he was not directly accusing Foskett but felt the lawyer had engineered the killing to gain access to the Oakes family's money.

Maloof further stated that he had been alerted by a woman that Foskett was planning to kill him. Soon afterwards, a man bearing a striking resemblance to himself was shot by an unknown gunman in a telephone booth.

Maloof, according to the FBI, said a man called Christy (sic), whom he described as a rum runner who had become a prominent citizen in Nassau, may have been in collusion with Foskett, since the two of them had been responsible for persuading Oakes to go to the Bahamas in the first place. During his talks with agents, Maloof described Foskett as an unscrupulous man who would stop at nothing to achieve his goals. Apropos of nothing particular, he also described him as a short, stocky character who was a neat dresser.

Maloof offered himself for interview with Scotland Yard and said he would like Lady Oakes to be present. However, so far as is known, no such interview took place.

In implicating Foskett, Maloof was not considered to be far off the mark. The lawyer, described by his own family as an unpretentious character, was in truth a ruthless go-getter with a remarkable knack for ingratiating himself with his social superiors.

The Foskett story was, in fact, very much in line with the American Dream, a zero-to-hero rise similar to that of Oakes himself, though on a much more limited scale. A small town boy from Indiana, son of a locomotive driver, Foskett began his working life as a railway clerk before struggling to pay his way through law school. Once qualified, he worked initially in his home state, then went to Seattle before settling in Florida in 1922. There, he formed a partnership with his long-time friend Bert Winter, and their firm, Winter Foskett, went on to establish itself as trust law experts among the state's movers and shakers.

With his railway background, Foskett would have had little difficulty finding a conversational entrée in the company of Wallis Simpson. For her uncle, Solomon Warfield, was a railway magnate with Indiana connections. Foskett could be relied upon to milk this link for all it was worth as he oiled his way into Florida high society. Soon he was a trusted legal acolyte of the rich east coast set, a man who specialized in drawing up wills, and exploiting legal loopholes, to safeguard other people's fortunes. In the case of Sir Harry Oakes, however, it seems his renowned avarice got the better of him. Once found out, he faced the enormity of ruinous exposure in the eyes of the self-serving milieu who provided his livelihood. Like Christie, he was now suspected by Sir Harry of double-dealing. The solution was to take an extreme course.

The files released from the British National Archives in June, 2005, also included a letter to the Bahamas Attorney General, L A W Orr, from investigator Raymond Schindler dated 8th June 1959. Bearing the letterhead "Schindler Bureau of Investigation", and an address in East 44th Street, New York City, the letter was Schindler's final attempt to get the Oakes case reopened. He died later the same year. In it, he claimed that, during his investigations in Nassau in 1943, he had found finger and palm prints on the walls of the room in which Sir Harry was killed. These prints were made by short, stubby fingers whereas de Marigny, the son-in-law acquitted of the crime, had long, slender fingers. Schindler told Orr that these prints were washed off and never identified, as were further prints and smudges in other rooms in the house. He was informed by authorities that this had been done "so as not to confuse the issue", but told Orr: "The party guilty of this should have been prosecuted for destroying evidence."

Schindler also made an extraordinary claim in the letter which has never been revealed in any of the accounts I have read of the Oakes affair. He said a gun was found in the drawer of the little table between the twin beds where Sir Harry slept. "I was advised that he did not own a gun. I tried to find out who owned this gun as Sir Harry might have explained to this person his reason for needing a weapon. Again, I was told that Sir Harry was not shot, and the gun was taken away so as not to confuse the issue."

Schindler said he had written asking the Duke of Windsor, early in 1944, to allow Scotland Yard in to reopen the investigation. He had also established that FBI Chief J. Edgar Hoover had volunteered to send agents to Nassau in an attempt to throw new light on the affair. In addition, Schindler himself had offered his services free of charge.

Subsequently, Schindler flew to Nassau in an effort to secure evidence for the Crown. But he claimed his hotel telephone was tapped, and that he was followed wherever he went.

"A very old friend named Charles Hubbard and I were playing golf the day after my arrival. During the game, he was called to the clubhouse. When he rejoined me on the golf course, he said the call was from Government House and they wanted him to advise them instantly if I discussed the Oakes case. They told him that if I did, I would immediately be deported from the island.

"I remained in Nassau a day or two longer, but everyone I phoned or talked to had received the same message Mr. Hubbard had received. There was some power emanating from Government House which stopped the reopening of the investigation and I have done nothing in the matter since then."

Schindler, however, said any competent investigator in 1944 would have found innumerable leads. "However, Nancy Oakes when interviewed in London a few days ago, stated that no-one had ever questioned her since her husband was acquitted, and the same applied to Alfred de Marigny," he added.

Typically, Schindler did not reveal why he had failed to follow up these leads himself at the time of the trial when he was drawing generous fees, and extravagant expenses from Nancy and her husband.

Nonetheless, his final question to the Attorney General was a valid one which still requires an answer: "What has prevented them from attempting to solve this case since 1944?"

Christie was a close friend of the Duke, while Foskett was the Windsors' US legal adviser. The imagination does not have to be tested to the limit to reach some fairly obvious conclusions.

Foskett died the same year as Christie – 1973 – at the age of 87. The pair of them almost certainly took to their graves all we ever needed to know about the strange and eternally intriguing murder of Sir Harry Oakes.

ABOUT THE AUTHOR

John Marquis

John Marquis is an award-winning British journalist who has worked on newspapers and magazines for more than forty years. He has been an investigative reporter, international sports writer and editor of both newspapers and magazines during a career which has included two long spells in the Bahamas, where he now works as Managing Editor of *The Tribune*, the nation's leading daily newspaper.

He has worked for several major news organisations, including *Reuters* and *Thomson* newpapers, and his work has appeared in many leading publications, including *The Scotsman*, the *London Evening Standard* and the *Boston Globe*.